PENGUIN BOOKS

FAMILY PORTRAITS

Carolyn Anthony grew up in North Carolina and
was educated at Salem College and the University of
North Carolina at Chapel Hill. She has worked in
publishing in New York for a number of years, as
editor, publicist, and journalist.

FAMILY PORTRAITS

Remembrances by
Twenty Distinguished Writers

EDITED BY CAROLYN ANTHONY

PENGUIN BOOKS

PENGUIN BOOKS
Published by the Penguin Group
Viking Penguin, a division of Penguin Books USA Inc.,
375 Hudson Street, New York, New York 10014, U.S.A.
Penguin Books Ltd, 27 Wrights Lane,
London W8 5TZ, England
Penguin Books Australia Ltd, Ringwood,
Victoria, Australia
Penguin Books Canada Ltd, 2801 John Street,
Markham, Ontario, Canada L3R 1B4
Penguin Books (N.Z.) Ltd, 182–190 Wairau Road,
Auckland 10, New Zealand

Penguin Books Ltd, Registered Offices:
Harmondsworth, Middlesex, England

First published in the United States of America by Doubleday, a division of Bantam
Doubleday Dell Publishing Group, Inc., 1989
Reprinted by arrangement with Doubleday
Published in Penguin Books 1991

10 9 8 7 6 5 4 3 2 1

"Great Aunts" by Margaret Atwood, copyright © 1989 by Margaret Atwood.
"My Mother, Priscilla Stanton Auchincloss" by Louis Auchincloss,
copyright © 1989 by Louis Auchincloss.
"My Father: Lawyer Sam Boorstin" by Daniel J. Boorstin, copyright © 1989 by Daniel J. Boorstin.
"Harvest Home" by David Bradley, copyright © 1989 by David Bradley.
"The 'F' Is for Fascinating" by Mary Higgins Clark, copyright © 1989 by Mary Higgins Clark.
"A Four-Blade Case" by Clyde Edgerton, copyright © 1989 by Clyde Edgerton.
"The Many Masks of Kathleen Godwin and Charlotte Ashe" by Gail Godwin,
copyright ©1989 by Gail Godwin.
"The Sweet Nechâma" by Alfred Kazin, copyright © 1989 by Alfred Kazin.
"Fragments: A Portrait of My Father" by Susan Kenney, copyright © 1989 by Susan Kenney.
"Facts, Visions, Mysteries: My Father, Frederic Oates" by Joyce Carol Oates,
copyright © 1989 by Joyce Carol Oates.
"Wild Women Out of Control" by Sara Paretsky, copyright © 1989 by Sara Paretsky.
"Looking Back at My Father" by May Sarton, copyright © 1989 by May Sarton.
"Bathsheba: A Sacred Memory" by Isaac Bashevis Singer, copyright © 1989 by Isaac Bashevis Singer.
"Revisiting Teoc" by Elizabeth Spencer, copyright © 1989 by Elizabeth Spencer.
"Letter—Much Too Late" by Wallace Stegner, copyright © 1989 by Wallace Stegner.
"Yellow Pages" by Morley Torgov, copyright © 1989 by Morley Torgov.
"Missing: A Man with a Briefcase" by Susan Allen Toth, copyright © 1989 by Susan Allen Toth.
"A Cunning Woman" by Jonathan Yardley, copyright © 1989 by Jonathan Yardley.

Grateful acknowledgment is made for permission to reprint material from
Outrageous Acts and Everyday Rebellions by Gloria Steinem. Copyright © 1989 by Gloria Stenem.

Grateful acknowledgment is made to Eudora Welty for permission to quote from
"One Writer's Beginnings," © 1983, 1984 by Eudora Welty.

Grateful acknowledgment is made for permission to reprint material from the
Introduction to **Lanterns on the Levee: Recollections of a Planter's Son** by William Alexander Percy.
Introduction copyright © 1973 by Walker Percy.

LIBRARY OF CONGRESS CATALOGING IN PUBLICATION DATA
Family portraits: remembrances/by twenty distinguished writers;
edited by Carolyn Anthony.
p.   cm.
Reprint. Originally published: New York: Doubleday, c1989.
ISBN 0 14 01.4357 2
1. Authors, American—20th century—Biography—Family.   2. Family—
United States.   I. Anthony, Carolyn.
[PS129.F28   1991]
818'.5403—dc20   90—20623

Printed in the United States of America

CONTENTS

For
Alethea B. Taylor
in memory of
Robert William Taylor

ACKNOWLEDGMENTS

There have been many who have helped make *Family Portraits* a book.

First, of course, the writers—it is *their* book—and I am grateful to all of them for their enthusiastic response to the idea and for allowing us to share their memories.

There were others who had a part in bringing this collection together.

My thanks to Nancy Evans, who was for this book from the start, and also to Shaye Areheart, William Barry, Alex Gotfryd, Leslie Hanscom, Eileen Jordan, Sybil Steinberg, and Maron Waxman for their good advice and wise counsel along the way. My husband, Robert Anthony, who shared my pleasure when things were going right and cheered me up when they weren't, receives for this and for much else my loving gratitude.

Carolyn Anthony

FOREWORD

> The memory is a living thing—it too is in transit.
> But during its moment, all that is remembered
> joins, and lives—the old and the young, the past
> and the present, the living and the dead.
> —EUDORA WELTY

Memory is the theme that shapes the essays in *Family Portraits*, as twenty distinguished writers reach back in time to recapture the families of their childhoods.

How remarkable is the human memory, that system of complex neurological connections that enables us to quote from Shakespeare, send a man to the moon, play a piece of music and recall in astonishing detail the people and places of our past. Complex and barely understood, memory also is unpredictable. It plays tricks. It is not always there when we need it. It is often there when we least expect it.

A few years ago, my memory played such a trick on me. Riding a bus in Edinburgh, I was overtaken by a sudden sense of *déjà vu*. I had never been to Scotland before. I knew no one. What was it that seemed so familiar? Of course, the *faces*. All around me were the rugged, bony faces of my mother's family, those descendants of Scottish farmers who had settled in North Carolina almost two hundred years before. Look-alikes all of us—me, the people on the bus, those North Carolina McDaniels, McCallums and McCalls, distant cousins no doubt, as well.

I hadn't thought about them in years, the family I once knew. Now I began to remember.

Going to see my grandparents was the highlight of my childhood summers. They lived less than two hundred miles away, but in those days before the highways and interstates the trip took us almost a full day. My mother and father in the front seat, me in the back, we drove, it seemed to me, endlessly through Eastern Standard time, stopping, often, for gas, another Coca-Cola, a breath of air for me, an antidote, all of us hoped, to the car sickness that plagued me every mile of the way. Then, finally, we were *there*, greeted with shrieks and hugs, in my grandparents' house, a house filled with the laughter and good-natured kidding of a large family—seven blood-related aunts and uncles, plus assorted wives and husbands, a dozen or more cousins and, of course, my grandparents. I was doted upon, admired, entertained and overfed. I was never more content and happy.

These visits came to an end with the death of my grandparents when I was entering my teens. The house was sold; aunts and uncles scattered. I grew up and seldom thought of that house and those people, vanished, like my childhood, forever. Or so I had thought until that rainy night, years later, in Edinburgh.

Reading the essays in *Family Portraits* as they began to arrive, I found myself again repeatedly reminded—by a writer's words, a thought, a conversation—of those people who had once been so important to me. But there was a difference now. Through the writers' eloquence and passion, I knew something else: those people are still important, always will be, for family feelings are the ties that bind. They endure—and make us what we are.

Carolyn Anthony
Brooklyn, New York
March 1989

GREAT AUNTS

by Margaret Atwood

Margaret Atwood is the author of several novels, most recently The Handmaid's Tale *and* Cat's Eye, *and has also published nonfiction and poetry. She was born in Ottawa and now lives in Toronto.*

In the early part of my childhood, I did not know any of my relatives, because they lived in Nova Scotia, two thousand miles away. My parents had left Nova Scotia during the Depression because there were no jobs there; by the time I was born, the Second World War had begun, and nobody traveled great distances without official reasons and gas coupons. But although my two aunts were not present in the flesh, they were very much present in the spirit. The three sisters wrote one another every week, and my mother read these letters out loud, to my father but by extension to me and my brother, after dinner. They were called "letters from home." "Home," for my mother, was always Nova Scotia, never wherever we might be living at the time; which gave me the vague idea that I was misplaced. Wherever I actually was living myself, "home" was not there.

So I was kept up on the doings of my aunts, and also of my great-aunts, my uncles, my cousins, my second cousins, and many other people who fitted in somewhere but were more distantly related. In Nova Scotia, it's not what you do or even who you know that is the most important thing about you. It's which town you're from and who you're related to. Any conversation between two Nova Scotians who've never met before will begin this way, and go on until both parties discover that they are in fact related to each other. So I grew up in a huge extended family of invisible people.

But it was not my invisible aunts in their present-day incarnation who made the most impression on me. It was my aunts in the past. There they were as children, in the impossible starched and frilled dresses and the floppy satin hair bows of the first decades of the century, or as shingle-haired teenagers, in black and white in the photograph album, wearing strange clothing—cloche hats, flapper coats up over the knee—standing beside antique motorcars, or posed in front of rocks or the sea in striped bathing suits that came halfway down their legs. Sometimes their arms would be around one another. They had been given captions, by my mother, in white pencil on the black album pages: "We Three," "Bathing Belles." Aunt J. was thin as a child, dark-eyed, intense. Aunt K., the middle sister, looked tailored and brisk, in a Dutch cut. My mother, with huge Pre-Raphaelite eyes and wavy hair and model's cheekbones, was the beauty, an assessment she made light of: she was, and remained, notorious for her bad taste in clothes, a notion she cultivated so she wouldn't have to go shopping alone. But all three sisters had the same high-bridged noses; Roman noses, my mother said. I pored over these pictures, intrigued by the idea of the triplicate, identical noses. I did not have a sister myself, then, and the mystique of sisterhood was potent for me.

The photo album was one mode of existence for my invisible aunts. They were even more alive in my mother's stories, for, although she was no poet, my mother was a raconteur and deadly mimic. The characters in her stories about "home" became as familiar to me as characters in books; and since we lived in isolated places and moved a lot, they were more familiar than most of the people I actually encountered.

The cast was constant. First came my strict, awe-inspiring but lovable grandfather, a country doctor who drove around the dirt roads in a horse and sleigh, through blizzards, delivering babies in the dead of night, or cutting off arms and legs, or stitching up gaping wounds made by objects unfamiliar to me— buzz saws, threshing machines. Under his reign, you had to eat everything on your plate, or sit at the dinner table until you did. You had to go to church, every Sunday. You had to sit up straight. ("Father laid down the law," said my mother. And I could picture him laying it down, on the dining-room table, in the form of two great slabs, like those toted around by Moses; only his were of wood.)

This larger-than-life figure, who resembled in my mind the woodcut of Captain Ahab in our copy of *Moby-Dick,* once threatened to horsewhip my mother for "making moon eyes at the boys." ("Did you?" I said. "I don't know," said my mother.) Although he never actually did any horsewhipping, the word made a vast impression on me. I didn't know what a horsewhip was, and such a punishment had the added attraction of the bizarre.

Then came my distracted, fun-loving, bridge-playing grand-mother, and my Aunt K., a year younger than my mother but much more intellectual and firm of will, according to my mother. Then Aunt J., sentimental and apt to be left out. These three were "the girls." Then, somewhat later, my two uncles, "the boys," one of whom was an inventor and blew the stove lids off the country schoolhouse with some homemade explosive hidden in a log, the other a laconic ironist who frequently had everyone "in stitches." And the peripheral figures: hired girls who were driven away by the machinations of my mother and Aunt K., who did not like having them around; hired men who squirted them while milking the cows; the cows themselves; the yearly pig; the horses.

The horses were not really peripheral characters; although they had no lines, they had names and personalities and histories, and they were my mothers' partners in exciting and, it seemed to me, life-threatening escapades. Dick and Nell were their names. Dick was my favorite; he had been given to my mother as a broken-down, ill-treated hack, and she had restored him to health and glossy beauty. This was the kind of happy ending I found satisfactory.

The stories about these people had everything that could be asked for: plot, action, suspense—although I knew how they would turn out, having heard them before—and fear, because there was always the danger of my grandfather's finding out.

What would he find out? Almost anything. There were many things he was not supposed to know, many things the girls were not supposed to know, but did. And what if he were to find out that they knew? A great deal turned, in these stories and in that family, on concealment; on what you did or did not tell; on what was said as distinct from what was meant. "If you can't say anything good, don't say anything at all," said my mother, saying a great deal. My mother's stories were my first lesson in reading between the lines.

My mother featured in these stories as physically brave, a walker of fences and also of barn ridgepoles, a sin of horse-whipping proportions—but shy. She was so shy that she would hide from visitors behind the barn, and she could not go to school until Aunt K. was old enough to take her. In addition to the bravery and the shyness, however, she sometimes lost her temper. This was improbable to me, since I could not remember any examples. My mother losing her temper would have been a sight to behold, like the Queen standing on her head. But I accepted the idea on faith, along with the rest of her mythology.

Aunt K. was not shy. Although she was younger than my mother, you would never know it: "We were more like twins." She was a child of steely nerves, according to my mother. She was a ringleader, and thought up plots and plans, which she carried out with ruthless efficiency. My mother would be drawn into these, willy-nilly; she claimed she was too weak of will to resist.

"The girls" had to do household chores, more of them after they had driven away the hired girls, and Aunt K. was a hard worker and an exacting critic of the housework of others. Later on in the story, Aunt K. and my mother had a double wedding; the night before this event they read their adolescent diaries out loud to one another and then burned them. "We cleaned the kitchen," said Aunt K.'s diary. "The others did not do an A-1 job." My mother and Aunt J. would always laugh when repeating this. It was, as Matthew Arnold would have had it, a touchstone line for them, about Aunt K.

But there was even more to Aunt K. She was a brilliant student, and had received her M.A. in history from the University of Toronto at the age of nineteen. My grandfather thought my mother was a flighty, pleasure-bent flibbertigibbet until she saved her own money from schoolteaching and sent herself to college; but he was all set to finance Aunt K. for an advanced degree at Oxford. However, she turned this down in favor of marrying a local Annapolis Valley doctor and having six children. The reason, my mother implied, had something to do with Great-aunt Winnie, who also had an M.A., the first woman to receive one from Dalhousie, but who had never married. Aunt Winnie was condemned—it was thought of as a condemnation—to teach school forever. She would turn up at family Christmases, looking wistful. In those days, said my mother, if you did not get married by a certain age, it was unlikely that you ever would. "You didn't think about not marrying," said Aunt J. to me, much later. "There wasn't any *choice* about it. It was just what you did."

Meanwhile, there was my Aunt K. in the album, in a satin wedding gown and a veil and a cascade of lilies identical to my mother's, and later, with all six children, dressed up as the Old Woman Who Lived in a Shoe in the Apple Blossom Festival Parade. Unlike the stories in books, my mother's stories did not have clear morals, and the moral of this one was less clear than most. Which was better? To be brilliant and go to Oxford, or to have six children? Why couldn't it be both?

When I was six or seven and my brother was eight or nine and the war was over, we began to visit Nova Scotia, every summer or every second summer. We had to: my grandfather had had something called a coronary, more than one of them, in fact, and he could die at any moment. Despite his strictness and, to me, his fearfulness, he was loved and respected. Everyone agreed on that.

These visits were a strain. We reached Nova Scotia from Ontario by driving at breakneck speed and for a great many hours at a time over the postwar highways of Quebec and Vermont and New Brunswick, so that we would arrive cranky and frazzled, usually in the middle of the night. During the visits we would have to be on whispering good behavior in my grandfather's large white house, and meet and be met by a great many relatives we hardly knew.

But the worst strain of all was fitting these real people— so much smaller and older and less vivid than they ought to have been—into the mythology in my possession. My grandfather was not galloping around the countryside saving babies and sawing off limbs; he was not presiding over the large dining-room table, laying down the law. Instead he carved little wooden figures, chess pieces and apple-blossom pins, and had to have a nap every afternoon, and his greatest exertion was a stroll around the orchard or a game of chess with my brother. My grandmother was not the harried although comical mother of five, but the wispy-haired caretaker of my grandfather. There were no cows anymore, and where were the beautiful horses?

I felt defrauded. I did not want Aunt J. and Aunt K. to be the grown-up mothers of my cousins, snapping beans in the kitchen. I wanted them back the way they were supposed to be, in the bobbed haircuts and short skirts of the photo album, playing tricks on the hired girls, being squirted by the hired man, keeping dire secrets, failing to do an A-1 job.

Much later, when I thought I had grown up, Aunt J. took me to my first writers' conference. That was in Montreal, in 1958; I was eighteen, and bent on being a writer. I had already produced several impressive poems; at least I was impressed by them. They had decaying leaves, garbage cans, cigarette butts, and cups of coffee in them: I had been ambushed by T. S. Eliot several months previously, and had wrestled him to a standstill. I did not yet know that it was the done thing, by now, to refer to him as T. S. Idiot.

I had not shown my seedy poems to my mother, who was the oldest of the three sisters and therefore pragmatic, since it was she who'd had to tend the others. She was not particularly literary; she preferred dancing and ice-skating, or any other form of rapid motion that offered escapes from domestic duties. My mother had only written one poem in her life, when she was eight or nine; it began: "I had some wings, / They were lovely things," and went on, typically for her, to describe the speed of the subsequent flight. The beauty of this was that whatever I came out with in the way of artistic production, my mother would say, more or less truthfully, that it was much better than she could do herself. But by this time I wanted professional advice. I knew that if I forced her to read my butt-and-coffee-grounds free verses, she would say they were very nice, this being her standard response to other puzzlements, such as my increasingly dour experiments with wardrobe. Clothing was not a priority of hers either.

But Aunt J. had written reams, according to my mother. She was a romantic figure, as she had once had pleurisy and had been in a "san," where she had made flowery shellwork brooches; I had received several of these treasures for Christmas, as a child, in tiny magical boxes with cotton wool in them. Tiny boxes, cotton wool: these were not my mother's style.

Aunt J. had to be careful of her health, an infirmity which seemed to go along with writing, from what I knew. She cried at the sad places in movies, as I did, and, as a child, had been known for impractical flights of fantasy. Her middle name was Carmen, and to punish what they thought to be her inordinate pride over this, her two older sisters had named the pig Carmen.

By now, Aunt J. was no longer lanky. She was rounded in outline, myopic (as I was), and depicted herself as a sentimental pushover, though this was merely a convenient fiction, part of the self-deprecating camouflage adopted by women then for various useful purposes. Underneath her façade of lavender-colored flutter she was tough-minded, like all three of those sisters. It was this blend of soft and hard that appealed to me.

So I'd shown my poems to Aunt J. She read them and did not laugh, or not in my presence; though on consideration I doubt that she laughed at all. She knew what it was to have ambitions as a writer, though hers had been delayed by Uncle M., who was a bank manager, and by their two children. Much later, she herself would be speaking at conferences, sitting on panels, appearing nervously on talk shows, having authored five books of her own. Meanwhile she wrote children's stories for the weekly Sunday-school papers, and bided her time.

She sent my gloomy poems to second cousin Lindsay, who was an English professor at Dalhousie University. He said I had promise. Aunt J. showed me his letter, beaming with pleasure. This was my first official encouragement.

The writers' conference Aunt J. took me to was put on by the Canadian Authors' Association, which at that time was the only writers' organization in Canada. I knew its reputation—it was the same tea-party outfit about which F. R. Scott had written: "Expansive puppets percolate self-unction / Beneath a portrait of the Prince of Wales." It was rumored to be full of elderly amateurs; I was unlikely to see anyone there sprouting a three-day beard or clad in a black turtleneck pullover, or looking anything like Samuel Beckett or Eugene Ionesco, who were more or less my idea of real writers. But Aunt J. and I were both so desperate for contact with anything that smacked of the world of letters that we were willing to take our chances with the CAA.

Once at the conference, we opted for a paper to be given by an expert on Fanny Burney. I goggled around the room: there were a lot of what I thought were middle-aged women, in flowered dresses—not unlike Aunt J.'s own dress—and little suits, though there was no one who looked like my idea of a writer: pallid, unkempt, red-eyed, poised for the existential jump. But this was Canada and not France, so what could I expect?

Up to this time I had seen only one Canadian writer in the flesh. His name was Wilson MacDonald and he'd turned up in our high school auditorium, old and wispy and white-haired, where he'd recited several healthy-minded poems about skiing, from memory, and had imitated a crow. I had a fair idea what Jean-Paul Sartre would have thought of him, and was worried that I might end up that way myself: wheeled out for a bunch of spitball-throwing teenaged thugs, doing birdcalls. You could not be a real writer and a Canadian too, that much was clear. As soon as I could, I was going to hit Paris and become incomprehensible.

Meanwhile, there I was in Montreal, waiting for the Fanny Burney expert with Aunt J. We were both nervous. We felt like spies of a sort, infiltrators; and so, like infiltrators, we began to eavesdrop. Right behind us was sitting a woman whose name we recognized because she frequently had poems about snow-covered spruce trees published in the daily Montreal newspaper. She was not discussing spruce trees now, but a hanging that had taken place the day before, at the prison. "It was so dreadful for him," she was saying. "He was so upset."

Our ears were flapping: had she known the condemned man personally? If so, how creepy. But as we listened on, we gathered that the upset man was not the hanged one; it was her husband, who was the prison chaplain.

Several gaps opened at my feet: the gap between the

sentimentality of this woman's poems and the realities of her life, between the realities of her life and her perceptions of them; between the hangers and the hanged, and the consolers of the hanged, and the consolers of the hangers. This was one of my first intimations that, beneath its façade of teacups and outdoor pursuits and various kinds of trees, Canada—even this literary, genteel segment of Canada, for which I had such youthful contempt—was a good deal more problematic than I had thought.

Years later, I went on a literary outing with both of my aunts.

This took place in the early seventies, when I was over thirty and had published several books. Aunt J.'s husband had died, and she'd moved from Montreal back to Nova Scotia to take care of my aging grandmother. I was visiting, and the aunts and I decided to drive over to nearby Bridgetown, to pay a call on a writer named Ernest Buckler.

Twenty years before, Ernest Buckler had written a novel called *The Mountain and the Valley*, the Mountain being the North Mountain, the Valley being the Annapolis Valley. He'd had some success with it in the States, at that time, in Canada, a surefire ticket to hatred and envy—though because he was an eccentric recluse, the hatred and envy quotient was modified. However, his success in the States had not been duplicated in Canada, because his Toronto publishers were United Church teetotalers, known for throwing launch parties at which they served fruit juice. (Modernization came finally with the addition of a bottle of dreadful sherry, doled out in a separate room, into which those who craved it could slink furtively for their hit while the fruit-juice drinkers pretended not to notice.) These publishers had discovered that there were what my mother referred to as "goings-on" in Buckler's book, and had hidden it in the stockroom. If you wanted to actually buy one, it was like getting porn out of the Vatican.

(My grandmother, before word of its depraved nature had spread, had bought this book as a birthday present for my grandfather, but had taken the precaution of reading it first. She took it out behind the barn and burned it. "It was not fit for him to read," she had remarked, which cast as much light on her opinion of my grandfather—veteran of dissecting room and childbed—as on her opinion of the book.)

I had read this book at the age of thirteen because somebody had given it to my parents, thinking they would like it because it was about Nova Scotia. My mother's comment was that it was not what things were like when she was growing up. This said a lot. I snuck this book up onto the garage roof, which was flat, where I swiftly located the goings-on and then read the rest of the book. It was probably the first novel for adults that I ever did read, with the exception of *Moby-Dick*.

I remembered Ernest Buckler's book with fondness; and by the seventies I'd become involved in a correspondence with him. So over we went to see him in the flesh. My Aunt J. was all agog, because Ernest Buckler was a real writer. My Aunt K. drove. (My Aunt J. never drove, having scraped the door handles off the car on one of her few attempts, according to her.)

Aunt K. knew the vicinity well, and pointed out the places of interest as we went by. She had a good memory. It was she who had told me something everyone else had forgotten, including myself: that I had announced, at the age of five, that I was going to be a writer.

During this drive, however, her mind was on other historical matters. "That's the tree where the man who lived in the white house hanged himself," she said. "That's where the barn got burned down. They know who did it but they can't prove a thing. The man in there blew his head off with a shotgun." These events may have taken place years, decades before, but they were still current in the area. It appeared that the Valley was more like *The Mountain and the Valley* than I had suspected.

Ernest Buckler lived in a house that could not have been changed for fifty years. It still had a horsehair sofa, antimacassars, a wood stove in the living room. Ernest himself was enormously likable and highly nervous, and anxious that we be pleased. He hopped around a lot, talking a mile a minute, and kept popping out to the kitchen, then popping in again. We talked mostly about books, and about his plans to scandalize the neighborhood by phoning me up at my grandmother's house, on the party line, and pretending we were having an affair. "That would give the old biddies something to talk about," he said. Everyone listened in on the party line, of course, whenever he had a call, but not just because he was a local celebrity. They listened in on everyone.

After we left, my Aunt J. said, "That was something! He said you had a teeming brain!" (He had said this.) My Aunt K.'s comment was: "That man was oiled." Of the three of us, she was the only one who had figured out why Mr. Buckler had made such frequent trips to the kitchen. But it was understandable that he should have been secretive about it: in the Valley, there were those who drank, and then there were decent people.

Also: there were those who wrote, and then there were decent people.

A certain amount of writing was tolerated, but only within limits. Newspaper columns about children and the changing seasons were fine. Sex, swearing, and drinking were beyond the pale.

I myself, in certain Valley circles, was increasingly beyond the pale. As I became better known, I also became more widely read there, not because my writing was thought of as having any particular merit but because I was Related. Aunt J. told me, with relish, how she'd hidden behind the parlor door during a neighbor's scandalized visit with my grandmother. The scandal was one of my own books; how, asked the outraged neighbor, could my grandmother have permitted her granddaughter to publish such immoral trash?

But blood is thicker than water in the Valley. My grandmother gazed serenely out the window and commented on the beautiful fall weather they were having, while my Aunt J. gasped with suppressed giggles behind the hall door. My aunts and my mother always found the spectacle of my grandmother preserving her dignity irresistible, probably because there was so much of it to be preserved.

This was the neighbor, the very same one, who as a child had led my aunts astray, sometime during the First World War, inducing them to slide down a red clay bank in their little white lace-edged pantaloons. She had then pressed her nose up against the glass of the window to watch them getting spanked, not just for sliding but for lying about it. My grandmother had gone over and yanked the blind down then, and she was doing it now. Whatever her own thoughts about the goings-on in my fiction, she was keeping them to herself. Nor did she ever mention them to me.

For that I silently thanked her. I suppose any person, but especially any woman, who takes up writing has felt, especially at first, that she was doing it against an enormous, largely unspoken pressure, the pressure of expectation and decorum. This pressure is most strongly felt, by women, from within the family, and more so when the family is a strong unit. There are things that should not be said. Don't tell. If you can't say anything nice, don't say anything at all. Was that counterbalanced adequately by that other saying of my mother's: "Do what you think is right, no matter what other people say"? And did those other people whose opinion did not matter include the members of one's own family?

With the publication of my first book, I was dreading disapproval. I didn't worry much about my father and mother, who had gracefully survived several other eccentricities of mine—the skirts hand-printed with trilobites and newts, the experiments with beer parlors, the beatnik boyfriends—although they had probably bitten their tongues a few times in the process. Anyway, they lived in Toronto, where goings-on of various kinds had now become more common; not in Nova Scotia, where, it was not quite said, things were a bit more narrow. Instead I worried about my aunts. I thought they might be scandalized, even Aunt J. Although she had been subjected to some of my early poems, coffee cups and rotting leaves were one thing, but there was more than dirty crockery and mulch in this book. As for Aunt K., so critical of the shoddy housework and drinking habits of others, what would she think?

To my surprise, my aunts came through with flying colors. Aunt J. thought it was wonderful—a real book! She said she was bursting with pride. Aunt K. said that there were certain things that were not said and done in her generation, but they could be said and done by mine, and more power to me for doing them.

This kind of acceptance meant more to me than it should have, to my single-minded all-for-art twenty-six-year-old self. (Surely any true artist ought to be impervious to aunts.) However, like the morals of my mother's stories, what exactly it meant is far from clear to me. Perhaps it was a laying-on of hands, a passing of something from one generation to another. What was being passed on was the story itself: what was known, and what could be told. What was between the lines. The permission to tell the story, wherever that might lead.

Or perhaps it meant that I too was being allowed into the magical, static but ever-continuing saga of the photo album. Instead of three different-looking young women with archaic clothes and identical Roman noses, standing with their arms around each other, there would now be four. I was being allowed into "home."

MY MOTHER, PRISCILLA STANTON AUCHINCLOSS

by Louis Auchincloss

My mother's father's family, the Stantons, came originally from Stonington, Connecticut, where some of them had been whalers and all of them can still be buried, but since the 1850s they have been New Yorkers, a polite, agreeable, urbane clan, of no particular distinction or notoriety, but boasting a general manager of the Metropolitan Opera and (today) a federal judge. The Stantons had no family fortune, though Priscilla's grandfather (a fact perhaps happily forgotten by society) had been Daniel Drew's broker; each generation had made or married enough money to keep it decorously going, and they were known in Gotham as people who had "always been there."

My grandfather, Louis Lee Stanton, who became an officer of Standard Trust Company, a minor but respected adjunct of the Morgan empire, married Pauline Dixon, daughter of a successful Brooklyn granite dealer. Their first child, Priscilla, was born in 1888, and their second, Louis, in 1894. Louis died in infancy, and the Stantons had no further children until 1897, so that Priscilla was an only child in her most formative years. She was far, however, from being a lonely one. She lived in a daily crowd of Dixon first cousins.

For it was the Dixons, not the Stantons, who provided the centrifugal force in her life. Her mother's four brothers and two sisters, who had all emigrated from Brooklyn to Manhattan, clustered together so tightly in neighboring brownstones that Forty-ninth Street between Fifth and Sixth avenues was dubbed by their friends "Dixon Alley." I let Mother describe them in a family memoir:

> Of course the seven varied greatly among themselves, but the ceaseless intimacy did establish a common sense of values, and I think it was a pretty sound one, probably more Greek than Christian. Anything in excess (except perhaps homesickness) was disapproved. Churchgoing was regular, but perfunctory, and any close religious ties discouraged as too emotional. I remember hearing that Alice Babcock was to be severely punished unless she stopped reading the Bible so hard. Considering that the family had only New England blood (as far as I know there was no mitigating mixture), this may have been a wise protection against the New England conscience—although the seven had this conscience under pretty good control. I don't mean that they were soft on the fundamentals, honor, truth, loyalty, or that they did not care about what was done and more about what was not done, but they did not expect too much of human nature. Their marriages were mostly happy, but they were less severe than their contemporaries on those who were less fortunate. We are constantly told how the world changes—and indeed it does—but I cannot see where, if they came back today [1960], they would find themselves ill at ease in today's world or have to change any of their basic ideas. Perhaps this is because their skepticism protected them against too much identifying themselves with the currents of their times, religious and humanitarian. I can remember no enthusiastic embracing of causes or any undue faith that much could be done to hasten progress. They were generally in sympathy with liberal ideas, but in a very mild way. Their constant supply of cold water to throw on the dreams of

youth was rather trying, but it was balanced by the warmest interest and helpfulness if there was anything you wanted to do for yourself: to travel, to give a party, to get new clothes. They all had good, alert minds but very little interest in the arts.

A family, or clan, that achieves power over its adolescent members does so in the same way as a mafia, not so much by fear—though that may be in it—as by the assurance of advantages to be gained in excess of the duties exacted. If Mother had to devote many afternoons to shopping with her aunts or sitting with some elderly bedridden cousin, there were handsome young male Dixons to keep an eye on a shy and nervous "Pris" when the time came for going to dances. Indeed it was Courtland Dixon who told his Yale classmate Howland Auchincloss that he had just the girl for him. He had. And the benefits conferred were not only social ones. When Mother's father died in 1911 of Bright's disease, leaving a widow and two sons not yet in their teens and with a sadly diminished income, it was her maternal aunt, "Pink" Barclay, who picked up the school bills.

As Mother has indicated in her memoir, the Dixons were not an intellectual crowd. But they had a cheerful tolerance, even a pleasantly ungrudging respect for those who were. If Pris was a great reader and had the best marks in her class at Miss Chapin's School, why that was just fine, that was nifty. Of course, it wasn't quite as exciting as winning the golf tournament at the Rockaway Hunt Club, or being the most beautiful debutante of the season, like Sally Dixon, but then Pris herself wouldn't claim it was, would she? No, indeed, she would not. For that is just where clans like the Dixons are most fatal to the development of any novel talent. They never repress anyone; they are too amiable for that. And the shy Priscilla yearned for the approbation of these attractive and easygoing relatives and was easily accorded it. And having once obtained it, she never, never wanted to let it go.

With their love and approval, of course, she had to some extent to accept their values. It was a package deal, as with any social entity. An example of how this worked is how my grandmother handled the question of Mother's college career.

Pauline Stanton was a strong-minded woman with a keen sense of human and a no-nonsense attitude toward life. She faced her early widowhood and the onset of the cancer that was to kill her at fifty-five with signal courage. She was tall and striking-looking, always smartly dressed, and she moved with a brisk efficiency through the crowded social life of her clan and group. She was considerably better read than her siblings and had an eye for a good picture. But that she was always a Dixon at heart is shown by the satirical sketch that she wrote for Priscilla called "My Daughter's Friends," where she made some rather tart fun of the new "liberated spirit" of these young women, showing one who liked to practice on a rifle range as still afraid of a mouse and another who aspired to be a philosopher as arriving for the weekend with a trunk of books it took the hired man and a friend of his to lug up to her room. Laughter was the Dixon way of dealing with the "pretentious."

Was it pretentious in 1907 for Priscilla to aspire, as she did, to go to college? Well, no, perhaps not. Pauline would not go that far. It was quite unnecessary, of course, for the domestic role that Priscilla would one day play, but there was no point in disappointing the girl unnecessarily, and if she went to Barnard she could live at home, so . . . well, why not consult Miss Chapin? Maria Bowen Chapin, headmistress of her eponymous school, was the acknowledged authority on such matters. The authority, consulted, agreed that Priscilla should go to Barnard, but suggested that she transfer for her twelfth grade to Brearley, a school better equipped to train girls college bound. It is not to be surmised that this implied, in Miss Chapin's opinion, the smallest academic superiority of Brearley to her own institution.

So Priscilla went to Barnard. But there was a catch. She had to take a maid with her, an Irish girl, Alice Morrissey (who would spend her whole life in Mother's employ), not so much as a chaperon—a domestic would not have qualified—but under the supposition that two females would be safer than one in the upper reaches of Manhattan. Poor Priscilla was much embarrassed when her new friends asked her who the little woman sitting in the back of the classroom was. But despite this social hurdle she received a bid from the sorority Kappa Kappa Gamma (which Father, with mild male chauvinism, would later refer to as "Wrapper, Wrapper, Pajama"), and she had every reason to feel that she had gained a firm foothold in her new life.

Then the blow fell. Her sorority initiation was scheduled for a night for which she had already accepted an invitation to a dinner party. When she asked her parents if she could get out of it, their attitude was one of mild astonishment that the question should even be put. "But you accepted it, dear child; didn't you just say you'd *accepted* it?" In pre-World War I Manhattan one either attended a dinner party or sent one's coffin. So Priscilla sadly gave up her initiation (the sorority, fortunately, took her *in absentio*) and went to the party, where she found herself seated next to a Yale senior called Howland Auchincloss. My grandmother always maintained this was her ultimate justification.

Mother never graduated from Barnard. Her engagement to Father, which lasted for two years, and her own father's declining health, with its calls upon her time, interrupted her studies. But she had few regrets. She was very much in love, and she fully accepted now the tribal mores that would confine a woman to the home she had freely chosen. The very intensity of her new feelings seemed to justify it. She could laugh to herself when Father's older sister told her that she'd rather see her brother in his coffin than married to a woman who denied the divinity of Christ (not that Mother did), but she didn't laugh at the awesome responsibility that she had undertaken to make Howland the wife she deemed him to deserve. She was assailed by wracking doubts about herself. "I'm going to write Howland and break our engagement!" she cried out one day to her mother. The latter, knowing how many times that letter would be rewritten, simply asked her not to use the best notepaper.

Father was, in all but one respect, to which I shall advert later, a perfect husband. He had charm and humor and a character of singular fineness and humility. He was an able and meticulous lawyer who was never prosy or long-winded, a gregarious mixer who could be happy in his own company and a natural athlete who never required anyone else (including his three unathletic sons) to be. He never wavered in his position that Mother was the greatest thing that had ever happened to him. Indeed, trying to explain it to me once, he unintentionally aroused my resentment. "Compared to what your mother and I feel for each other," he said, "you children hardly exist." In his confused sense of what a great emotion he was attempting to put in words, he forgot how this would sound to a boy. But even then I think I realized there was enough love left over for me.

Father had suffered depressions as a boy, but they did not recur until he was almost fifty, and the first twenty years of his married life were marked by his steady rise in his profession. Graduating from Harvard Law School in 1911, the year of his marriage to Mother, he entered the firm of Stetson Jennings & Russell (Russell was his maternal uncle, Jennings his sister's father-in-law) and became a partner in 1921, after the death, within months of each other, of the three founders. The new, reorganized firm was what is still familiarly known as "Davis Polk." The Davis was John W. Davis, the losing candidate to Coolidge in 1924, and the firm's principal client was J. P. Morgan & Co. As with "Dixon Alley," Mother was confronted with social entities to which she had no difficulty in giving all her loyalty.

Davis Polk in those days was a small fraction of its present size, but its position was just as distinguished, and the senior partners whom I best remember, Davis, Frank Polk, and Lansing Reed, were all men of remarkable charm. Mother was always congenial with their wives; it was the most natural thing in the world for her to endorse Father's devotion to a firm that was as much his club as his place of work. When in later years the more ordinary wife of a younger partner told Mother that the one thing in the world she really wanted was a mink coat, Mother's disgust was occasioned less by snobbishness (though that was in it) than by the inappropriateness of so shallow a sentiment in a member (even by marriage) of a partnership that Mother had come to dignify as a force in public leadership. And always behind Davis Polk were the Morgan partners, known to Mother, though less intimately, whom she had no trouble in casting in the role of guardians of the highest moral standards in the world of finance.

What I am trying to bring out is that there was never a point where the rebel in Mother (and I am assuming there is the germ of one in all of us) was given anything substantial to feed on. The Dixons were charming, as were Father's partners, as even were the staid and distant Morgan partners. And they were all very nice to Priscilla and Howland. "Don't get Dixonized," Grandmother Auchincloss had growled to Father when he became engaged. But Dixonized was precisely what Father wanted to be! He was delighted with the life he shared with Mother. And why should she not have been equally satisfied with it? There were children and charities and the pleasant busyness of summer communities and a sense of useful work underlying it all. She felt herself liked and admired. Why should she have wanted anything more?

Only because her life used so little of her capability. *She* was the one of our family who should have been the writer. Or a teacher. Or a scholar. It seems quite possible to me that the all-embracing role that she ascribed to motherhood in the life of a woman may have been a self-justification for the little use she had made of her own natural talents. If the family was the be-all and end-all of life, as she seemed to have deduced from her increasingly idealized memory of Forty-ninth Street, if creating and maintaining that warm, pulsating exchange of love and confidence was the point of human existence, then shouldn't the family be as large as possible, large enough anyway to put out of the question any other serious occupation for a female parent? Priscilla had wanted eight children; it was Howland who drew the line at four.

Mother carried her theory of multitudinous progeny in the very teeth of those who argued the dangers of overpopulation. "There's plenty of room for more people," she told me once, in a rare moment of irrationality, as we were driving along a Westchester expressway. "Think how many cottages you could build on that landscaped park!" She came to regard childlessness as a major tragedy for a couple, and she would have been appalled today by the number of young wives who elect it in deference to a more vigorously pursued career.

The duty to have children obviously encompassed the duty to see that they were safely reared, and this secondary obligation soon became paramount to Mother, even exceeding the duty to a beloved spouse, who would presumably bow to the priority. When Mother was told of the young Franklin Roosevelt's polio, she is supposed to have exclaimed, "How glad his wife must have been it wasn't one of the children!" And from the duty of keeping her children alive—or at least from her conception of it—sprang the morbid preoccupation with death that was to dog her middle years and sap so much of her vital energy.

I believe that Mother came to fear her responsibility for the possible death of a child more than the death itself. I have no doubt that her anxiety about me when I served in the amphibious navy in World War II was substantially less than her anxiety when I was driving home in the early morning, after many drinks, from debutante parties. The war was in no way chargeable to her account, but hadn't she and Father paid for the automobile in which I whizzed to dances, and wasn't it their home from which I started and to which I returned? I do not mean to imply that Mother didn't love her children or wouldn't have been devastated by the demise of one of them (all four in fact survived her). But I do mean to suggest that her dread of responsibility was carried to an obsessive degree. I remember her comment about a newspaper account of some children who, having been refused permission to fly and been taken to a railway station where tickets to their destination had been purchased, had awaited the departure of their parents to hop a plane which had crashed, killing them all. "Well, those parents were certainly off the hook!" she exclaimed.

It was obviously Father's role to intervene and insist that the children be allowed to take the ordinary risks of life. Mother might not have even minded—so long as he assumed the entire responsibility. But he never knew this, and he dreaded the terrible misery of her fits of worry, which could indeed be appalling. So when we went to a ranch in Wyoming we were not allowed to go on an overnight pack trip (suppose one of us suffered an attack of appendicitis?); we were discouraged from sailing; flying, even as passengers, was out of the question, and motoring was restricted as much as possible in an age of automobiles. Mother even contemplated putting speed governors on the family cars and was only dissuaded by the argument that speed might on occasion avoid an accident. I can remember a grotesque incident on a trip abroad, when, approaching the edge of the Moher Cliffs in Ireland, the Auchinclosses intrigued the other tourists by dropping to their hands and knees at Mother's shrill command to crawl for greater safety.

Once, years later, when I asked Mother if she had ever considered the damage done to her offspring by these constant warnings of danger, and contrasted her behavior to that of her great friend Madeleine Pell, who had allowed her fine athletic children to career about the earth in the fastest of machines, she retorted: "But Madeleine lost a child!" It was true that Nelson Pell, Mother's godson, the most charming of men and an able pilot, had mistaken a giant incinerator for an airport light in an impenetrable fog. But he had had a good life.

Why was she so afraid? We don't know. I remember the

reply of a famous psychiatrist, Dr. Ludwig Cast, who used to walk with her on the mountains of Mount Desert Island, when she told him proudly that, without the benefit of his profession, she had raised a family and led a good life: "Ah, but the woman you might have been!" There was only one incident that she recalled that struck me as possibly having a bearing on her neurosis, and that was the death of her younger brother when she was six years old. She had been envious of the stylish mourning of some of the Dixon cousins for a relative who wasn't one of hers, and she hoped that her sick little sibling would die so she could be similarly attired. Then the poor boy did die, and the young Priscilla saw in the shattered faces of her parents what death really was. Did she try for the rest of her life to make up for that infantile death wish?

I realize that in laboring my point I have made Mother seem a very different figure from that which she presented to the world. Her fears for her family were always a private occupation. She was not one of those boring mothers who never stop prating about their children. In the wide circle of her friends where she was justly loved and admired, she seemed the very reverse of what she could be in a crisis at home. Handsome, trimly dressed, seemingly self-assured, she was one of the best of conversationalists, incisive, witty, shrewdly, often brilliantly, intelligent. Her pungent, realistic advice was eagerly sought on the charitable boards on which she conscientiously served. One cultural institution elected her a trustee for a single task: to bring about the resignation of a beloved but too-long-in-office director. They knew that Mother had the courage and charity to do the job quickly and well, and she did.

The friend who knew her best, Gabrielle Chandler, observed to me once: "I'm so glad I'm not your mother's child. She has helped me enormously, again and again, with just the right advice. If I'd been her child, and therefore a 'responsibility,' I wouldn't have had the benefit of her free intelligence."

Mother was always an omnivorous reader, and when I started to write for the students' magazine at Groton School, and later at Yale for the *Lit,* she was intensely interested in my stories and gave me helpful advice. I shall never forget her saying, of my describing the tumbril that took the unfortunate Marie Antoinette to her execution as a "repulsive vehicle," that it might have been a greasy aeroplane. And I remember the lesson she gave a would-be-writer cousin who had taken a year off to build with his own hands a sailboat to document the chapter in his novel where his hero would do just that: "But don't you know, that's the chapter everyone will skip?"

Writing was one thing; publishing quite another. When at Yale I wrote a novel and submitted it to Scribner's, Mother was alarmed. Was I seriously considering becoming a novelist? This was the greatest act of pretentiousness, of "hubris," against the deities of a Dixon or a Davis Polk world, unless one were clearly a genius. Society would always make an exception for a genius. But in the field of art, who needed any but the very best? Would any Dixon think it was "nifty" to be a second-rate scribbler? And then there was the question of money. The family means were not sufficient to support a nonproducing son for a lifetime. If I was to take my place in the world where Mother and Father had found theirs, I would have to earn a decent living. There was some sense in this; what I couldn't forgive was that Mother did not consider me a genius. I have had plenty of critics since who would have agreed with her desire to spare me the disgrace of being a minor writer, but what child wants an unbiased opinion from a parent?

The problem was solved, at least temporarily, when, to Mother's relief, the novel was rejected. I decided, in a fit of angry disappointment, to leave Yale, give up writing forever, and go to law school. Father objected to my leaving Yale, but Mother wanted to take advantage of my mood. If I was too old to be subject to her veto of death-risking actions, I could still be persuaded to avoid the social death of choosing a career beyond my capacities. She approved my resolution to give up writing and only worried when, in my law school summers, I started another novel. But I destroyed it, became an editor of the *Virginia Law Review*, and on graduation accepted a job with Sullivan & Cromwell, easily the equal of Davis Polk. Both parents were delighted. I was safe.

Then came the war, in the last year of which, aboard an LST in the Pacific, I started writing again. After VJ Day my parents were again alarmed when I delayed my return to Sullivan & Cromwell for three months while I finished my novel. After I had gone back to my firm, however, I was to put them to a much worse trial. The novel, submitted to Prentice-Hall, was accepted for publication!

Now Mother behaved, for the one and only time, really reprehensibly. Granted that she sincerely believed that the book was a bad one and that what she considered its vulgar passages would hurt me with my employers, might she not have tried to take some pride in the accomplishment of a son in getting a novel published at all? Instead she nagged me until I made the ridiculous mistake of using a pen name at a time when too many people already knew that the book was mine. It enjoyed a considerable success for a first effort, and even Mother was proud of some of the reviews. When my second book, *The Injustice Collectors*, came out under my own name, she at last came around, and when I decided to leave the law to try the experiment of writing full-time (which didn't work out), she and Father very generously staked me to it.

But we were not yet out of the woods. After I returned to the law and became a partner in another law firm, there was no longer the argument that what I wrote might offend my employers. I was my own employer and financially independent of my parents and anyone else. But the field I had carved out for my literary endeavors, the New York business and social worlds in which I had been raised, was precisely the establishment to which Mother, and to a lesser degree Father, felt themselves bound by the deepest loyalties. Had I criticized these worlds in what Mother regarded as a serious work of nonfiction, she might have accepted it. But novels and short stories, with characters who might be (and often were) identified (however erroneously) with persons whom Mother respected, and sometimes a little bit feared, were anathema to her. It seemed to her that her son was betraying an allegiance from within the citadel. If he wanted to attack such persons, it should be openly, directly, though how she would have reacted even to that was not clear.

I dreaded the hassles that accompanied the submission of each manuscript to Mother's inspection. She would implore me to alter this or that character so that it would be less like X or Y. I always refused. Why then did I subject us both to the ordeal? Because I wanted her approval more than anybody's. To me she was the ultimate critic. And she was beginning to think there might be something to my writing. For this I was willing to forgive anything.

I will admit that *The Rector of Justin* was a tough one for both her and Father. Virtually the entire Groton "family," including the children of the late and infinitely revered headmaster, insisted on identifying my central character with Endicott Peabody, and loud was the outcry. Father, a Grotonian himself, and Mother had almost worshipped "the rector," as he was known, and it was not a happy time for them. But Mother thought it was a good book, and she actually began to defend it.

But the climax of her change of attitude came with *The Embezzler*. This novel was based, not on the personality of Richard Whitney, but very much on his famous embezzlements in the 1930s. The crime had been one of the great dramas in my father's downtown world. Whitney had been a president of the New York Stock Exchange, and his brother George the president of J. P. Morgan & Co. It came at a time when the old forces of laissez-faire were under the sharpest attack from FDR's New Deal government, and Whitney was widely regarded by Father's world as a "traitor to his class." The whole business had been intensely interesting to me as a Yale undergraduate and later as a novelist, and I knew that sooner or later I would have to "do" something with it. Eventually I saw how I could treat it. I read the whole record of the case to get my facts straight and then proceeded to put it in a novel with a totally fictional cast of characters.

But George Whitney's widow got wind of what I was doing, summoned me to her apartment, and appealed to me to abandon the project. When I pointed out that the case had passed into history and that I was using nothing that was not notorious, she replied: "Yes, but people are beginning to forget about it, and you'll stir it all up again." I did not feel that this was an argument for killing a book on which I had worked long and hard and that ultimately turned out to be a national best-seller, so I politely declined. Mrs. Whitney was big enough not to hold it against me.

The point, however, was Mother. She had herself received her friend's appeal. If any one person could have represented everything that Mother most valued in the "establishment," it was Martha Whitney. Not only her husband but her father before him had been Morgan partners, and she herself was a kind of Roman matron, with great presence and personality. Even before *The Embezzler,* Mother had admitted that when she apprehensively turned to one of my manuscripts and tried to imagine what the world would say of it, "Martha's are the eyes that I feel reading over my shoulder." And now! Martha was not only reading it; she was vociferously protesting! The nightmare had come true. First the Groton family and now the House of Morgan were reacting exactly as she had feared they might.

Perhaps there is nothing like a nightmare's coming true to make one see what threads and patches it is made up of. Suddenly there was Martha Whitney, understandably concerned over any renewed interest in an ancient scandal, but who really had nothing to lose from the appearance of a novel based on a crime of which all the world was only too well aware, and there, on the other hand, was her own son, in whose professional career as a novelist *The Embezzler* might well (and did) prove an important step. Mother came down strongly on my side, and never again (and she lived to be eighty-three) was there an issue between us over my fiction.

I sometimes think that having produced a writer of whom she ultimately approved may have made up a tiny bit for the career she missed. I hope so.

MY FATHER:
LAWYER SAM BOORSTIN

by Daniel J. Boorstin

I never knew anyone quite like my father, but then I never really knew my father either. He was a man without a single vice, but with a hundred foibles. He was a "devoted" husband in a miserably unhappy marriage. He was embarrassingly proud of me, and advertised my small academic triumphs by stopping fellow Tulsans on the street to show them newspaper clippings, and he thermofaxed my letters home to give to passing acquaintances. Yet he never once praised me to my face. When I won my Rhodes Scholarship to go from Harvard to Oxford, he had no comment, but noted that a neighbor boy had been given a scholarship to send him from Tulsa Central High to the University of Oklahoma. My mother was one of the world's best cooks, not in the gourmet category, but in the Russian Jewish style, spending endless hours in the kitchen to make her cheesecake or her blintzes just right. Then when my father came to dinner from his office (always later than expected) he seldom failed to say that he "would just as soon eat a bale of hay." "Man should eat to live, and not live to eat."

Still, there was never any doubt that my mother ruled the roost, and her tribal feelings confined the family's social life. For most of our years in Tulsa we lived in a "duplex" apartment, with my mother's sister Kate and her husband and daughter living below. My mother's only friend was this sister, but my father was everybody's friend, and spent his spare hours in the lobby of the Tulsa Hotel, and later the Mayo Hotel, chatting with acquaintances or strangers, or simply reading the newspaper and hoping to be interrupted by a strange or friendly voice. My mother was suspicious of anyone who was not a blood relation (including especially her brothers' wives), while my father's suspicions (with some reason) fell especially on the blood relations themselves. Except for two or three occasions when we entertained at dinner a local merchant who was my father's prize client, I cannot remember a single occasion when we had nonfamily guests in our house or were in another Tulsa home.

Everything about our life—including our coming to Tulsa—seemed dominated by my mother's family. I never understood how two people so ill suited to each other could ever have married. But the story of how my father and mother first met was supposed to explain it. And behind that was the story of the last years of my father's independence, back in Atlanta.

My father always spoke with a warm and soft Georgia accent. His father was one of the many Jews who emigrated from the Russian pale in the late 1880s to escape pogroms, military service, and persecution. This Benjamin Boorstin came on his own, and for some reason, never explained, settled in Monroe, Georgia. His brother came about the same time. But the immigration officers spelled his brother's name Boorstein, and so he remained. The two brothers had stores on opposite sides of the street in Monroe, where their differences of name were constant reminders of their recent arrival. Benjamin Boorstin sent for his wife, who came over with their infant, Sam. My father went to school in Monroe. While working in a general store in his spare time he managed to collect the premium tags attached to the little bags of cigarette tobacco he was selling. He sent off a stack of these tags and received one of the primitive plate cameras.

This camera changed his life, for he used it to earn his way through college. Arriving in Athens, Georgia, the site of the state university, he quickly found his way into the office of the president. He showed the president his photographs of the cracked walls and peeling ceilings of the university classrooms. These pictures, and more like them, he said, would persuade the state legislature to grant appropriations for repairs and for new university buildings. With that he applied for the novel job of university photographer, and got it on the spot. Then he worked his way through by helping the president with his campaign for larger appropriations and by taking class pictures.

In those days law was an undergraduate subject. When Sam Boorstin received his LL.B. degree he was still under twenty-one, and when he appeared before the judge to be admitted to the bar, it was objected that he was underage. He won his first case when he persuaded the judge to admit him anyway, and so became the youngest member of the Georgia bar. In Atlanta he began practice as junior member of one of the most prestigious old law firms. He spent his spare time joining every fraternal organization that would let him in. These included the Elks, the Odd Fellows, the Red Men, and the Masons. I still have the fine Hamilton gold watch with the Masonic emblem engraved on the back which was given to him when he became the youngest Worshipful Master in the United States. He kept his hand in as a beginner in Georgia Democratic politics, which became easier when Governor John Marshall Slaton engaged him as his private secretary. One of Sam Boorstin's qualifications—in addition to personal charm and an outgoing manner—was his elegant handwriting. He had acquired a beautifully rotund and flourishing hand by attending a penmanship school. His flamboyant signature was one of the first mannerisms that I tried to imitate—without any success.

He might have had a career in Georgia politics, even though he was a Jew. But unpleasant events—surrounding the infamous Leo Frank case—intervened, and made this impossible. The innocent pencil manufacturer Leo Frank was railroaded on a charge of raping and murdering one of his employees after a turbulent trial that roused the ugliest passions of racism and anti-Semitism that Georgia had ever seen. The case became a newspaper sensation. My father, though still one of the most junior members of the bar, lent a local hand to the defense, as aide to several eminent imported Eastern lawyers, including the distinguished Louis Marshall. When, to no one's surprise, Frank was convicted, my father had the bitter assignment of carrying that word to Frank's wife. Then Frank was seized and lynched by a raging mob, who had the shamelessness to have their photographs taken standing proudly beside the dangling body of the innocent Frank. There followed in Atlanta one of the worst pogroms ever known in an American city, an unpleasant reminder of the Russia from which the Boorstin-Boorstein brothers had fled. My mother's brothers then owned a men's clothing store in Atlanta, whose store windows, like those of other Jewish merchants, were smashed in the aftermath of the Frank case. The prospects were not good for a young Jewish lawyer interested in politics.

Meanwhile my father had married my mother under legendary circumstances. She had come down from New York City to visit her brothers in Atlanta. The handsome and promising Sam Boorstin began courting the attractive Dora Olsan from the "East." The society section of the *Atlanta Constitution* carried a picture of the pretty visitor with the story of a dinner held at the hotel in her honor. Governor Slaton was present, and at the end of the dinner he arose, offered a toast, and said, "Sam Boorstin, if you don't marry that beautiful girl, I'll see that you're disbarred." Sam married Dora.

The Frank case impelled my mother's three brothers—along with my father and the husband of her sister—to leave Atlanta. They went to Tulsa (then still pronounced Tulsy), Oklahoma, a frontier town in what only nine years before had still been Indian Territory, set aside for the so-called Five

Civilized Tribes. In 1916 Tulsa had few paved streets and fewer paved sidewalks. My three uncles opened a bank, and the husbands of the two sisters tagged along, with Kate's husband joining the bank. My father opened a law office, slightly separating himself from the family, and he soon became one of Tulsa's most energetic boosters.

After settling in Tulsa—which my mother despised (and never stopped despising)—my father never really took a vacation. He made a few business trips, and once came to England to visit me when I was at Oxford. But he thought Tulsa was a good enough year-round place. Meanwhile, my mother (usually with her sister) left town at the first crack of summer heat, usually to go to Atlantic City or some other resort.

It is still hard for me to understand—much less explain— my father's love affair with Tulsa. He thought, or at least said, it was the greatest place on earth. In fact, Tulsa was a frontier village translated into the architecture and folkways of the 1920s. With endless prairies stretching around, there was no good reason for skyscrapers. Still, Tulsa built the Philtower, the Philcade, and the Exchange National Bank Building which cast their twenty-two-story shadows across the barren plain. That was where I first understood the American booster's defense against critical overseas visitors. "No reason not to boast, just because the great things have not yet gone through the formality of taking place."

As for culture, there wasn't much. Only a Carnegie library, the annual visit of the Metropolitan Opera Company—heavily sponsored by the best lady's "ready-to-wear" clothing stores— and Kendall College, a Baptist missionary school to which none of the wealthy local citizens sent their sons and daughters.

My father joined in the manic optimism for the future of Tulsa, which soon called itself "the Oil Capital of the World." Oil was mother's milk to all of us raised in Tulsa. And the gambling spirit infected my uncles, who played for, and won and lost, fortunes in oil. Would their next well be a "gusher" or a "dry hole"? Was it possible to open a new "oil field" on this or that farmer's land? This was the adult jargon most familiar to me.

While my father was a booster for Tulsa, he never became an oil gambler. Instead he became a species of lawyer now nearly obsolete. He was a lone "general practitioner." He never had a partner (my mother never would have tolerated it!), but through his office came a stream of young lawyers just out of law school whom he trained in the old apprentice style. They adored him, but found him difficult to work for. Many of them became district attorneys and judges, or founded prosperous law firms that far outshone him. He had his own way—his *very* own way—of doing everything. This included the way you use an index, the way you hold a pen, the way you talk to clients. Each of these apprentices stayed for a few years and then went on—much wiser in the law and how to practice it, but relieved at not being told how to do everything. I personally suffered more than once from my father's insistence on doing things his way. After I had been shaving for many years my father still insisted on my running the razor *against* the grain of my facial hair, as "the only way to get a close shave." His golf lessons, offered in a warm spirit of paternal helpfulness, made me hate the game, and I've never gone near a golf course since.

My father would have been happy to see a "Samuel A. Boorstin and Son" shingle outside his office, and to that end he really hoped I would go to the University of Oklahoma. My mother's insistence that "only the best" was good enough and that I must "go East" to Harvard helped save me from all that.

Still, my father's law practice was exemplary for those who believe that the law is a public service profession. The big money was in oil, and he had a share of corporate oil practice. But what he enjoyed most, and talked about most, was his "general" practice. This was more like the work of a village curate than that of a city lawyer. He was especially proud of the occasion when he saved a hapless girl from disaster. He prevailed on her mother not to seek annulment of a quickie marriage until several months had passed—and so ensure the legitimacy and the financial provision for the baby he wisely suspected to be on the way. This despite the mother's and the girl's protests that "nothing had happened." There were countless occasions when he prevailed on irate husbands and wives not to go for a divorce. And there was the time when he helped secure the acquittal of one of his clients on a murder charge for shooting a rival merchant on Main Street.

As a prominent Democrat he was naturally the best general counsel for the *Tulsa Tribune,* an outspoken, violently rightwing Republican daily. He defended the *Tribune* against numerous libel suits, and despite their provocative and belligerent postures, he never lost a case for them.

He never got rich in the practice, but he had one profitable piece of good luck. A representative of Amtorg (the Soviet oil combine), who had come to Tulsa to improve his knowledge of oil-well technology, was run over by a truck and had to spend weeks in a local hospital. My father took his case and won one of the largest personal-injury verdicts on record in Tulsa until that time. The damages awarded were in the neighborhood of $75,000. This was by far my father's biggest case—which still gives me a warm feeling for the Soviet Union. But from a family point of view there was a price to pay. I don't think my father ever told my mother how much of a fee he had received in this case. But I do remember my mother's frequent question: "Whatever happened to all the Kapalushnikov money?"

My father's law office was a piece of Americana. The place of honor went to a pen-and-ink drawing of a mythical judge representing the Majesty of the Law—which my father had me trace from a picture that impressed him—and a photograph of the justices of the hallowed Supreme Court of the United States. On the walls and under the glass on his desk were mottoes, uplifting aphorisms, and lines of verse. The most poignant message (and now the most obsolete) in those days of breachof-promise suits was the framed commandment: "Do Right and Fear No Man; Don't Write and Fear No Woman." There were some Edgar Guest poems and Kipling's "If—" in an ornate version printed by Elbert Hubbard's press. And then: "When the One Great Scorer comes to write against your name—He writes—not that you won or lost—but how you played the game." His favorite modern literature was Elbert Hubbard's "A Message to Garcia."

My father still seems to me to have been the most unmercenary man in the world. He took cases because he thought he could somehow help someone. He never pressed for his fees, and took cases without thinking whether the client could ever pay him—which of course infuriated my mother. He also loved to give gifts, and never worried about the cost. There was a particular kind of loose-leaf address book bound in leather which he thought (and insisted) that everyone should use. If a celebrity came to lecture at Town Hall, afterward he would send him one of these books and try to begin a correspondence. Each address book must have cost over ten dollars and they added up. He treasured the letters of acknowledgment he received from the celebrities, which he pasted in a book and showed to visitors to his office.

His law practice required a good deal of reading—in the extensive law library which he maintained in his office at considerable expense. He invited other lawyers—especially the young ones just beginning—freely to use this library, which must have been one of the best and most up-to-date law libraries in town. His nonlegal reading was myopically focused. If he found a book that he really liked he would give it Biblical status. One particular biography of Judah P. Benjamin—the first professing Jew elected to the U.S. Senate (1852; 1856), who held high office in the Confederate States of America and at the end of the war emigrated to England, where he prospered as a barrister—caught his fancy. He never failed to refer to it whenever any question of history or literature arose, and pressed me to read and reread it.

He was an early champion of gummed and printed name stickers and Scotch tape, which he affixed to everything—books, golf clubs, hats, tennis rackets. He could never understand why I preferred the pristine book. This was only one expression of his love of gadgets, his booster faith in the next way to do anything, including laxatives and the latest electronic belts and exercise machines to cure all ills. As an optimist he was a ready victim for visiting book salesmen and their multivolume subscription sets, often in "simulated leather." I remember particularly the unbroken (and mostly unopened) sets behind the glass doors of our living-room bookcase, which included the Works of Theodore Roosevelt, the World's Great Orations, Beacon Lights of History, and the speeches and writings of the notorious atheist Robert G. Ingersoll.

My father's enthusiasm for Robert G. Ingersoll did not interfere in the least with his public stance as a Jew. We were members of all three Jewish synagogues—the Orthodox on the impecunious North Side and the Orthodox and Reform synagogues on the prosperous South Side. My father was active in the Anti-Defamation League and in various inter-faith activities. But I can never remember his presence at a religious service. Very different from my paternal grandfather was my mother's father, who lived with us for many years and was scrupulously Orthodox. Jacob Olsan went to "shul" every day, did no work on Saturdays, and was the reason for our maintaining a kosher kitchen with a separate set of dishes for Passover. The status of Jews in Tulsa was curious. For Tulsa was a headquarters of the Ku Klux Klan, which was responsible for burning down the Negro sections of town in one of the worst race riots of the 1920s. The Klan had no patience for Tulsa Jews, but the Jews somehow paid little attention to their gibes. My father and his Jewish friends looked down condescendingly on them and their like as a bunch of "yokels."

I don't know how much life in Tulsa had to do with it. But just as my father was totally without vice—he never smoked, drank, or to my knowledge womanized—so he was an irritatingly tolerant man in his opinions. I could never get him to express an adverse or uncharitable judgment on anyone—including the Klan bigots and the rising Nazis. He always tried to make allowances for why people did what they did. He was a living example of how immigrant mobile, westward-moving Americans wore off the edges of their convictions—how the West saved some people from bigotry but provided a fallow ground for bigots. I will never forget his contagious enthusiasm for the novelties of American life, and for the undocumented halcyon future.

HARVEST HOME

by David Bradley

David Bradley is the author of two novels,
South Street *and* The Chaneysville Incident,
*which was awarded the 1982 PEN/Faulkner
Prize. He is professor of English at Temple
University.*

Thanksgiving 1988. In the house my father built
my mother and I sit down to dine. A snowy cloth and ivory
china give wintry background to browns of turkey and stuffing
and gravy, mild yellow of parched corn, mellow orange of
candied yams. Amidst those autumnal shades cranberry sauce
flares red like flame in fallen leaves, and steam rises like scentless
smoke. Head up, eyes open, I chant prefabricated grace (Father,
we thank Thee for this our daily bread which we are about to
partake of . . .) and long for the extemporaneous artistry of my
father, now almost a decade dead. His blessings—couched in
archaic diction ("Harvest Home," he called this holiday) and
set in meter measured as a tolling bell—were grounded in a
childhood in which daily bread was hoped for, not expected;
his grace had gravity, unlike this airy ditty I now mutter.

Still, it seems there is even in this doggerel dogma (. . . May
it nourish our souls and bodies . . .) an echo of his voice. Hope
flutters in me, rises as I come to the end (. . . in Jesus' name
and for His sake . . .), then hangs, gliding in the silence, as I
pause and listen. My mother sits, head bowed, patient and
unsurprised; for nine years I have paused so, just short of

"amen." What I wait for she has never asked. And I have never before said.

Once there were more of us. For once we were a mighty clan, complete with house and lineage. As we are dark (and sometimes comely), outsiders might expect us to trace that lineage to Africa, but we have benign contempt for those who pin their pride to ancestries dotted by the Middle Passage or *griot*-given claims to Guinean thrones. For what is Africa (spicy groves, cinnamon trees, or ancient dusky rivers?) to a clan that knows, as we know, the precise when and where of our origin: on March 10, 1836, in Seaford, Delaware. Then and there a justice of the peace named Harry L-something (the paper is browned, the ink faded, and ornate script all but undecipherable) certified that a "Col. man by the name of Peter Bradley" was henceforth a freedman. This Peter was our progenitor.

Outsiders might wonder that we do not fix our origin in 1815, the year of Peter's birth. The reason: the slave laws— what oxymoron that!—decreed that a bondsman had right to neither property nor person. Peter could not own a family, for he did not own himself. But on March 10, Peter's master gave Peter to Peter for Peter's birthday; this not only made him, legally, his own man but entitled him to purchase a (black) woman. He could have owned her, and any children he fathered on her. But he did not. Peter wed a free woman; thus the two sons he sired were free from the moment of their birth. But Peter, by that time, was not. For after being given by his master to himself he gave himself to his Master, and became a minister of the gospel.

Such service became a clan tradition. Both Peter's sons became ministers, licensed by the African Methodist Episcopal Zion Church, the first denomination organized by American blacks who chafed at the unequal opportunity offered by the Methodist Episcopal Church. One son was "M.A."—we do not know his full name, or date of birth. The other was Daniel Francis, born in 1852. Through him our line descends.

Daniel Francis became a minister at the age of nineteen. Although we know nothing of his early assignments, we are sure that they were plentiful, for Zion Methodists followed the dictate of John Wesley that ministers should never stand long in any pulpit, lest they become too powerful. And we know that the Presiding Bishop eventually sent him to Williamsport, Pennsylvania, where he met Cora Alice Brewer. Though in those rigid times, Daniel Francis, at forty-four, would have been called a confirmed bachelor and Cora Alica, at twenty-seven, old enough to be called a spinster, love blossomed into marriage in 1896. The first fruit of the union was a man-child, John, born in 1898. A daughter, Gladys, followed in 1900. More sons, David and Andrew, were born in 1905 and 1906, after the family left Williamsport for Sewickley, Pennsylvania, outside Pittsburgh.

The house came in 1911, when Daniel Francis, who had been reassigned at least five times since Williamsport, was sent to a church called Mt. Pisgah, in the town of Bedford, in the south-central part of Pennsylvania. As Mt. Pisgah had no parsonage, Daniel Francis went ahead of the family to find a place to live. On the train he met a man named Bixler, who offered to sell him an eleven-acre homestead two miles west of Bedford, near the hamlet of Wolfsburg. The price was steep (seven hundred and fifty dollars), the terms usurious (one hundred dollars down, one hundred per year plus annual interest and a widow's dower), but Daniel Francis found both price and terms acceptable, perhaps because there were no other terms at all. And so, in the spring of 1912, our clan took up residence in our first permanent home.

But Daniel Francis did not see the Wolfsburg property as just a home. In early 1915 he announced plans to create what the local weekly, the *Bedford Gazette,* called a "an attractive summer resort for those of his race who will gather here from Pittsburgh and Western Pennsylvania." His future plans called for the building of a "large tabernacle for divine services, lectures and entertainments" and in time a normal school for the education of black craftsmen modeled on Tuskegee Institute—Booker T. Washington, Daniel Francis told the *Gazette,* had promised to come to Wolfsburg to speak. Although Booker T. Washington never did appear, a camp meeting was held in August on a sylvan portion of the homestead (christened "Green Brier Grove" in printed advertisements) and the next year a loan from the Bedford County Trust Company liberated the deed from Bixler's clutches and brought Daniel Francis's dream closer to reality. But Zion Methodists, like Wesley, feared empire-building pastors; later that year the bishop kicked Daniel Francis upstairs, appointing him Presiding Elder, the spiritual and financial manager of a group of churches in Pennsylvania and eastern Ohio.

But though the promotion killed a dream, it established our clan's mark of achievement: a successful son is he who follows in his father's footsteps and goes a step further. And though it forced us once again to wander, we never forgot the homestead. Somehow we made mortgage payments. By 1921 the homestead was ours, free and clear. A year later we returned to it. It was not, however, a joyful repatriation. On October 15, 1922, Daniel Francis died of "diabetes mellitus." His first son, John, now at twenty-one our chieftain, paid one hundred dollars for a funeral and secured a permit of removal. We escorted the body of Daniel Francis back to Wolfsburg, he to be buried in Mt. Ross, the local Negro cemetery, we to live.

The homestead did not long save us from wandering. Bedford, which to Daniel Francis seemed prosperous enough to support even black ambitions, soon proved capable of supporting few ambitions at all. White youths who wished to do more than sell hats to each other had to leave, if only to get higher education. Black youths, regardless of ambition, were virtually exiled; Bedford had no place for blacks skilled with pens rather than push brooms, and its small black community offered opportunity for exogamy. Some blacks made do. Bradleys do not make do.

And so we dispersed. Gladys married a man named Caldwell and settled in Cleveland, Ohio. David finished high school, won a scholarship, and went South to college. Andrew, after graduation, attached himself to the local Democratic party—a quixotic alliance, as Bedford blacks were fewer and less powerful than Bedford Democrats—and then went east to Harrisburg, the capital. John, who supported the clan until Andrew's graduation, married and settled in Sewickley, and fathered three daughters. But though we dispersed, the homestead remained—a haven in time of trouble, a gathering place for feasts, a totem signifying that, though we were wanders, we were not Gypsies.

That is what it signified to outsiders. And so it was that in 1956, our clan's one hundred and twentieth year, the *Gazette*, by then a daily, found our clan of local interest. "The rise of the Bradley family from the enforced degradation of slavery to dignity and high achievement is not unparalleled in the history of the American Negro," wrote reporter Gene Farkas. "But it is certainly one of the more outstanding examples of hard-won Negro accomplishment in the nation and the state. In the annals of Bedford County, the story of the Bradley family is without precedent . . . for it was from these hills and valleys, from the one-room schoolhouse at Wolfsburg and the old Bedford High School . . . that the Bradley boys emerged to eminence and respect."

Cosmopolitans and outsiders would have said that it was Andrew who had risen highest; in 1954, he became State Budget Secretary and the first black to sit in the Pennsylvania Governor's Cabinet. But local interest, and perhaps a sense of our clan's traditions—he even used the phrase "the footsteps of his father"—caused Farkas to give more space to David, who in 1948 had been elected an AME Zion General Officer—a step beyond Daniel Francis's final rank of Presiding Elder. Though his new duties called for travel, he was free to fix his base where he chose; David purchased land adjacent to the homestead and built what Farkas called "a modern stone bungalow," in which he housed both his own family and Cora Alice, who spent her days in the spartan familiarity of the homestead but at night enjoyed the sybaritic comforts of indoor plumbing and central heating.

Farkas did a good job for an outsider. Although he did not specifically mention another of David's contributions to the clan, that he alone of the third generation sired a son to carry on the name, the photographs that accompanied the story did depict the lad, David Jr., then six. And though Farkas did give short shrift to John, not mentioning the names of his wife and children (as he did with David and Andrew) and referring to his occupation with a euphemism (". . . he has worked for a private family for 25 or 30 years"), in this he only reflected the values of outsiders; men who hold advanced degrees and cabinet posts are commonly deemed more noteworthy than those who held rakes in "private" service. Farkas cannot be blamed for this affront to our dignity. How was he to know that the man so slighted was the chief among us? For the tale as Farkas told it was the tale as we told it to him. Sadly, it was the tale as we were telling it to our children. Except at Harvest Home.

Even when I was too young to comprehend a calendar I knew Harvest Home was coming; I could tell by the smell of my grandmother, Cora Alice. Usually she spent her days in the old homestead crocheting, reading the *Gazette,* and listening in on the party line. But the week before Harvest Home she abandoned leisure, stoked up her big Majestic coal stove, and got busy baking: tangy gingerbread, golden pound cakes, and pies of pumpkin, sweet potato, and mince. In the evening she would come back to the house my father built perfumed with molasses and mace, and I would crawl into her lap and lick surreptitiously at the vestiges of brown sugar that clung to her upper arms. The night before the feast she would not return at all. That would be my signal; I would sneak to my window to keep watch on the homestead a hundred yards away. At last I would see a sweep of headlights. I would press my ear against the gelid glass and listen. The sounds of car doors slammed, greetings shouted, would not satisfy me—I would stand, shivering, until I heard an odd and mighty booming. Then I would know the clan was gathered.

The next afternoon would find us in the rear chamber of the homestead, arrayed around a dark Victorian table with saurian legs and dragon feet. To an outsider the order of our seating might have seemed to loosely reflect Fifties customs—most of the children placed at a separate table and all the men at the main table, while the women served. In fact, it reflected our deep reverence for name and blood. The segregated children had the blood—they were of the fifth generation—but had it through their mothers; none had the name. The women who served—including Cora Alice herself, who, although she presided over the gathering, did so from the sideboard—had the name by marriage. The only woman at table not of the blood was my Uncle Andrew's wife, Gussie, who made it clear she waited on no one. She also smoked and drank in public. (My grandmother had declared her mad; she was left alone.) My cousins—the women of our fourth generation—although they'd lost the name through marriage, had the blood and so had seats. Their husbands had seats only as a courtesy to the chief of a related clan—once a husband tried to displace his wife; Cora Alice took away his plate. The men of the third generation had both blood and name, and so had seats of honor. And I too had a seat of honor: a creaky chair, made tall with cushions, set at the table's foot. For I was David, son of David, the only male of the fourth generation, the only hope for the continuation of the name.

I, of course, did not then understand why I alone among the children had a seat at the table. But I was glad I did. For

when all closed eyes and bowed heads to listen to my father
bless our gathering in fervent baritone extempore, I could raise
my head and look down the table, a virtual continent of
sustenance—Great Lakes of gravy, Great Plains of yams,
tectonic plates of turkey slices thrust upward by the bulk of
the bird itself, which rose like Rushmore. But in the place of
the visage of Washington or Lincoln this Rushmore was
crowned by a huge dark head with massive jowls, pebbly with
beard, a broad flat nose, a gently sloping forehead, grizzled
brows: the visage of our clan chief, my Uncle John.

Uncle John was titanic. Below his head was a neck thick
with muscle and a broad chest, powerful and deep, on which
his huge hands prayerfully rested, the fingers like a logjam.
When the food was duly blessed the jam burst. For Uncle John
did not eat—he fed. His plate—actually a spare meat platter—
was filled and refilled with turkey, potatoes, and stuffing all
drenched with tureens of gravy, and garnished with enough
corn on the cob to fill a field—once I counted a dozen ears
lying ravished by his plate, and always I watched his trench
work with apprehension, convinced that one day he would
explode.

He made all the noise of an explosion. He did not talk—
he roared. He roared with jokes—always corny and often in
poor taste—and aphorisms—"You can live forever if you don't
quit breathin'!"—and responses to conversational gambits—
once Uncle Andrew twitted him about his shabby clothing.
"Rags to riches! I ain't rich yet!" Uncle John roared, off and
on for the next twenty years. Mostly, though, he roared with
a laugh as big as he was, so concussive it subsumed all ordinary
vibrations. Halfway between a boom and a cackle, Uncle John's
laugh was like a bushel of corn husks rustling in a hundred-
gallon drum. It was not precisely a pleasant sound, but to me
it was a Siren song—or perhaps the call of the wild.

When I was small I would leave my place as soon as I
could to go and stand beside him. He would be busy devouring
dessert—quarters of pie, one each of pumpkin, sweet potato,

mince—like Cronus consuming his children, but would catch me up in the crook of his arm and balance me effortlessly on his knee, where I would sit in greatest contentment, remarkably unoffended by his smell—sweat, smoke, and bay rum (which he used for no good reason, since he rarely shaved). When I grew too big for that I would simply stand beside him while he finished eating. Then we would go to kill his car. He didn't call it that, of course. He termed it "blowing out the pipes" and claimed that without it the car—a spavined station wagon—would never climb the mountains between Bedford and Sewickley. But to me, at six or seven, it seemed like bloody murder.

From the back of the wagon he would take a quart jar of kerosene—he called it "coal oil"—and give it to me to hold while he started the engine, raised the hood, and removed the air cleaner. Then he would take the jar and begin to pour the coal oil into the unsuspecting intake manifold. The engine would pause in shock, then sputter, bark, and bellow at the same time, while from the tail pipe issued gouts of greasy black smoke. Meanwhile Uncle John poured more coal oil into the carburetor, his expression like that of a father administering foul-tasting medicine to an ailing child. When the jar was empty he would leap behind the wheel and pump the throttle; the engine would scream and thrash madly on its mounts, while the smoke from the tail pipe would take on bile-green overtones and show tiny flicks of flame. After a while Uncle John—at some clue known to him alone—would stop pumping. The engine would rattle, almost stop. Then the kerosene would clear through the cylinders; the grateful engine would settle into a smooth, fast idle, and Uncle John would smile.

Years later I marveled at all of this, not because the car survived it, but because we did. For it took no mechanical genius to see that we had toyed with tragedy, that that abused engine could easily have exploded, covering us with burning fuel, shredding us with shrapnel, generally blowing us to Kingdom Come. And I marveled that, even had I known that then—which I of course did not—it would have made no difference. Because then—and now—those dangerous pyrotechnics seemed a fitting prerequisite for what followed. For when the smoke showed clean and white I would sit beside Uncle John as he gently blipped the throttle—helping, he said, the pistons settle down—and recounted chronicles of the clan.

Clan history was nothing new—I heard it every day. But what I heard daily were parables, intended to indoctrinate me with the values and courage that had let us rise up from slavery. At Harvest Home, Uncle John told a different story—unpretentious, earthy, human as an unlimed outhouse. Cora Alice told me about Daniel Francis, after the barn was struck by lightning, burning his hands in the steaming ashes as he searched for nails with which to rebuild. Uncle John told me about my grandfather misjudging the dosage when he wormed the mule. David told me about the Christmas Eve when he, knowing his family was too poor for presents, asked for nothing and cried himself to sleep—but woke to find a hand-carved train, three walnuts, and one incredible orange. Uncle John told me about the time my father had the back of his pants gored by a roving bull. My grandmother and father told me of the glory of my people. Uncle John told me that we *were* people. This was vital. For it was something we were forgetting.

On Harvest Home 1957 I was drummed out of my clan. My crime was lying—a peccadillo, outsiders might say, especially as all children tell lies occasionally, some frequently. But I lied almost constantly, even when there was nothing to be gained. My father said I'd rather crawl up Fib Alley than march down Truth Street; this drove him crazy. For he believed a sterling reputation was some shield against the sanctions society—both American and Bedford County—could bring to bear on a Negro male. He was proud that we were held in high repute and feared what would happen to me—to all of us— were our name to lose its luster because of my lying. He announced that he would break me of it.

But he did not realize how good a liar I'd become—so

good I took him in. For a while I told him many obvious lies, let him catch and punish me. Then I tapered off. Catching me less often, he assumed I was lying less. But on that morning he discovered . . . well, I don't recall exactly what he discovered; some silken web of half-truths I had been spinning out for weeks. He confronted me, hard evidence in his hands, hot fury in his face.

Corporal punishment was not his way. His cat-o'-nine-tails was a Calibanian tongue wetted with Prosperian vocabulary, his lashes sad scenarios starring the local sheriff. That morning he seemed so angry I expected J. Edgar Hoover to make a cameo appearance; I could not imagine what salt he would rub into the wounds—I doubt the usual "thou shalt never amount to anything if thou keepest this up" would suffice. But he was too angry for anything like the usual treatment; he simply looked at me coldly and in a frighteningly quiet voice said, "Bradleys don't lie."

That statement rocked me. For I knew—at least I thought I knew—that it was true. My grandmother did not lie. My father surely did not lie. In the Church he had a reputation for truthfulness—and was in some quarters hated for it. His historical writing was marred by a concern for literal truth; he wouldn't say that two and two were four unless he had a picture of both twos and did the arithmetic three times. And God knows he preached what he saw as truth, and practiced what he preached. So I believed him when he said Bradleys did not lie. But I also knew that I did lie.

On any other day the conclusion of the syllogism—that I was not a Bradley—would have disturbed me. But that day was Harvest Home. I sat in my favored place, accepting accolades and choicest bits of feast food—the heel of the bread, the drumstick of the turkey—that all thought were my due, as sole heir to the name, but I knowing in my heart I had no right to them. I could barely eat.

Later, in the car, I only half listened to Uncle John's chronicle, wondering if I could ever explain to him that I had no right to listen at all. But in the midst of my dilemma I detected a variation from an earlier telling. "Wait," I said. "That's not what you said before."

"No," he said easily. "But don't it work out better this way?"

"Well, yeah," I said—and it did work out it better—"but it's not the truth."

"Oh yeah," he said. "The truth. Well, truth is funny. Because you never know it all. So you end up makin' things up to fill in the blanks. Everybody does that. But some folks always makes things up that's make folks sound good, make things sound clean and pretty. Trouble is, the truth usually turns out to be whatever makes the most sense. And if you think you got the whole truth, if it don't make sense, you better make a few things up. And even if you're wrong, it makes a better story." He paused, looked at me. I can't imagine what was on my face—amazement, probably, to hear the head of my clan drumming me back into it as firmly as I'd been drummed out. "Now don't you dare ever tell your daddy I said that," he admonished. And then he sent his laughter rustling and booming around the car.

It is interesting to speculate what would have happened if the *Gazette* had done a follow-up on The Bradley Family Twelve Years Later. By 1968 Andrew had served a second term in the cabinet and served there no longer* only because the Democrats had lost the Statehouse—he remained a force in the Party, and had had influence with both the Kennedy and Johnson administrations. He had also followed in at least one of Daniel Francis's footsteps, becoming a trustee of Lincoln University, an institution originally dedicated to the education of blacks. David, meanwhile, retraced his father's footsteps even as he stepped beyond; still a General Officer, he was rumored to be a strong candidate for Bishop, the highest office in the Church, and also preached at Mt. Pisgah, which was now too small to pay its own pastor. David Jr. seemed poised to follow. A senior in high school, he had been admitted to the University of Pennsylvania and awarded several national scholarships. Occasionally he too occupied the pulpit of Mt. Pisgah. Such facts could have led a reporter to believe the Bradley family was still upward bound, might even have caused him or her to see a rising track in tragedy; though Cora Alice had died in 1960, her funeral was resplendent with dignitaries: two ministers and a Presiding Elder of the AME Zion Church, and—the Democrats were then still in power—several state cabinet secretaries and the governor himself. Had such a story been done—it wasn't—the reporter might have written that, after a hundred and thirty-two years of freedom, the Bradleys continued to rise.

To say that, though, the reporter would have had to ignore clippings from the *Gazette* itself—a 1962 story describing the destruction of the Bradley homestead by a fire, a photo of the ravished house, its windows like blackened eyes, its clapboard siding stripped away, revealing underlying logs. But to be fair, few reporters would have seen the fire as metaphor. Fewer still would have explored the implications of the fire's aftermath: that for months the house stood unrepaired; that the eventual repairs were minimal; that they were financed by a note co-signed by only David and Andrew; that money to repay the loan was to come from rental of the homestead—to whites. And none, probably, would have understood that the *Gazette*'s account of Cora Alice's funeral reiterated an ancient insult. For although the second paragraph noted the careers of David and Andrew, the clan's chief was not mentioned until the final paragraph, and in passing: "She is survived by another son, John Bradley of Sewickley."

I was only nine when my grandmother died, and so recall little of the pomp and circumstance that surrounded her death. I do recall the lavish spread of ham and turkey and covered dishes brought by neighbors to assuage our grief. I recall that Uncle John ate little. And I recall that at the end of the day I stood beside him on my father's lawn while he looked sadly at the homestead. "I guess that's that," he said, and turned away.

And I do recall my grandmother's final Harvest Home. I remember overhearing my elders in council. The only items on the agenda were her failing health and her refusal to give up her days in the homestead. It was moved and seconded that Uncle Andrew take her to Harrisburg to see a specialist. During discussion the opinion was stated (loudly) that no doctor could cure the fact that my grandmother was ninety years old, but the countermotion ("Let her live the way she wants until she dies") was ruled out of order. The motion carried on a two-to-one vote. Council was adjourned, *sine die*. I remember the meal itself—the mood: heavy, the food: dry, the laughter: absent without leave. And I remember how quiet Uncle John was as he watched my father and Uncle Andrew get my grandmother settled in Uncle Andrew's Chrysler. Mostly I remember how, after my grandmother was driven away, Uncle John went to work with coal oil and a vengeance; I can still hear the sounds he tortured from the engine, the fan belt screaming, the valve lifters chattering like dry bones, the exhaust bellowing like nothing known to man.

Mostly I recall the burning of the house. For if our homestead was once a totem, was it not a totem still? Was not the burning a harbinger of greater doom? For months I would go, sometimes in the dead of night, and circle the hulk of our homestead like a satellite in orbit, pulled down and thrown up simultaneously. In daylight I would peer into the now exposed basement, full of detritus, alive with rats, in darkness sniff the scorched and rotten timber, seeking a message in the rubble and the stench. And when the house was lost to me—repaired and occupied by people my grandmother would have dismissed as poor white trash—I sought a message in the keepsakes of our clan—chipped photographs, browned bills and deeds, yellowed newspaper clippings. When I combined those mementos with my memories I found discrepancies. And when I thought about what made most sense I found a devastating truth: Bradleys did lie.

Most of our lies were common cover-ups of minor moral failures. Others drove to the heart of our history—it seemed doubtful, for example, that Booker T. Washington had ever heard of Daniel Francis. But no lie was as destructive as the one we'd told about my Uncle John.

There are many ways to say it. Then, when clichés were new to me and irony was *terra incognita,* I would have said that Uncle John was our black sheep. Now I say he was the nigger in our woodpile, proof that though Bradley blood flowed in dreamers, power brokers, and preachers, it also flowed in a hewer of wood, a drawer of water, a man content to work in service all his life. This embarrassed us, especially as he was not the least among us; he was the first. And so, while we did not deny him, we denied him his place. We allowed outsiders to see him as a minor footnote to our grand history. And then, made bold by headlines and column inches, tokens Society respects, we had forgotten the rules by which a clan exists and survives. Our junior elders—my father and Uncle Andrew—had rebelled against our rightful leader. This, I decided, was the message of the burned boards and beams of the house of Bradley. Our house had fallen because we had fallen away.

I did not want to fall away. For the years between the burning and my graduation were hard, lonely, desperate years. I needed my people. I needed my clan. I needed my chief. And though I despaired that we had fallen too far from our ways, I hoped that we had not.

I hoped hardest when those years were ending, when to the world outside I seemed poised to take my clan to greater heights. I feared those heights. And so, on the night of my commencement, as my class assembled for its final march, I stood quietly despairing. They chattered about parties and graduation gifts. I wanted only one gift: the presence of my chief. I doubted I would get it. I had sent him an invitation, but Uncle John was almost seventy and Sewickley was more than a hundred mountainous miles away. To make it worse, a violent thunderstorm was raging. Only a fool would make the trip.

But as we marched up to the auditorium door I saw him standing outside the hall, his threadbare coat and tattered sweater soaked with rain, his eyes searching for me in the line of robed seniors. "Who's *that?*" one of my classmates whispered. "My Uncle John," I said. In that moment he saw me. And even in the auditorium they heard, over the pounding of the processional, his booming, rustling laugh.

On Wednesday, September 26, 1979, the *Gazette* recounted the tale of Bradley clan much as it had in 1956 as part of the page-one obituary of the Reverend David H. Bradley. The burial at Mt. Ross Cemetery would be private, but, later, friends would be received at the Louis Geisel Funeral Home. Memorial services set for the next day, the *Gazette* anticipated, would be appropriately impressive; two AME Zion bishops— mentioned by name—were scheduled to appear. Among the surviving family was listed "John, of Sewickley."

Uncle John was too ill to attend the burial or memorial service, but I prevailed upon the husband of some cousin I did not recall to drive him to the wake, even though his legs were too weak to carry him inside. And so I saw him for the last time when I sat beside him in the car.

He seemed small, shrunken. He joked, but feebly, and when I teased him about the new clothes he was wearing he said, "Rags to riches! Guess I'm gettin' there," but with no force behind it. And he did not even try to laugh. That depressed me, to be honest, more than my father's death, for it told me that my uncle's death would not be long in coming. The death of a father causes grief; the death of a chief causes fear. I was especially fearful. For when he died the chieftainship would descend to me. I was not ready. I was not worthy. And so I sat beside him and cast about for something that would conjure up his laughter.

Inside, I told him, there were two wakes, in adjacent rooms. In our room there was no casket—we'd buried my father that morning. But in the other, in a grand, flower-bedecked coffin lined with crinoline, a rail-thin ancient white lady was laid out. Bedford being a small town, many visitors paid respects in both rooms. Seeing this, the undertaker, to make things more convenient, had opened the doors between the rooms. This caused no problem—until some of my father's ministerial colleagues arrived. Although ignorant of the specific arrange-ments, they knew just what to do on such sad occasions. Gliding as if on casters, they went to my mother and murmured comfort, then came to give me that two-fisted handshake of condolence before moving on to their next target: the deceased. When they saw no casket they did not panic—they said more comforting words while shaking their heads in sadness, their eyes covertly scanning. Eventually they locked onto the casket in the other room and launched themselves in that direction.

"I should have let them go," I told Uncle John. "But I just couldn't. So I said, 'Gentlemen, please don't go over there. Because if you do you're going to think he suffered a lot more than he did.' " I laughed, hoping that he would laugh too. But his reaction was but a polite chuckle. "Damn," I said. "I should have let them go."

He looked at me and smiled. "Well, don't let it bother you, son. Next time you tell it, you will." And then he did laugh. Not long, but long enough. Not loud, but loud enough.

He died nine months later. I did not attend the funeral. It would have been too quiet. Oh, there would have been sound aplenty—slow hymns, generous lies, even laughter—

of a sort. But it would not have been his laughter, a laugh that could shake the earth. And hearing other laughter would have made me know that he and his laugh were gone.

I will never be made to know that, I've decided. I have the right to that decision, for I am clan chief now. I do not have all the wisdom that a chief needs, but I have come to understand some things. I understand that the hypocrisy and hubris that brought our house to ruin were inevitable dangers. For any fool could see that black people in America could not rise on wings of doves. To even think of rising we should have quills of iron, rachises of steel. Of course, we do not have such mighty wings. And so we stiffen our pinfeathers with myths, flap madly, and sometimes gain a certain height.

This my clan did. We told ourselves good stories, said we were destined for the skies and launched forth. It worked. We rose. But as we rose we learned that flight is a risky and temporary thing, that there are powerful downdrafts in American air. Our solution was simple: don't look down. That worked too. But it brought us to another danger; we lost contact with the ground.

We were not wrong to dream of rising. Nor were we wrong to keep our eyes fixed ever upward—we did not make the air so treacherous. We were wrong because we ceased to listen for the echoes from below. This, I have decided, we will do no longer. We will rise no further until we do. And so I pause and listen, each year at Harvest Home, as now I pause and listen, while the steam rises from the cooling feast food and hangs accusing in the air. My mother grows impatient; I hear her chair creak with shifting weight. And it comes to me that I could lie about this. Could say I heard laughter booming, or heard, at least, an ancient echo. But truth makes a better story. And so I say, "Amen."

THE "F" IS FOR FASCINATING

by Mary Higgins Clark

*Mary Higgins Clark was born in Manhattan and
grew up in the Bronx and is the author of a
number of best-selling mystery novels, among
them* Where Are the Children? *and* While My
Pretty One Sleeps.

On our first date I asked Warren Clark what his
middle initial "F" stood for. Without batting an eye he
answered, "Fascinating." Two hours later over a nightcap in a
Greenwich Village pub he began scribbling names on a cocktail
napkin. At my surprised expression, he said, "I'm making a
list of the people I'll have at the wedding," then added, "Now
don't get all girly and cute. You know we'll be great together."

I had just begun a new job as a Pan American stewardess.
Warr completed his proposal by saying, "You can fly for a
year. Get it out of your system. I'll take my mother to drive-
in movies."

That was April 29, 1949. He was twenty-nine. I had just
turned twenty-one. We were married on December 26. It was
a day of gale-swept rain. Rather than arrive at the church
looking like a drowned rat, I waited for a break in the torrent
before rushing for the car. I was twenty-two minutes late. As
my brother handed me over to my intended at the foot of the
altar, Warr's romantic question was: "What kept you?"

We had five children in rapid succession and lived merrily
together until his death fifteen years later in 1964.

When I was asked to contribute to this collection of memoirs I knew it was time to write about Warr. But a dozen false starts later I was positive I wouldn't capture what I wanted to tell about him. The piece couldn't be maudlin. He was far too much fun for that. Even now when his name is spoken by family or friends, the immediate reaction is a burst of laughter. And so I studied some of the glittering remembrances other people have written about loved ones to see if I might get some ideas.

He led his class in every subject every year.

That wouldn't do at all. Warr was one of the brightest human beings I've ever known but his school record was totally undistinguished. His final mark of 17 in the chemistry course at Fordham Prep was in his opinion a sign of remarkable generosity on the part of the professor. "When those equations starting showing up on the blackboard, I looked up the movie schedule," he'd explain. "I hated the smell of the lab. My Bunsen burner exploded and I figured I'd do everyone good by staying out of the way."

In Spring Hill College, the Greek professor looked over the IQs of his students and tapped Warr for his class. He *did* enjoy Greek.

A war hero, he came home covered in glory.

Warr was in service for five years but never got overseas. He was in the first peacetime draft just before Pearl Harbor, washed out of pilot training because of a slight color blindness, spent the next sixty-one months in various units, and emerged sporting a good conduct medal. From what he told me, I know he was intensely disappointed not to get in the thick of the war as many of his friends had been but with that remarkable cheerful philosophy accepted what was beyond his control. When others told war stories, he talked about defending the domestic shores of Kentucky, Oklahoma, New Jersey, and Iowa.

Remember the war movies with the joyous reunions of soldiers and their loved ones during the war? The sighs, the brave smiles, the tearful embraces? One afternoon when Warren had not been home for over a year, he was given an unexpected holiday leave and decided to surprise his family. He arrived home when the house was empty, stashed his bag and himself on the floor behind the living-room couch, and fell asleep. Always a sound sleeper, he never heard his mother, father, and younger brother come home. They were in the midst of dinner when he rose from his hiding place like the phoenix from the ashes and nearly gave his parents joint heart attacks.

The Donald Trump of his day, his rise in the business world was meteoric.

Well, as a matter of fact it wasn't. After the service, Warr took a job selling silver flatware to prospective brides. He explained the sales pitch to me. "You open the case slowly. Reverently you pick up a fork. This finger here . . . this one there. You hold the fork up to the light so the gal can see the pattern. *You* gaze at it. Your eyes get moist. You murmur, 'Lovely, lovely.' "

He stayed with that job for about a year and for the next two years did not get around to returning the box of samples. Finally, when the letters became truly insistent, he took the sample box to the national meeting of the silver industry which was being held at a Manhattan hotel. He addressed the box to the president of his company with a note thanking him for the opportunity of selling his lovely, lovely silver.

His next job was as a salesman for American President Lines. That was where he was working when we met. The problem was that even though he was a born salesman there were no commissions and the pay was minimal. As he explained: "The side benefits are great. We can take a round-the-world cruise first-class every couple of years if I stay here. The only trouble is, I won't be able to afford to tip the steward."

His office was elegant and wonderfully located, fronting Fifth Avenue at Rockefeller Center. As he pointed out, another unremunerative benefit was that it was a great place from which to view the St. Patrick's Day parade.

Warr quit American President Lines a year after we were married. Unfortunately he took the first job offered him, selling hearing aids. The sales pitch made the job seem like a combination of humanitarian philanthropy and glittering commissions. "We have the names of hundreds of people who need to be shown how much their lives can change with proper hearing. You can bring that knowledge to them. Your commission will be fifty dollars for every aid you sell. Ten, twelve, fifteen units a week is not too much to expect as your immediate goal."

That kind of money, five hundred-plus a week, was a fortune in 1951. Besides, it was nice to have a position where you could help someone. With my enthusiastic backing, Warr took the job. Our first sign that something might be amiss was when he came home with a mortar and pestle, a one-burner heater, a jar of wax, and some lengths of string. What he had not been told was that he would be the one to take a wax impression of a potential buyer's ear. Remembering his chemistry experience, we tried to conceal our uneasiness. Obviously he had to practice taking wax impressions, so I became his subject. Marilyn, our firstborn, was then six weeks old. I would sit on the couch feeding her while Warr placed his equipment on a tray and began experimenting. "Try not to move," he'd caution as he stuffed my ear with globs of melting wax. After the wax hardened, he would pull the string and in theory a perfect impression of my ear would be made. It seldom worked. It was particularly interesting the evenings when his mother and mine would come down to adore their new granddaughter. Both sat with worried expressions, not wanting to interfere. About the third time she witnessed the event my mother said, "I'm just afraid that maybe your hearing might become affected, Mary."

I looked around, trying to seem bewildered. "Is someone whispering?" I asked plaintively.

We knew that both grandmothers were casting apprehensive eyes on the baby in my arms. *He wouldn't try taking an impression of her ear, would he?* The unspoken thought was practically a shout. When Warr said, "Okay, now it's Marilyn's turn," her two watchful guardians almost ripped her from my arms.

That job lasted about six months. The "hundreds" of leads turned out to have a common address, St. Raymond's Cemetery. The prospects who were still exercising the privilege of breathing already had hearing aids. The device Warr had been given to test those aids and show how inefficient they were bordered on fraud. In almost every case new batteries did the trick. He sold exactly one hearing aid, to a man who did honestly need the device, then turned in his burner, mortar, pestle, wax, and strings. "I guess I'm job hunting again." *Death of a Salesman* had just opened. At the end, Willy Loman, the salesman, dies. Warr whispered, "Do you think I should apply for his job?"

Soon after that he went back to the travel business, where he'd always belonged. At the time of his death, he was regional manager of Capitol Airways, one of the first charter lines. Afterward they told me, "He was irreplaceable. Three different men might do his job but no one single man can be that effective." I remember a specific example of what they meant. Because of engine trouble a charter flight was twenty-four hours late in departing overseas from La Guardia Airport. Someone phoned the newspapers and the *Daily News* ran the story: "distracted passenger weeps, 'I've waited twenty-four years to see my brother and now this.' " Warr read it and said, "And the old biddy couldn't wait another twenty-four hours." It was the kind of problem that usually cost an airline an account. But to the travel agent who'd booked the flight, and called in a fury, Warren said, "Come off it. We put those passengers in good hotels. Most of them never saw the inside of a hotel in their lives. They ate and drank on us for twenty-four hours." They all developed a taste for lobster and Johnnie Walker Black. When it was time to round them up for departure, we practically had to call in Pinkerton. We found one of them asleep in the laundry room. The one who screamed the loudest was so plastered she got on the plane barefoot." He and the travel agent went out to lunch and Warr came back with bookings for a dozen more groups.

He was a husband and father beyond comparison.

Now we're getting warm. Warr was a husband and father beyond comparison, but not by today's standards, whereby the mother and the father share the shopping, the housekeeping, the diaper changing. There was no such thing as the Lamaze method in our childbearing years, and even if there had been, I suspect Warr would have been among the missing. Marilyn was born thirty-eight years ago. In those days, the husband delivered his wife into the dark recesses of the hospital's obstetrical area and was sent home to get a good night's sleep. "First babies take a long time," the nurse chirped cheerfully to my better half. "A man needs his rest."

It was a long, hard labor. The following morning, when my well-rested spouse returned, there was still no end in sight. The doctor decided to bend the rules and allowed Warr to keep me company. He came into the labor room, obviously worried but determined to be cheerful. I was experiencing three-minute labor pains with thirty-second intervals. Warr sat there about fifteen minutes searching for comforting words. He found them. During one of the respites he said brightly, "Well, at least, *it doesn't hurt between the pains.*" I pulled myself up on one elbow. "Out!" I ordered. The following year when Warrie was born, it was another long siege. Once again Warr was sent in to be my comfort. That time he came in shuffling a deck of cards. "How about a hand of gin?" he asked hopefully. Once again I pulled myself up on one elbow. "Out!"

He offered to get up for the two o'clock feeding but the offer was as far as we got. When Marilyn was about six weeks old, he said, "Look, you're tired. All you have to do is heat the bottle, change her, and I'll take over." I took him at his word. The baby changed, the bottle heated, I tried to awaken the man I called my sleeping beauty. After ten minutes of hard work I succeeded. I handed baby and bottle to him and gratefully fell asleep. A few minutes later, I was awakened by an insistent wail. Warr was fast asleep, the baby in his arms and the bottle dripping somewhere near her ear. Muttering to the saints, I fed our firstborn and put her back in her crib.

The next morning Warren told me about waking up a couple of hours later and realizing that the last thing he remembered was holding the baby. "I started feeling around the bed for her," he said. "I was afraid of waking you up. Then I got down on my hands and knees and started feeling around the floor and under the bed. Finally, I knew I had to look in the crib. If she hadn't been there, I was planning to get dressed, tiptoe out, and disappear."

He wasn't a mother's helper but he was a wonderful father. He taught his children the gift of faith, the gift of laughter, the gift of generosity, the gift of taking life as it comes and living it with joy while it lasts. A natural athlete himself, as they became older he became involved in their sports. He was manager of the boys' Little League team, the kind of manager men are supposed to be. He wanted his team to win, but no matter how talented or untalented, every kid played in every game. His exasperated exchange with Fausto Moraglio, recently arrived from Milan, who struck out with awesome consistency, became town folklore. Warren said, "Fausto, I'm going to have you deported." Fausto hooted with laughter. "Mr. Clark, what makes you think they'll take me back?"

His wife had a dream and he encouraged that dream.

Well, we'll have to give that some thought. As soon as we were married, I told Warr that I wanted to start taking courses, that I just had to become a professional writer. His concern was genuine. "Honey, you're very smart, but you haven't even gone to college. I've known Ph.D.s who are banging their heads against the wall trying to get published. Sure, take any courses you want. Just try to think of writing as a hobby. I don't want you to get your heart broken."

No one was more delighted than he when six years later I began to sell short stories. He went around bragging to one and all but I never let him forget the "think of writing as a hobby" line. Whenever the news of a sale came I'd call his office and ask his secretary to say, "Mary Higgins Clark is on the phone." My first one-thousand-dollar sale was to *McCall's* magazine one week before Patty, our fifth child, was born. While in the hospital I read that the entire fiction staff of *McCall's* had been fired. Warren's comment was: "Maybe it's because they're buying such lousy fiction."

It was eight months later that the chest pains began. For three weeks we blamed it on a strained muscle. He had helped a neighbor pull out the stump of a dead tree. But the uneasiness that had been creeping into my subconscious sounded alarm bells. Warren looked far too tired at the end of the day for a forty-year-old man. Maybe there was a real problem. Unwillingly I remembered something he had told me when we were engaged. He had said, "When I was twelve, a feeling came over me that I wouldn't have a long life. I believe that's going to be true."

I insisted Warren see a doctor about the "strained muscle." Tests followed. He got the results one morning on his way to work. He was told that the arteries leading to his heart were almost totally clogged; that the pains he was experiencing were severe angina; that it was a miracle he hadn't had a fatal seizure when he strained to pull out the tree stump; that down the road there might be surgery for his condition but now he must consider himself a likely candidate for a heart attack. Always have nitroglycerin tablets in your pocket. Never run for a bus. Don't carry a heavy suitcase. Don't roughhouse with the children.

On a separate visit that day I heard the same news. That night when Warren came home from work, the kids jumped all over him, the baby crawled to him, and I held out the cocktail I had waiting. We toasted each other. Whatever time we had left, we'd make it great.

He was an inspiration to all who knew him.

Now we're on target. Three heart attacks in the next five years. Always the nitroglycerin tablets in his pocket. And the sense of humor never stopped. "I don't worry about you," he'd say when we talked about the future. "You could be in rags in Detroit at midnight and by sunup be well dressed with a hundred bucks in your pocket and you would have done it honestly. Just one thing. Don't be a blooming widow. I mean, try to look real gaunt." No one loved life more and no one was more graceful in living it and leaving it.

Warr hated to see me wear black. When I bought a black dress he would ask if I was planning to attend a funeral. After that final, fatal attack, in his honor I wore black for nearly a year, knowing that in his eyes I would look anything but blooming.

He is always with us.

Yes, he is. It will be twenty-five years since he is gone. The children are raised. But it has always seemed as though he walked with them. Three years after his death, when the boys were in high school, they came home obviously delighted with themselves. Their explanation: "Dad would be so proud of us. We took aptitude tests today and in mechanical ability we both came out untrainable."

The two oldest, Marilyn and Warren, are lawyers. As young children they had heard their father say, "You know, after the war I just didn't want any more regimentation. But if I hadn't been in the service five years, I'd have gone to law school." I believe that influenced their decision. All five, Marilyn, Warren, David, Carol, and Patty, have inherited his quick, sunny wit.

The Bible offers the prayer that we live to see our children's children. Like everyone who has lost a loved one too soon, I play the game "if only." How he would have loved to see the children grown. How he would have enjoyed the grandchildren. How much fun it would have been to share my success as a writer with him. But what joy it was to live those years with him, to have these children and grandchildren who are blessed with his genes.

We shall meet him in the hereafter.

I certainly believe that. St. Thomas More's last words were: "We shall merrily meet in heaven." When I get there, I'm going to listen for the sound of laughter. Warren F. (for Fascinating) Clark will be in the midst of the merriment. Our reunion will not be that of Heathcliff and Cathy racing toward each other on the moors. Much more likely, he'll drape an arm around my shoulders and ask me the same question he asked when I arrived at the altar of St. Francis Xavier Church twenty-two minutes late all those years ago. "What kept you?" will be his greeting to me.

A FOUR-BLADE CASE

by Clyde Edgerton

Clyde Edgerton is the author of Raney, Walking
Across Egypt, *and* The Floatplane Notebooks.
He lives in Durham, North Carolina.

I t is a Sunday morning, and he's coming to *visit*.
He's driving through in his tractor-trailer truck on the way to
New York, from Florida, where he lives. He can stop for only
an hour or so. My mother, who is his sister, has reluctantly
agreed that the family may stay home from church for his visit.

It's 1949. I am a five-year-old boy, an only child. I live
with my parents in a small house in rural North Carolina.

His giant tractor-trailer truck is now parked a short way
from my house, down in front of the community store. I walk
the distance with my parents, and there he stands near the
truck, talking, laughing, a toothpick in his mouth. Uncle Bob.

He sees me, picks me up, sets me on his shoulders, and
starts walking around the truck, talking to me. His undivided
attention is mine. Uncle Bob's undivided attention will always
be different from that of other adults, because it will exist in
a context of adventure. Here before me is a tractor-trailer
truck: a dinosaur beast. And it belongs to him. My blood kin.
He, my Uncle Bob, drives it.

Now he is sitting with me, and only me, up in the cab. He
has his hand on the gearshift and is explaining how it works.
He's doing this for me alone; only I am with him. He talks to
me about the inside of this cab *as if I were a grown man*. He

pulls back the curtain up behind the seat and there, right there in the cab, is a bed—where the driver sleeps when he is away from home. The fact that someone could be away from home, sleeping warmly and comfortably in the cab of a truck, is almost more than I can imagine.

Back on the ground, he talks and laughs with a brother, sisters, in-laws. He has narrow shoulders, but he's tall and sturdy. There's a tattoo on his forearm. He turns and looks at me, while saying to my mother and father, "How about if I take the boy on up to New York. He can sleep with me in the cab. I'll have him back in two days."

My heart leaps up into the sky, where it loops, rolls, spins.

Mother and Father look at each other.

"We'll have to think about that," they say.

The conversation changes. I see something called New York in my mind—a strange place with tall trees. I will ride in that giant truck and then at night I will sleep up in that cab—in the bed behind the seat—far away from home, safe with Uncle Bob.

I almost drown in a deep, sweet lake of anticipation.

He's preparing to leave. The conversation comes back to me and the trip. My parents have decided.

I cannot go.

We hold to vague, yet powerful perceptions about certain long-past conversations, even after the exact words are forgotten. Hearing a tape recording of one of those conversations probably would not change our perception—the feeling left by the conversation—regardless of what the words really were. We would trust the feeling over the words. Such a conversation took place after Uncle Bob drove off without me that day in 1949. And during that conversation, someone said, "You can't be sure about what Robert's hauling." In the air—and left with me forever—was a feeling of lawlessness about the trip. Clearly my parents thought the trip would be dangerous. I couldn't imagine how that might be so.

Years later, Uncle Bob told me something that explained, in part, my parents' reluctance that day in 1949. Starting in 1941 he had hauled nontaxed whiskey up and down the East Coast in his truck. He was paid two dollars a mile. In 1944 he abruptly retired from that line of business, bought some land on Highway 301 just north of Ocala, Florida, put some money in the bank, built a store and home, and settled there with his fourth wife and his daughter. He was forty-eight. I was born that same year.

Uncle Bob stayed in the trucking business for a few more years, hauling fruit and vegetables only. In the meantime, he turned his store and land into a combination café–bar–grocery store–service station–trailer park called Martin's Corner Trailer Park. Years before—I was not to learn why until I was grown—he had changed his name from Robert Ridley Warren to Walter Clarence Martin.

After settling down in Florida Uncle Bob wrote to my father, telling him that some of the best quail hunting in the world was within driving distance of Martin's Corner. Uncle Bob owned several bird dogs and a jeep equipped for hunting. Yearly Christmas pilgrimages to Florida began—my parents and I visiting Uncle Bob and his family.

Soon I was old enough to go hunting with my father, Uncle Bob, and Uncle Bob's hunting partner, Clarence Bethea. First, without a gun. Then, when I was twelve, with a gun. The traditions in my father's family—and in my mother's—were that a boy was allowed to start hunting with a shotgun at age twelve. I was no exception. The hunts, in a jeep and on foot through pine and scrub oak woods, with English pointer bird dogs, usually on a 25,000-acre ranch (posted) near Ocala, Florida, were the source of story after story I would tell to my friends in North Carolina as soon as I got home.

These hunting trips stand in my memory like gold. Two elements of the hunting trip ritual, especially.

First, the way Uncle Bob woke me up in the mornings. I would have gone to bed early the night before, excited, knowing that the next day would bring on the dogs, the jeep, shotguns, woods, the hunt. But night had to pass first. I would fall asleep, and then in the dark of the early morning I would feel through the covers a hand around my foot. I would awaken, move, lean up onto my elbows, and in the darkness hear Uncle Bob say, "Time to go, boy." That hold on my foot—gentle, patient, waiting for me to wake up—is something I often think of now when I wake before light. It seemed important to him not to jar me awake—to hold my foot as long as it took—before bringing me the best news in my world: "Time to go, boy."

The next part of the ritual is Uncle Bob cooking breakfast in the kitchen over in the store—bacon, eggs, grits, and toast. He cracks an egg in the frying pan and begins singing, "I with I wath an apple, a-hanging in a tree, and every time my Thindy pathed, she'd take a bite of me." Then he says, "Come here, thun, take your thoothing thyrup." He is becoming his favorite uncle, Uncle Alfred, who died seventeen years before I was born, who always spoke with a lisp, and who was a family favorite. Uncle Bob cooks in silence for a minute, sings a bit, and then says again, "Come here, thun, take your thoothing thyrup." Silence. "Come here, you little thun of a bitch!—and take your *thoothing thyrup!*" Uncle Bob is Uncle Alfred, singing at breakfast, calling one of his children in to take their "soothing syrup." Then he laughs and says, "Ah, Lord, what a dandy he was. All them children, and when he whipped one, he'd whip them all—to be sure he got the right one. I do think about him often. He'd be coming in from the field, and he'd say, 'Muh [Nora, his wife], Muh, put on the coffee.' And then that coffee would be just a perking up a storm. You'd hear it going *blu-lup, blu-lup*"—here Uncle Bob turns and looks at me and gets the sound just right, *blu-lup*—"and he'd pick up that pot of coffee and sip it right out of the spout. I seen him do it many a time. You might not believe that, but it's a fact. I seen him do it many a time."

Uncle Bob might then tell another Uncle Alfred anecdote—all the while cooking and serving breakfast—perhaps about Uncle Alfred and the red-eye (white lightning), or maybe the one about Uncle Alfred and the fire poker, or Uncle Alfred and the revival meeting. The very same stories over and over and over. I got to know Uncle Alfred better than most of my living uncles.

I'm glad Uncle Bob was unconcerned with "redundancy" and told those stories over and over. I never tired of them. They were about someone in my family, and thus also about me. In defining my family's history, Uncle Bob was defining me. Without him and his stories, I would be different than I am.

He was the best storyteller I ever knew. He would look me in the eye and go to talking, describing with beautiful, simple metaphors (". . . and that hawk had a wingspread wide as that stove over there"), using his hands, raring back to laugh before he bore in again, taking me down finally to the end of a story about Uncle Alfred, or Aunt Etta, or maybe about his Uncle Burke, or his father—a man named Israel and called "Izzy"—or maybe a bird-dog story about Old Joe, Leaping Lena, or some other dog he owned or once owned. He told me stories when I was six, or eight, or ten, told them with no less emphasis and relish than when he told them to me thirty years later.

There was a summer trip to Ocala when I was fourteen.

Confidence that I would be safe in Florida with Uncle Bob and Aunt Berdena, my parents let me ride the train—the Silver Meteor—from Raleigh, North Carolina, to Ocala.

Uncle Bob put me to work. But oh no, a thousand times no—no, it didn't seem like work. It seemed like one grand adventure after another. He let me "pump gas" for his customers—take their money and make change. He let me drive his jeep over from his house, across a side road, to the store and back. He let me cut the grass around the store and trailer park with his new riding mower. It had a rotary blade under a large, round, flat metal cover, handles like a garden tiller, and a seat which was pulled behind like a cart pulled by a horse. Driving it was a joy. And I still remember Uncle Bob's warning. He was sitting behind the bar in his store, rolling his own cigarette—with one hand, as he liked to do, showing off. He said, "Watch out on the turns now, or one of them handles will catch you in the balls." This was not the language of grown-ups I was used to, and I loved it, remembered it, and though I was not surprised by it—Uncle Bob was a master of unparliamentary language—I marveled that such language could be spoken by my own blood kin.

That summer, while I visited, Uncle Bob and I cleared the overgrown, weedy lot behind his house. First a chain was looped around the back axle of the jeep. Then the ends of the chain were fastened around a small sapling or wild hedge. I would be behind the steering wheel—a fourteen-year-old boy in love with cranking and driving an automobile, if only for five feet. Uncle Bob would stand behind the jeep and at the proper time yell, "Hit it." With my tongue through my lips I'd give it the gas and pop the clutch. The jeep would lurch forward and up would come the tree. We worked off and on for several days. I wouldn't have been happier driving a bulldozer. When we finished and the lot was clear, Uncle Bob said, "You tell your daddy you were driving the jeep, pulling up trees as big as your arm."

One morning that summer, before light, Uncle Bob came and held my foot. "Time to go, boy." We were going fishing on the Silver River—the river that fed Silver Springs, the tourist attraction. He explained that he had "fishing rights," but that if we heard a boat coming we should reel in, place our rods out of sight inside the boat, and become sightseers.

He had taught me to cast with an open-faced reel the day before, and then had given it to me, along with an old rod.

We were on the river before dawn. As it became light we started fishing. Uncle Bob took a pork-rind tail from a little jar and attached it to his lure, then showed me how to do it. "That'll make it smell so good they can't resist it." Soon it was light enough to see the lure beneath the surface of the clear water—and after the cast, as I reeled in, I'd see several bream following along behind it before one rushed to take it. We fished for half a day and caught fifty large bream and two small bass. I remember the numbers because back home in North Carolina I told my friends all the details, over and over.

I still hear my uncle's voice, the cadence, specific words and sentences he spoke when I was a boy. One winter, during a Christmas visit, we had been hunting on posted land all day—Uncle Bob, Clarence, and I. I was around fifteen or sixteen. My father was not along because of his emphysema.

Just before sundown, Clarence, Uncle Bob, and I had driven along a path across a big field. We had finished hunting for the day. The tired dogs rested in back. Ahead, we saw a jeep with two men leaning against it. The jeep was sitting crossways in the path just in front of the gate which led out onto the highway.

"What do they want?" I asked.

"Us," said Clarence, who was driving.

"Why?"

"We been hunting on their land."

"It ain't their land," said Uncle Bob, "but they're supposed to keep everybody off it."

We were approaching the men, driving slowly along the path.

"What do you think, Bob?" said Clarence.

"Well, hell—drive around them."

"Believe I will."

As we approached slowly—as if to stop—the men straightened up, took a step or two toward us. Clarence simply drove around them and their jeep, through the gate, and onto the highway. They got into their jeep and followed us. Suddenly Uncle Bob said, "Pull into that service station, Clarence. I'll whip either one of them's ass with me and him both standing on my coat."

I don't recall being nervous. I knew Uncle Bob would be in charge no matter what happened. I hoped the other men would be as afraid of him as I knew I would be. Apparently they were, for they kept driving down the road, and I've never forgotten Uncle Bob's words: "Pull into that service station, Clarence. I'll whip either one of them's ass with me and him both standing on my coat." One reason I remember, of course, is that I repeated them so many times to my friends back home.

There were other stories to take back home. Another Christmas when my mother, my father, and I arrived in Florida, Uncle Bob's hand was wrapped in a cast. He had broken it on another man's jaw. There was a hole in the counter in his bar, where the man—before or after being hit, I don't remember which—had shot at Uncle Bob, and missed.

There were stories told by others (and still are) of his gold mining in California, of his being in such and such a fistfight, of his driving cross-country in his tractor-trailer truck with a little white dog named Snowball.

But there were also stories with a different feel, a different flavor: stories about the bootlegging, and the business of his changing his name. Voices, looks, words, postures, gave rise to a cloud of mystery, a feeling of hush-hush. Something, some things about him, were not being told. He had been in some kind of trouble—some kind of exotic trouble, it seemed. But this mystery about Uncle Bob only increased my admiration for him. He came to exist among my heroes: Roy Rogers, "Lash" LaRue, the Lone Ranger, Connie Mack Brown, Hopalong Cassidy, Zorro, and Uncle Bob. Later, my pantheon changed—there were Rocky Marciano, Ty Cobb, the Dukes of Dixieland, Ray Charles, Stephen Crane, the Red Baron, Ernest Hemingway, and Uncle Bob. And now: Eudora Welty, Flannery O'Connor, Mark Twain, and Uncle Bob. He's been there all these years because of, and in spite of, what I've come to know about him, and because of the way he laughed with me, wrestled with me, taught me to shoot, fish, sharpen a knife, and drive his jeep, and because of the way he talked to me and told me stories, stories sometimes for me only.

Late in his life, when I was grown, he began to open up to me with new stories about the old days, personal stories. Secrets were revealed—others left concealed. By then I had learned more about him directly and indirectly through stories from other relatives. Some of his new stories I already knew, most of the more personal ones I didn't. He told them all with the same old fierceness, humor, and animation, but in some of these new stories were undertones of rage and regret.

His father died of typhoid in the epidemic of 1911 when Uncle Bob was sixteen. Six weeks later his eighteen-year-old brother died of the same disease. His mother, another brother, and three sisters left their small sharecropping farm in rural Wake County, North Carolina, and moved to town. His mother married a man whom Uncle Bob quickly came to dislike.

He left home, was married at nineteen, but discovered that his wife's child was not his. He left her. He never told me about this when I was a boy—but he told me several times in his later years. Soon after leaving his wife he was working on a chain gang. He never specifically explained the "trouble" he got into, the trouble which led to his changing names, but several times in talking around it he said, "I never killed nobody."

He escaped from the chain gang in almost the same way Paul Newman's character escaped in the movie *Cool Hand Luke*—he told a guard he had to go to the bathroom, hid behind a bush, finished filing through his ankle chains, crawled, then ran, away. Then he went "on the road," into "show business," working county fairs throughout the Southeast. Somewhere along the way he sewed some money into his necktie, drove a Model T Ford across the United States, and mined gold in California. Months later he arrived home on the train with one nickel to his name.

In 1978, when he was eighty-two, he drove his new yellow Nissan pickup from Ocala up to North Carolina for a short family visit. Somewhere along the way he had run over a road sign. Including all the details—how it popped up in front of him, how it sounded when he hit it—he told the story several times.

He also told us all about a small red dashboard light coming on several weeks earlier for no reason that he could figure out. He had taken the truck back to the dealer, he said, and the dealer told him that the light signaled work to be done. Uncle Bob would have to pay money to get the work done, else the light would not go out. Well, he's never heard of such a thing, he told the man. He needed to have a conference with the manager. I could see Uncle Bob standing in the service department at the Nissan dealer's, leaning forward talking to the manager, a fierce confidence, a kind of laughter in his face, refusing to budge from his position. Pay money to get a light turned off! Why, who the hell thought that up? I saw the manager realizing quickly that this was not an ordinary man, that this was one of those exceptional cases he'd learned about in training. We'll take care of it, Mr. Martin. I see your point.

This image of Uncle Bob, of his confidence in the face of a formidable but senseless foe, stays with me, and in a controversy at a college where I once taught, I carried this image into meetings with administrators who, because of a novel I'd written, had decided to withhold my teaching contract. Finding no written grievance procedure, I pressed—unsuccess-fully—for an impartial hearing on the issue of academic freedom, and finally resigned. Along with other friends and family, Uncle Bob, though not physically present, was with me throughout an agonizing three-month struggle.

And besides all he gave me when I was growing up, my knowledge of his energy in old age will serve me well. In 1982, at age eighty-six, he had a severe heart attack. He was on a respirator in intensive care for ten days. Two weeks after being released from the hospital, he was on top of his house, repairing his *roof*.

By then he had long since sold Martin's Corner Trailer Park. He and Aunt Berdena had moved into a mobile home near a lake. He had built rooms onto the mobile home, and then built a garage and shop out back. He often told me that when he ran out of things to do he was going to tear down that garage and shop and then build them again.

During our last conversation, just before he died, we were walking in his yard and he was talking about his shop and his garden. His mind seemed to be coming and going. He kept pointing to a corner of the yard and saying something about "his land." What he said was jumbled, rambling, and had no meaning for me. Then he would again be coherent for a while. It was sad and frightening. I was losing him. He was beginning to slip away.

And then, there in his yard, he suddenly stopped, stood still, and pulled out his pocketknife, his old worn-down, four-blade Case. With it, years before, he'd taught me the skill of knife sharpening. It was one of his main tools. He held it out to me in his hand, a hand I now remember and see as I remember and see a familiar face.

"I want you to have this."

My first impulse was to say no, I have a new Swiss Army knife—it'll do everything. But then I understood what was happening. I took the knife—it felt heavier than it looked—and said, "Thank you. I'll always keep it." I put it in my pocket.

We walked around in the yard for a while longer, talking.

As he always had, he talked straight to me, as if I were an old friend, not just a nephew. Then we went inside. He was tired.

The knife lies now along the top of a ten-by-ten silver picture frame that hangs on the wall beside me. In the frame, bordered by a wide, dark maroon mat, is a business card. Along the top of the card in small letters are the words "Groceries, meats, gas, oil." Along the bottom is "Hwy. 301 North, Ocala, Florida." And in the middle, beneath the symbol of a flying wing, are the words "Martin's Corner Trailer Park."

In one of his last letters to me, filled, as all his letters were, with phonetic spelling, wild metaphors, warmth, sentiment, he said in shaky handwriting, "You no of all the off springs you always was my favorite." He signed that letter "Just old Bob, your favorite uncle." That I was his favorite means mountains to me. I'm glad he knew he was my favorite. And I'm glad I wrote him back and told him that I loved him.

THE MANY MASKS OF
KATHLEEN GODWIN
AND CHARLOTTE ASHE

by Gail Godwin

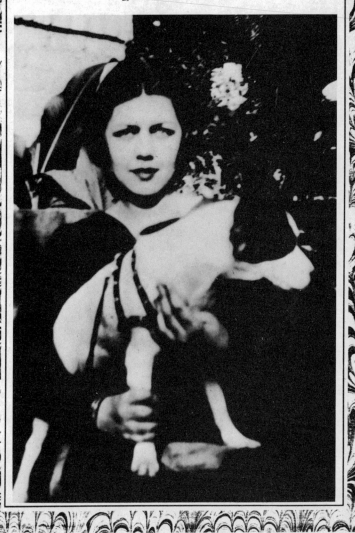

*Gail Godwin is the author of nine novels,
including* The Odd Woman, Violet Clay, A
Mother and Two Daughters, *(all three of which
were nominated for the National Book Award),
and* The Finishing School *and* A Southern
Family, *which won the Thomas Wolfe Award
and the Janet Heidinger Kafka Prize). Her
forthcoming novel is* Father Melancholy's
Daughter. *She grew up and was educated in
North Carolina and now lives in Woodstock,
New York.*

Several years ago, my mother began giving me unusual birthday presents. Wrapped in conventional gift paper, they pose as innocent surprises, but every one of them is capable of detonating. She always gives me two or three.

One recent birthday she must have been feeling especially . . . What's the word I want here? What's the word to describe someone who both stirs things up and plays a deep game? Inciter? Igniter? Provocateur? *Evocateur? Evocatrix?* I like the pun in "-trix," but that still leaves out the aspect of her that always plays her cards close to her chest. That's the trouble. I always leave out aspects when I try to describe this elusive presence I have been studying all my life. "Elusive presence" isn't a bad description. It expresses her contrarieties: always there, but never completely grasped. But that still leaves out so much.

Anyway, one recent June 18 she presented me with a whole box of these time bombs from the past. Inside was a puzzling gold medal for athletics, which took me a while to figure out; I have never been athletic. There was a handmade notebook, decorated with drawings and cutouts, into which my younger hand had laboriously copied out advice from various sources about how to look good and behave shrewdly during a romance. There was a platinum wedding band studded with small diamonds. And a little yellowing pamphlet, *How to Make a Confession,* put out by Holy Cross Press, West Park, N.Y., 1948, in which an eleven-year-old girl in Asheville, N.C., had checked off her sins in the categories conveniently provided by the Episcopal monks. She checked eight out of ten under Pride, none under Idolatry, one under Profanity, two under Irreverence, five under Disobedience, quite a few under Hate, some under Impurity, almost all of the ones under Deceit, two under Theft ("Have you been stingy?" "Have you wasted time?"), and four under Discontent, although she should have checked five. (I know you, little girl. You ought to have checked "Been dejected because of the position, talent, or fortune of others?" We haven't changed all that much down the years, you and I.)

Other items in the birthday box included:

—A brown envelope containing a 107-page Master of Arts thesis submitted to the Faculty of the University of North Carolina at Chapel Hill in 1935 by Kathleen May Krahenbuhl and approved by Robert B. Sharpe, her adviser. Title of thesis: "The Influence of Inigo Jones on Ben Jonson's Masques." (Well, of course she passed. She was a master of masks and masques even then, my mother. People don't change all that much down the years.)

—The December 1945 issue of *LOVE Short Stories.* Its format has been extinct on the newsstands for decades. "Pulps," these magazines were called, because of the inferior paper stock made from wood pulp. On the cover is an illustration of a woman looking out of a window. She is framed by cozy yellow curtains with polka dots in them; there is frost in the corner of the window, and, just outside, a branch of evergreen with a touch of snow. She is pretty in the pert airbrushed style of the time, she is all dressed up, with earrings and upswept hairdo, and it's clear from the dewy eyes and the smile on her heart-shaped mouth that she is expecting Someone any minute to come through the sparkling frost to claim her.

Turning to the table of contents, I see that Kathleen Godwin has a story beginning on page 24 ("Romance for Three"—*means heartbreak for one*) and, looking further down, that Charlotte Ashe has a story beginning on page 82 ("Bride in Hiding"—*a bride ran away from scandal—into the arms of love*). Beside the name Charlotte Ashe has been penciled in "Kathleen." As if I might not remember who Charlotte Ashe was.

When this issue of *LOVE Short Stories* came out, we were living on Charlotte Street, in Asheville. My mother was the most glamorous person I knew. I was not completely sure of her, the way I was sure of Monie, my grandmother, who in our household performed the tasks associated with motherhood while Kathleen Godwin went out in all weathers to breadwin for us like a man and her alter ego Charlotte Ashe concocted the extra romance for two cents a word on the weekends. (One story per author to an issue was the magazine's policy.)

She was more like a magical older sister, my mother, in those impressionable days when the soft clay of my personality was being sculpted. She came and she went (mostly went, it seemed to us two stay-behinds). She dabbed perfume behind her ears and, checking her stocking seams in the full-length mirror, dashed off to her jobs, returning after dark in elated exhaustion, wearing the smoky, inky smells of her larger world.

She brought stories from the different jobs. ("I saw the awfullest thing at the Veteran's Hospital . . ." "Well, Mrs. Wolfe called the paper today, she had remembered something else about Tom, so of course I rushed right over there . . ." "Who would ever have guessed I'd be teaching Spanish? But as long as I keep a lesson ahead of them, no one will be the wiser." "Do you know what that dreadful little Mr.—— had the nerve to say to me?")

Even in this Era of the Working Mother, she would have been considered something of a heroine. Or "role model," as we say now. Up before sunrise. Off to the Plonk School of Creative Arts, where she taught Drama or Poetry or Creative Writing, or whatever the autocratic Miss Laura Plonk, who thoroughly believed in Kathleen's versatility, decided needed teaching that day. Then across town to St. Genevieve's Junior College (English Composition; Beginning Spanish); then grab a quick drugstore lunch (pack of cheese crackers with peanut butter and a Coke with a squirt of ammonia in it) and on to the newspaper, where her regular beats were interviewing wounded servicemen at the VA Hospital out at Oteen; transcribing any and all sudden recollections of the town's famous novelist as soon as they were vouchsafed to his mother; and keeping track of celebrity visitors like Béla Bartók, who was composing his last orchestral work in a boardinghouse on Edgemont Road (and putting into the music the birdsongs he heard outside the window), or Mrs. Roosevelt, who finally succeeded in charming my mother out of her Roosevelt hatred by remembering to ask, every time she visited Asheville, "And how is your little girl, Mrs. Godwin?"

Mrs. Godwin was long since divorced by then, but in her characteristic style was playing her cards close to her chest. "When people ask, I say your father's in the service. It's true. He's in the Navy. The rest is nobody's business." Many years later, she told me, "People still frowned on divorcées then; they were much more likely to give jobs to wives of servicemen."

Or widows. After the war ended, she was obliged to kill

him off. Once he came up from Florida to visit us, and she made us all say he was my uncle. I obeyed, my grandmother obeyed, *he* obeyed—he was very good-natured about it. I remember. I was sorry not to be able to claim him to my friends, because he was so handsome and amusing. But Kathleen was running the show and we all accepted it. She was also the star of the show, in the role of plucky war widow supporting her mother and little girl. Even Mrs. Roosevelt thought my father was dead, so who were we to spoil everything now?

His Navy letters to her were in that same birthday box of explosives that included the *LOVE Short Stories* and my eleven-year-old sins and the athletic medal and her thesis on masques and the wedding band. ("I went out and bought it myself, with my own money. Your father was broke at the time. It might still fit you.")

These selected birthday offerings, I was beginning to understand, were not just a way of cleaning out her closets and divesting herself of outworn masks, or even of doling out to me selected artifacts from our shared past; they were also an art form, and one at which she was singularly adept. They were cunning little stage sets through which someone who recognized the "pieces" could then reenter the past and watch reruns of the old masques being played out in those days. Only now, that same someone would have grown out of the emotional dependencies of her childhood (one would hope!) and was therefore ready to appreciate the masques *artistically,* as interesting embodiments of the human drama . . . could therefore even *enter* the masques, if she liked, and play the parts of the other mummers and see what it might have felt like to be behind their masks . . . and the masks behind *those* masks.

And begin to make all sorts of connections about who these people were, and who she is, and what came from where, and what they all had in common.

My father's Navy letters, written first from a Reserve Aviation Base in Memphis and later from the Headquarters Squadron of Fleet Air Wing Eleven in Puerto Rico, turned out to provide invaluable insights for my later exegesis of the stories by Kathleen Godwin and Charlotte Ashe in the December 1945 issue of *LOVE Short Stories*.

What a threat, you devil, to stop writing me. Sometimes I think you are kind of peculiar, after all. Once I thought that you were just mamma's little girl, but I have about decided differently.

Your letters put me to shame. I just re-read your letter of yesterday and it was snappy and quite cheerful. Your work must be very interesting and I know that is the kind of thing you always wanted to do.

You sounded as though you wish to discontinue our correspondence. If that is what you wish, do it by all means. Certainly I would not care to read your letters if I felt that you were wasting perfectly good time and energy trying to be patriotic and build up morale for the armed forces—that is poppycock.

I want to thank you for the nice long letters you have written me lately and ending them with love. I really hope you are sincere when you end your letters with love.

Dear Kathleen: Sure nuff, honey, apologies for the delay and this is not a letter but only a short message to assure you I am with you always in spirit and body. Have enjoyed the letters but I am not in the mood yet to come out with a wordy epistle. I will not go into detail to explain why I have been off the beam, but you are familiar with those things, having been through Milton's travels some as myself.

I must write you a few lines this morning while I have that peculiar feeling—rather good—as a result of a most pleasant dream about you last night. I have had dreams of you since we parted but they never were quite so pleasant or turned out so well. Of course this one was all away from reality in some respects. We fussed a little and sarcasm flew but all on the surface and then I kissed you and that was *wonderful*. I don't remember having seen Gail in the dream.

The little picture was cunning as hell but you could do better if you would. You are just afraid I will think you are ugly. You don't have to worry about that for you know that I know that you are not beautiful 'cause I always told you that when we were together. But you are sweet and have something maybe—just that invisible, intangible something (a little of it) that is fascinating and by now I'll wager that you have a lot more of it . . .

I just sit and dream about what might have been and then get very unhappy and blue. When you say that you do not say anything to Gail about me because she does not ask anything—oh how that hurts. I am certainly reaping the bitter now. I am glad that you are staying busy and doing the things you like to do. I believe you are happy—and I am glad.

Thus the prevailing tone of the letters. The dominating *tempo,* one might better say. Two mummers engaged in a dance of . . . what? Power? Need? Attraction? Mutual torture? Or a little bit of all of the above? Who are these people behind their masks of pathos and bravado and come-ons and turn-offs? You don't even need her letters to follow the dance. You can deduce her last move and her next move from his responses. I think she was running the show most of the time, but that's not to say she didn't suffer some knocks and bruises ("Not beautiful"!). Who were these two people? They were both pretty agile purveyors of words. They were neither of them novices of masquerade. Each knew how to push the other's buttons and understood the importance of timing to achieve their effects.

But what effects, exactly, were they after? Did they themselves know? Did some strategic misstep cause them to run past each other when they really wished to be together? Or were they after different things from the start?

Let's see what light the stories will shed, those two "love" stories, one by Kathleen Godwin and the other by Charlotte Ashe, in the December 1945 issue of *LOVE Short Stories*.

Reading them carefully, dispassionately, more as a literary critic on the scent of biography than as a daughter with axes still to grind, I have to wonder how they ever made it into this magazine. They aren't like the other stories. They are too complex for the form into which they have been squeezed. There are outbursts of impatience and parody in just the wrong places to sustain the reader's belief in a simple, straightforward love story. Peripheral characters (in particular, older women) seem more genuine than the lovers. There are sly shadings of those devices Shakespeare so reveled in: disguises, mistaken identities, the theme of the Double. There is too much loving attention lavished on details. The writer often seems more interested in metaphor than marriage.

> The three houses in the Alabama town stood like a cozy little group of friends, apart from the rest of the street, with their wide green lawns, spacious terraces and clipped hedges.

That is the opening of "Romance for Three," by Kathleen Godwin. It has been given second place of honor, right after the lead story ("Recapture Yesterday," by Karen Cookson), and a prominent full-page illustration. The illustration features two young women in the foreground: a blond all-American type with a Lauren Bacall hairstyle and a sporty dress, and a dark-haired female with an "upsweep" and à la mode outfit. *"You are the family friend, yes?" Madelon said, her dark eyes flicking from Larry's retreating figure to Nancy,"* reads the caption. In the background on the left, a uniformed man turned away from us in three-quarter profile seems to be hanging up something in a closet just out of sight; in the right background is a handsome dark-haired man in a suit and tie who is concentrating intently on blond Nancy, who is unaware of his gaze.

"Nancy stood before the center house," begins paragraph two of the story,

> looking at her own home on the one side and Dr. David Forsythe's on the other. She waved at David who was sitting on the side

terrace in the late afternoon, lazily reading a newspaper. Then she approached the door of the middle house.

It was silly to feel apprehensive, she told herself, just because Mrs. Winthrop had left word for her to drop by as soon as she got home. She and Mrs. Winthrop were wonderful friends. They had been even before she had become engaged to Larry Winthrop just before he went away. Mrs. Winthrop had been the one who had cookies and lemonade in summer or hot cocoa and sandwiches in winter for three children tired out with play—Nancy, Larry and David.

With admirable economy, the stage has been set. And given the visual aid of the illustration on the facing page, the observant reader can make a pretty good guess as to the parameters of the story. But hasn't reckoned on the wild-goose chase Kathleen Godwin, Master of Arts and Disguises, has in store along the way.

Mrs. Winthrop, the interesting older lady who knows just how to furnish her house, whose graciousness and sympathy enlists us from the first, has sent for Nancy because she has just had a telegram from her son, Larry. He is coming home from the war—but with a French fiancée. He asks his mother to "prepare" Nancy, adding cold-bloodedly, "No use hurting Madelon with what's gone and forgotten."

Mrs. Winthrop, the true lady, breaks the news forthrightly, at the same time letting Nancy feel her own continuing affection. Nancy is shocked and hurt, but when the older woman tries to comfort her, the masque begins. Nancy, telling herself she can't bear to hurt and disappoint *Mrs. Winthrop,* "confides" in Larry's mother that . . . well, actually, Larry has been away three whole years and, in the meantime, she, Nancy, has grown very attached to David. Mrs. Winthrop seems relieved, and, at that moment, Dr. David Forsythe himself drops providentially into the Winthrop living room and, having overheard Nancy's lie, backs her up most generously. Nancy is first embarrassed, surprised, then very grateful to her childhood friend she has always taken for granted. When Nancy and David are alone, they make more elaborate plans to pretend to be engaged in order to save "Aunt Laura's" feelings, though David is put out with Larry for his double-dealing.

The treacherous Larry soon arrives with his fiancée in her smart suit and hat that "simply shrieked Paris." Madelon is a real beauty, but when Nancy, as "the family friend," is helping her to get acclimated, she is touched by Madelon's simple friendliness. The French fiancée squeezes her hand and says it's nice having another girl her age and wants to hear all about *Nancy's* wedding plans.

The two couples double-date a lot. Admirably does Dr. David plays his role as Nancy's lover. He even kisses her in such a way that she has to admit to herself she never felt anything like this with Larry! But Nancy also enjoys being drawn into flirtatious little sparring matches with her old love, Larry. He seems miffed by her "engagement" to David and taunts her that she still loves him. The ambivalence and the sarcasm fly:

> "Dave's my best friend," Larry said. "And you were always my girl. You couldn't change that quickly."
> "It's been a long time, Larry. You seem to have managed to change."
> "But your letters. You still love me, Nancy."
> "Do you think I should?"

(The kind of dialogue I was weaned on, incidentally. Never Reveal Your Whole Hand. Don't Burn Your Bridges. Keep 'Em Guessing! No wonder I made such a mess with those two brothers in high school. While one loved me, I hankered after the other. Only to find, after I'd won the other, and wore his athletic medal as a trophy around my neck, that I loved the first. But it was too late. He had pledged himself to the grocer's daughter.)

In "Romance for Three," meanwhile, David begins to pay more attention to the neglected Madelon, while Larry and Nancy are busy sparring. Who really loves whom in this dizzying postwar masquerade? The dancers whirl faster and faster, knocking and bruising inadvertently or with swift, purposeful jabs, kicking dust into one another's eyes to cover up their feelings. Overcome with sudden affection for her pretend fiancée, Nancy flings herself into his arms, then recovers herself and teases David: "I'm just practicing, you know, to make it seem real in front of the others." Then Madelon, hurt by Larry's neglect, pretends to be falling in love with David, and Nancy, interpreting his kindness to the French girl as reciprocation, realizes her own heart at last and is bitterly unhappy, though she acknowledges she has only her pride, vanity, and fear of being hurt to blame for this whole charade. It takes an attack of angina on the part of the accommodating Mrs. Winthrop to stop the music and sort out the rightful partners. While Dr. David is taking "Aunt Laura's" pulse and the unhappy Nancy is breaking an ampule under that good lady's nose, Mrs. Winthrop says to Nancy, "It took you a long time to learn that David loves you so. I've known it for so long. It was always Larry I worried about because I knew he must find someone else." Nancy has been educated through true feeling, and, lucky for her, Dr. David Forsythe has not left in defeat or disgust, or pledged himself to the grocer's daughter, but has waited patiently for her to outgrow her need for masks and see what has been in front of her face the whole time. Yet he can't resist a last wicked counterthrust of ambivalence just before he puts an end to this masque:

> "Do we have to pretend to be engaged, Nancy?"
> "What do you mean?" she asked, frightened again.
> "Let's make it real," he said, and for answer she lifted her face and her kiss was all the answer he needed.
> It is real, she thought blissfully. Better than any dream.

"Bride in Hiding," by Charlotte Ashe, at the tail end of the magazine, is granted a mere single-column half-page sketch of a pensive girl with a very large shadow. The text of the

story is disrespectfully broken up by full-page ads for engage-
ment rings and skin cream, or flanked with distracting sidebars:
"Reduce or Money Back" . . . "Lilian Russell Knew It: In the
Gay 90's FORBIDDEN FRUIT Liqueur Was the Toast of the
Town" . . . "Learn Nursing at Home" . . . "Hair off Face, Love
at Last" . . . "Thrilling Work Coloring Photos at Home."

"Bride in Hiding" is not, stylistically, as shaped or as sharp
as "Romance for Three." It reads, a lot of the time, as if it was
being dashed off by someone rather weary with the whole farce
of girl meets boy, gets mad, makes up, gets married; someone
whose thoughts keep wandering somewhere else; someone
irked by the necessities of the marketplace: having to remember
to make the girl's fingers "slender and nimble" when they are
arranging books on a library shelf, sick of having to make the
man's white teeth "flash" and the skin around his dark eyes
"crinkle."

Yet there is a dark energy and unsuppressed subversity
about this story that makes it my favorite, even though the
execution is less polished and the happy ending rushed and
unconvincing. This story, if I may detour into simile for a
moment, is like a girlfriend I have admired for a long time for
always being stylish and witty and self-satisfied, who suddenly
passes her hand over her face and, revealing an utterly serious
countenance, announces in a thrillingly rebellious voice: "I am
getting damned sick of this charade of my life, there is more
to me than you think . . . just you wait!" And then she passes
her hand over her face again and the mask of the stylish
sunshine girl is back, leaving me to wonder if I imagined that
brief disturbing vision.

When the reader meets Ginna Lee, in "Bride in Hiding,"
she is working in the Cranfield Public Library, rearranging
books that have been pushed out of place by "restless, seeking
hands." She is fitting the newly arrived daily newspapers into
their long wooden poles when her own picture jumps out at
her from her hometown paper. "Miss Lee Craddock, last seen
at Trinity Church on her wedding day, is missing," the caption

reads. She quickly clips and destroys the offending item and is just replacing the mutilated newspaper on the rack when a nice-looking man with a sunburnt face asks to see that very paper because it has news of the legislature. He has just been discharged from the Army, he tells Ginna Lee (whose real name is Lee Craddock), and is starting up his law practice again. He invites her to lunch, but not before the head librarian, Miss Toppett, has roundly shushed them. Like "Aunt Laura" Winthrop in "Romance for Three," Miss Toppett is the presiding Older Woman of the piece, but whereas Mrs. Winthrop benevolently watched and waited, Miss Toppett wastes no time in warning her new employee off Jim Cranfield, the lawyer. He is already spoken for by Janice Gordon, the banker's daughter, Miss Toppett explains to Ginna. "This is a small town. You are a stranger and don't understand our ways. Janice has waited nearly four years for Jim to return. Everyone expects them to be married."

The requisite Obstacle and/or Misunderstanding has been punctually set in place, according to the conventions of the *LOVE Short Stories* format. Is our poor heroine to be hurt twice, then? For we know, having been inside her head, that she has fallen in love with Jim after one lunch and one evening out, when he has told her, "You are everything a man could dream of or want." And we know that her pride, if not her heart, is still smarting from having been left at the altar by the base Rod, who decided at the last minute he loved Sally better.

Everything gets resolved nicely, of course. Otherwise, *LOVE Short Stories* would have rejected "Bride in Hiding" by Charlotte Ashe. Even the villain Rod reexamines his heart, repents, tracks the runaway Lee Craddock down, and blows her cover. Two men want her, but she wants only Jim. But what about Janice Gordon, the banker's daughter?

Well, Janice turns out to be a peach about the whole thing. But much more than that: if you read behind the masks (and the insider reader knows that Charlotte Ashe, a.k.a. Kathleen Godwin née Krahenbuhl, M.A. in Dramatic and Literary

Subterfuges, is an old hand at such devices), you understand that Janice Gordon is none other than Lee Craddock/Ginna Lee's *other half*. Shortly, Janice Gordon will be off on her own, to fulfill her professional yearnings, leaving Ginna behind to do what everyone expects: marry the GI and settle down.

In the second part of this sneakily unconventional story, Ginna Lee is sought out and befriended by Janice Gordon. The writing devoted to their alliance crackles with an aliveness denied to the mating-dance passages between Ginna and Jim.

"You look so familiar," Janice Gordon tells Ginna. "I feel as if I'd known you always. . . . You've run away from something. Not anything bad, just unpleasant, maybe. I've wanted to run away many times but I've never had the nerve. I want to live in a big city where there is noise and bright lights are shining. I want to study designing."

And then, the tacit exchange:

> Janice looked at Ginna, her dark eyes probing. "Tell me, are you in love with Jim?"
>
> "I've known him exactly twenty-seven hours and thirty-one minutes," Ginna told her, laughing a little to cover her confusion.
>
> "I've known him practically all my life but is that any reason, really, why I should love him more than you?" Janice asked frankly, and then continued without waiting for an answer. "And if something doesn't happen I'll be married to him. Everybody expects it. Then I'll stay in Cranfield all the rest of my life. And I'm too tired to fight it."

The men came back from the war and wanted their jobs. Women, bowing to the pressures all around them ("Learn Nursing at Home" . . . "Thrilling Work Coloring Photos at Home"), retreated behind the polka-dot curtains, put on makeup for their next masque, and waited for that Special Someone to come through the sparkling night and claim them. Kathleen Godwin resigned from the newspaper ("I did not get fired. I resigned because I knew he was going to fire me. There's a difference"). She did not retreat behind the curtains immediately, however, because her skills were still needed. For three years she taught Composition and Romantic Literature to GIs at Asheville-Biltmore College. Several of her students proposed. She finally bowed to the Spirit of the Times disguised as a young firebrand who quoted Freud and professed himself to be an admirer of independent women. They eloped one weekend in '48, and she spent the next thirty-nine years of her life masked as a submissive wife. ("Soon after we were married, he caught me in the bank one day, putting something into my savings account, the savings account my daddy had opened for me when I was a child. And he was so hurt, then angry. He said I had kept this from him and he thought marriage was sharing everything. So I shared most of what was in the account with him, and I didn't put any more into it after that. But I never closed that account. I always left just a little bit in it, just enough to keep it open.")

Charlotte Ashe, that spirited, subtle, troubled creature, discontinued her publishing career. But not by any means did she expire. She sent herself into a sort of creative hibernation at the behest of her other half, who kept shushing her and saying, "Lie down and be good, damn you, and let me get on with this life I have allowed to choose me, with these promises I have made." Yet there were outbursts, again and again. She kept waking up and sending her spirit into Kathleen Cole, wife and mother of more little children. Between the two of them, Charlotte and Kathleen, they produced three more novels, Kathleen Cole taking all the credit, but Charlotte Ashe, that repressed Double who had turned wrathful, managing to ignite and then wreck every one. She put fire and spite and rebellion and fantasy into them and ruined their chances of posing as Uplifting Narratives; her thwarted, pulsing individuality set parts of them aglow like dangerous tumors. Publishers were made uneasy, or offended, or confused. "This is neither fish nor fowl," one wrote. "Take out the steaminess, and we'll try it on a religious publishing house," advised the agent. "Or leave in the steam and take out the religion. In that case, however, you might want to use a pseudonym."

Charlotte Ashe, quite a bit of her, found her way into Gail Godwin. I have learned to recognize her—and to salute her (warily!), that discontented trickstress of multiple disguises, whenever, after thinking I have been writing about one thing, I discover behind it her covert designs.

For instance, to bring this Exploration of an Influence up to date, what on earth possessed me, a year ago, after finishing a long, painful, very much autobiographical family novel told from all the "masquers'" points of view, to embark on a "completely made up" novel in which a little girl, the daughter of an eloquent, moody clergyman and a vibrant, rebellious woman much younger than he, is abandoned at the age of six by this vibrant mother? I was never the daughter of a clergyman; my mother never abandoned me—she still hasn't. (The "real" Kathleen, in fact, finally shed the mask of submissive wife two years ago after it almost choked her to death; she has opened two more bank accounts and, it turns out, has been embroidering for years this most elaborate of new masks which she wears now: a Janus-faced one doubling as Solitary Spiritual Searcher and Involved Community Enabler.)

So, Charlotte Ashe, your current devious designs are making themselves clearer. With whom does this mother in my new novel, this wife of the respected Status Quo, run away? With *another woman*, with a *stage designer*, named—of all things—Madelon.

I didn't realize until I was deep into the writing of this essay just what is going on here. I must let it go on; the new novel is still very much in progress. But what I am doing, it seems, in getting these two women together, even though it destroys the father and splits the child down the middle, is getting something important back together: two warring sides of the same woman.

Wish me luck, Kathleen, Master Designer and Giver of Birthday Presents. Giver of Birthdays. One of these days, if, by hook or crook, we manage to keep all our accounts open, we're going to skin down to our last masks. What will be behind them? Do we really want to know? I think not just yet.

United States Atlantic Fleet
Fleet Air Wing Eleven
Headquarters Squadron

2030 Saturday Night March 27, 1943

. . . Honey, there are pages and pages of things to write you but my index finger is invalid. I caught a big Moray eel yesterday off one of the ramps during one of my interludes and while skinning him my hand slipped and struck one of his teeth or fangs and split the end of it and it is too sore to pound on it too long tonight. That devilish eel fascinated me, tho. He was about 5 lbs. big and 3 feet long and as green as a lizard and I opened him up after he became desperate and choked himself to death, to see what was in him. Sure enough there was my fish which I had on the hook for bait and *his* heart was still beating like everything when I threw him overboard. I took the eel down to the water's edge to wash him off after I had taken out his stomach and I'm a son of a gun if he did not almost get away from me, jerking around. So then I peeled or skinned him up to the head and cut his head off. He had such a big mouth and pretty teeth I decided to skin his head and take what little meat there was off and examine his jaw bones and the hinges on them when my hand slipped and like to cut my finger off. I gave up then and threw his old head over in the grass and thought maybe I would go back sometime and get it after my finger gets well. I will send you one of those nice teeth to put on your bracelet . . .

THE SWEET NECHÁMA

by Alfred Kazin

Alfred Kazin was born in Brooklyn and now lives in Manhattan. He has taught at Harvard, Cornell, Berkeley, New York University, and Notre Dame and is the author of On Native Grounds, A Walker in the City, A Writer's America, *and—soon to be issued—*Our New York *(photographs by David Finn).*

I have never been able to lose the feeling that I was raised not by my actual father and mother but by a pack of women. My mother was a "home" dressmaker in the Brooklyn tenement where I spent the first twenty years of my life surrounded by Russian Jewish immigrants, all of them in the working class. And how everyone worked! Our kitchen, with my mother's old Singer sewing machine in the corner nearest the window, was practically a dress shop. Women being fitted, women waiting to be fitted, women and girls of all ages in various stages of undress, spilled all over our overcrowded little apartment, leaving me with the impression that the world was mostly female. When men appeared, which was seldom, for my father had no friends of his own, they were there to collect the rent or to clatter in with a fresh box of seltzer. Men were definitely less flavorsome than women, lacking in the vital human juices.

In addition to her daily customers, my mother had a following all her own, some relatives, some just friends of the relatives, all dressmakers like herself, and all of them unmarried. They had somehow turned my active mother and our kitchen into the center of their lives. They were forever streaming in, without so much as a pull at the bell (our door was always open), to gossip and drink tea in the one corner of our kitchen not spilling over with dress material, pattern books, empty hangers, extra spools of thread.

Almost any evening my housepainter father, who was shy and silent by nature, easily ruled by my mother, and who was never happier than when he went off at daybreak to paint bridges and subways, retreated with the *New York World* to a corner of the "dining room" (where we never dined), leaving the kitchen, with its steaming female conviviality to my mother, her admiring circle, and me. I was the first "American" child, the pet of the household, forever entranced by so much abundant sweet-smelling female flesh, the shrieks of laughter, the sheen of Polish amber beads all these ladies fancied, the musky fragrance of their face powder, and the rosy Russian blouses that swelled and rippled in terraces of embroidery over opulent breasts.

My parents never chatted easily together, never went off on outings, never laughed or argued together. The life between them was usually silent and quite formal. Whatever her own disappointments, my mother was proud to have married at all; she thought little of her looks, spoke reverently of a beautiful sister left in Poland. I somehow knew that her furious labors at the sewing machine and her many women friends made up for the strangeness of life with my handsome but always silent father. Still, marriage was essential, marriage was *it*. My mother thought it an absolute disgrace, unnatural and unbearable, for a good Jewish woman not to be married. Marriage was the end and purpose of life for a woman.

Insatiable in this as in her work, my mother was the world's busiest matchmaker, proffering advice to Becky or Pauline on how to catch a certain dentist on Sackman Avenue, bringing up alternative candidates. She seemed to keep a

Rolodex in her head of every bachelor and widower still available between New Lots Avenue and Eastern Parkway. She lectured and admonished the ladies with a ferocity that left some in tears.

One of the "circle," however, invariably laughed. This was my favorite, Nechárma Heller, whom I liked to think of as more a relative than she was. She was just a cousin of my mother's, but dear to my mother because they were from the same Polish village, Dugzitz, bordering on White Russia. "*Die zusser Nechárma*," my mother called her, "the sweet Nechárma." We all loved and admired her, but my mother, a little too commanding, would have liked to *be* Nechárma. And I would have liked Nechárma to be my mother.

Nechárma laughed at all this talk of marriage. She *was* married, so to speak. She and her "common-law husband" (this came before "companion"), a master baker named Berl, had certainly lived in a state of marriage for many years. They had three sons, had lost a fourth, Robert, to the terrible flu epidemic at the end of the "Great War." Legally—a constant topic and amazement in our stiffly proper family—they had never submitted to the bourgeois yoke and legal hypocrisy of a marriage ceremony. They were by belief, you might say by profession, Anarchists—rebels and idealists of the most un-yielding kind, so contemptuous of the Jewish orthodoxy that had surrounded them in youth that their sons were not circumcised, had never been bar mitzvahed (confirmed) at thirteen. Anarchists were against the state in every manner and form, against every legal trapping and coercion set up by the wicked capitalist oppressors to ensnare the downtrodden working class. The future, the radiant Anarchist future, was to be made by spontaneous groupings and cooperatives of people, joined "from the heart," as the slaves and victims of capitalism were not.

Such idealistic revolutionary talk—in *our* dress shop of a kitchen!—won me to "the sweet Nechárma," the gentlest of rebels. It was to interest me even in her difficult mate, Berl, the most opinionated and argumentative of men, who invariably sought a political discussion with my father only to crush him. But he was Nechám's mate. They were so heatedly involved with each other as man and woman, as fellow rebels, that they were forever separating, leaving the sons to be boarded with other families. What a thrill this was to me! There was not enough between my parents even to separate them. They did not even talk to each other very much.

Nechám was a certified rebel because she was legally unmarried. More than this, she actually smoked cigarettes, and read not tame Yiddish papers but one rousingly called *The Voice of Free Labor*. "Free" was the word for Anarchists, for Nechám and Berl, for the Haymarket Anarchists martyred in Chicago in 1887, for Emma Goldman, Alexander Berkman, and Prince Kropotkin. Free, to live forever in a state of true human freedom! Nechám smilingly expressed herself in perfect freedom on subjects my mother—and even my timidly "Socialist" father—would never have thought of—women's rights, the thrill of being part of the great worldwide pioneering movement of Anarchism, along with audacious comrades in Spain, Italy, Mexico, and Russia.

No one else I knew, no other woman, above all no other *couple,* seemed to me such *fighters,* so staunch, independent, and brave, as Nechám and Berl. Nechám herself, round and slightly dumpy, looked like every other working-class woman and relative, had that slightly Oriental look around the eyes often found among Russian Jews. Yet in spirit, above all in demeanor, she seemed to me lighter, more humorous, than the other women I knew, beginning with my mother. Although her actual life with Berl was stormy beyond words, and after at least ten separations over the years she insisted on living alone (Berl usually occupying the same neighborhood), she kept an *air,* a detachment, refusing ever to let her sons say a harsh word about their father.

And then there was her name, Nechám, her beautiful Hebrew name, meaning "Comfort," as in the great biblical verse from Isaiah near the opening of Handel's *Messiah:* "Comfort ye, comfort ye my people, saith your God." Nechāma would have denied that God ever spoke at all, that "God" could have said any such thing to "His" people. What a determined atheist she was until her death! What a rebel she remained even in her coffin! She had given strict orders that there was to be no religious service. The funeral home director, shocked at such goings-on, had the traditional lighted candle put at the head of the bier.

As a boy it charmed me that the only vocal atheist I knew had a name—and what a name!—right out of the Bible. This was no Ida or Bertha, Mildred or Yetta. Although she professed not to love the religious tradition, she was part of it for me, just as she had always been part of the great secular tradition of Jewish rebelliousness and concern for life's victims.

Like more famous rebels, Nechāma was actually a child of privilege who had begun her revolutionary career by separating from her own privileges. Her father was a country doctor who was able to provide her with a personal maid. Typically, she spent most of her time in the company of a poverty-stricken family, pained by their meager rations. Her parents had to send the maid to get Nechāma back to them, if only by bedtime. The poverty everywhere around her started her lifelong interest in the working class. Her father even bought a food store for her to manage. Just as she was always giving away her best clothes, so she gave away so much of the stock that it had to close.

Under the Czars, the greatest number of Russian Jews were segregated in a "Pale of Settlement." They had few civic rights, were excluded from the great cities, from higher education, were constantly harassed by officials and the local population. In every political crisis, the government instigated "pogroms," murderous attacks on Jewish settlements.

In self-defense, and inspired by the emerging ideal of a Socialist world without class exploitation in which all nationalities in the Russian Empire would respect each other's cultural autonomy, working-class Jews organized the "Bund," the General Jewish Workers Union. The Bund was officially against all nationalism, even Jewish nationalism in the form of Zionism, but insisted on Yiddish, the common language of most impoverished Jews, over the Russian known only to educated Jews of the middle class.

Of course the young Necháma became an active member of the Bund. The police were soon on her trail, and she escaped to London, where in the East End poor Jewish immigrants worked impossible hours but still had time to ponder the rival appeals of Anarchists and Socialists. In London, Necháma met her fate, the headstrong, eternally argumentative, passionately militant Anarchist Berl Heller. He was a baker by trade, had done time in Czarist prisons, was a zealous political animal perfectly at home, despite his fractured English, in the militant atmosphere of the rising Labour Party, the great mass demonstrations in Hyde Park and Trafalgar Square.

Berl was a passionate man in everything, very fond of the ladies. Before he and Necháma met in London, he had taken up with a lady named Dora. It was typical of the sweet and smiling Necháma that she easily won Berl away from Dora. Typical of Necháma, too, that she made a friend of Dora. In the enthusiastically radical atmosphere of the Jewish East End, it was natural for Necháma to make an alliance without benefit of clergy. The first of their four sons, Robert, was conceived before they left for America.

Everybody was going to America in the first years of this century, or so it seemed. It was a tense, thrilling time. On one record day in 1907, 21,000 immigrants came into the port of New York alone; in one week, over 50,000. The total for the year would be 1,200,000. The United States was living through a "Progressive Era" that would end only with what John Dos Passos called "Mr. Wilson's War." There was a rapidly growing Socialist party, with one representative in Congress from the German workers of Milwaukee and one from the Jewish workers of New York.

Berl had been a baker in Russia and in London, and of course was one in New York, returning home early in the morning from his night shift with a great bag of bread and rolls for his family. Part of my fascination with the Hellers, I have to admit, had to do with Berl the baker, who was as proud of his bread and rolls as he was of his political opinions, though these last underwent as many vicissitudes as his life with Nechúma. There was something about *all* the Jewish bakers I knew in my childhood! What originals! A widow baker who lived a floor above us in our tenement would, on her return from her night shift and just in time for my breakfast, leave outside our door an enormous onion roll shaped like a cart wheel. Nothing in my childhood ever tasted like the bagels, bialys, onion rolls, pumpernickel, and onion rye one bought for a few pennies from the many bakery shops in our neighborhood, the Brownsville district in eastern Brooklyn, far removed from "New York."

Brownsville was almost entirely Jewish up to the Second World War, and was still full of empty land, "New Lots," old farmhouses once occupied by the Scottish farmers who gave their names to the streets before they abandoned the place. Rents were cheap, new apartments always available. My parents managed to stay in the same four rooms for forty years. The Hellers, on the other hand, evoked my admiration, my absolute envy, by managing to move at such frequent intervals that we never quite knew where they had landed next until Nechúma came around to our kitchen to report to my mother and the women around our kitchen table.

Part of my fascination with the Hellers had to do with their frequent separations and the moves they seemed to make every year. Although Anarchists were going to make the great new world of the future through spontaneous groupings of workers "joined from the heart," without coercion of any kind, Berl and Nechúma were forever breaking up and then getting together for new experiences. At one point they became part of a utopian colony in Stelton, New Jersey, named after the martyred Spanish Anarchist educator Francisco Ferrer. How I would have liked to live in Stelton, New Jersey! I was lost in admiration for the Hellers' audacity, their idealism, their very lack of the furniture and domestic piles that would have hindered such a move for any anxiously protective family like my own. But such was the spell that the Hellers provided for my mother as for me that while I was still a boy I knew all about *their* quarrels and separations, every detail of the terrible flu epidemic of 1918 in which Robert died. I knew more about the Hellers than I ever did about whatever it was that kept my melancholy parents glued together in the same apartment for forty years.

The Hellers were very, very dramatic. The fiery center of the eternal drama was Berl the hothead, Berl the revolutionary zealot with more love for humanity in general than for any misguided wretch who happened to disagree with him. He was an executive of the Bakers Union (they still conducted all meetings in Yiddish), always traveling about—still an occasional philanderer. What a passionate, stormy, driven man! He talked with the force of a shovel slamming into soft earth.

What got to me was his sense of detail about everything and anything that had ever happened to him. He was so fierce in polemic, in his automatic political self-righteousness, that it never occurred to him that what kept his audience tied down was not his argument but his temperament. He would have been perfect for the old silent movies—everything was black or white, every gesture was picturesque, meaningful beyond words, *profound*. It was really something to hear him announce some current political position or idolatry. For a time he leaned toward Marxism, then became a totally outraged and intolerant opponent of Marxism in every form, constantly railing against the Soviet Union as "Red Fascism." He could not talk back to an opponent without going up in flames, so to speak, storming around the room in his rage, dramatically slamming the door behind him as he left our apartment. No one else ever took my father so seriously as to shun him after some political argument.

And then, it has to be told, Berl kept his eye for the ladies, was capable of amorous exchanges with a boarder or family friend right in the next room. This periodically broke Nechama's heart. If they had separated the month before because of some burning, absolutely fundamental political disagreement, when Berl was still an Anarchist but Nechama had reverted to plain old Socialism, they would now have to separate still again. Then there were the hot reunions, with Berl rushing back to Nechama to fall on his knees and plead forgiveness.

How did I know all this? From my mother, who was clearly fascinated by goings-on unknown to her experience, from Nechama's own talk around the kitchen table, from the Heller children themselves, who though they suffered from the instability that rocked their lives, were understandably caught up in the undeniable excitement. Wife and sons were all forced to become extensions of Berl—of his sleeplessness, of the state of his bowels, of his current rages political and personal, which to no one's surprise always tended to be identical.

A terrible egotist, he discouraged his sons from going to college on the grounds that with the Depression hovering over everything, it was probably more sensible to learn a trade. Yet the very emphasis of his authority, unknown to my father, appealed to me by reason of its force. I wanted the Jewish workers surrounding me everywhere in my youth to be strong, to become part of American life, not to remain "poor immigrants."

Although Berl misused the English language, as most Yiddish-speaking workers did, he was not afraid to use it just as he liked to travel everywhere in the country for the Bakers Union. When he was in his eighties, and obsessed with the rise and fall of the radical ideology that had been his whole life (except for Nechama), he was persuaded by his sons to make tapes, hours at a time, recounting the history of Jewish militancy in Russia, England, and the United States. The unfaltering flow of reminiscence and the most meticulous detail was absolutely remarkable. He had clearly never forgotten a single detail of his experience, not a single shift in his many opinions. It all went on and on in his crude but vital English, went with a force, a velocity, a maddened energy that explained his effect on his family—and on me.

But where would he have been, where would any of this have been, without Necháma? Although they drove each other crazy and she finally refused, absolutely refused, ever to live with him again, he remained in her neighborhood and was constantly on the telephone to her. The last time I saw her alive, the last time I ever heard *his* voice, was when I was taking some photographs of her. At that very moment Berl telephoned her to remind her that Isaac Bashevis Singer, their idol, was to appear on television that night. After all, they had been allied for half a century. When Necháma asked me to greet him, he responded: "So what do you think of my wife's horrible Marxist dogmatism?"

It was my mother who had the last word. When I laughed with her over Berl's performance on the telephone and said how much I had always admired the couple for their fervor and for having the guts to stay unmarried, she suddenly became jealous and even a little spiteful. "You silly," she said to me. "Didn't you ever guess that they *were* married but were afraid to admit it to their Anarchist friends, to their own children? They were married in London before they took ship for America, and by a *rabbi!* Necháma's father back in Russia insisted on this. And Necháma couldn't refuse him!"

FRAGMENTS: A PORTRAIT OF MY FATHER

by Susan Kenney

Susan Kenney was born in New Jersey and grew up in Pennsylvania, Ohio, and New York. She graduated from Northwestern University, and later earned a Ph.D. from Cornell University. She is the author of four novels, Garden of Malice, Graves in Academe, In Another Country, *and* Sailing, *as well as numerous articles and reviews. Since 1968 she has taught English literature and creative writing at Colby College in Waterville, Maine, and was the Visiting Writer at Amherst College in 1988–89.*

My father, James Morrow McIlvaine, died suddenly when he was forty-eight and I was twelve.

He died of a massive heart attack in a Port Huron, Michigan, hospital while away from home on business, at 4:20 A.M. on Friday, June 19, 1953, nine days after his birthday and two days before Father's Day, a bitter irony that struck me even at the time. My mother had given him a new leather suitcase embossed with his initials for his birthday the week before, and his parting words as he went down the stairs and out the door were: "I love my new suitcase." He got in his car, smiled and waved, drove away, and never came back.

In two of my novels, *In Another Country* and *Sailing*, I wrote about his death and its impact on me through the eyes of a fictional narrator named Sara, whose father's sudden death at age forty left a lifelong impression on her so strong she was still reliving the event some thirty years later. But when in my own forty-eighth year I looked back over what I had written about the death of fathers, both Sara's and mine, it suddenly struck me as sad to think that, though in many ways my father's death has been the single most significant event of my life, what I had so far recorded as his greatest impression on me should be his death—not his too short presence in my life but his long absence from it.

In the first chapter of *In Another Country,* Sara says of her father's death:

> I never stopped feeling bereft; knowing him only as a father, I had not known him at all as a man, and I never would. . . . I blamed him for never writing down his thoughts. He never wrote me a single letter, so there was no trace of him in his own words. . . . I tried to reconstruct the fragments he had left me, tried to make remembered words and movements, bits of conversation, take on coherence and show him whole. But I couldn't do it, and after a while I put my fragments away, old unsorted photographs yellowing in a dusty attic box.

After rereading these lines, I decided to hunt out my own version of the dusty attic box, in reality the catchall bottom drawer of an old desk where I keep my own collection of fragments pertaining to family life—clippings, papers, old letters, photographs, kids' drawings, locks of baby hair, and so forth—to see what there was. I hadn't looked at or even thought of any of its contents in many years—usually whenever I need to put anything else in, I just open the drawer a crack and shove it in like a letter through a mail slot—but as I hauled open the drawer and began to remove the accumulated layers, I was surprised to find how much was actually there. In fact, my father—unwittingly of course, for he, like Sara's father, never dreamed that he would die and leave me wondering—had left behind more than just "odd bits of conversations, movements, old unsorted photographs," more than just my memories of him, the hearsay memories of those who knew and loved him. And without really thinking very much about it, I had kept it all, moved it from house to house in the same old desk drawer. I can't even remember the last time I looked at any of it over the last twenty-five years.

Yet here it all is, with what I once called the mindless persistence of objects, a two-pound Candy Cupboard box of oddments. Here are the yellowed photographs, here too others, newer, not so yellow, also old report cards, a few letters from and to him and about him, newspaper clippings, a job dossier, a 16mm movie reel, a few other things; this and that. Still not much, in fact not a great deal to show for forty-eight years of life. Words and pictures, the odd object or two, memories, associations, stories passed on from one generation to the next. Fragments, puzzle pieces. After all these years, can I reach into the silence, the stillness of both voice and movement, reconstruct the fragments, and show him whole?

It's almost a foot square, the old Morrow family Bible, and the embossed leather cover is completely detached from the rest of the three-inch-thick volume; otherwise it's in pretty good shape, considering it's dated 1865. "The Holy Bible," says the title page, "translated out of the original tongues, and with the former translations diligently compared and revised."

It was presented, according to the inscription inside the detached cover, to my great-grandmother Clara Johnson by her mother, on the occasion of her wedding to James E. Morrow, on September 19, 1867. Clara (or perhaps it was James; the entries are in several different hands), finding the appropriate and traditional spaces for family records in the middle of the huge volume, instantaneously and dutifully began to set down all relevant births and marriages, starting with hers and her husband's. Deaths too, but they come later. There they all are, the old ones, their names and dates written in a fine upright script, beginning at the top of the page following II Maccabees. At the bottom of the first column under "Marriages" the entry reads: "Rev. Edwin Linton McIlvaine and Hilda Morrow were married July 10, 1900 at no. 1519 Irwin Av Allegheny, by Rev. David M. Skilling, assisted by Rev. Dr. James H. Snowden." And on the next page facing, under "Births," near the bottom: "James Morrow McIlvaine was born at Emlenton, Pa, June 10, 1905."

Words and pictures, stories and associations. Here is a small photograph, two by three, of a fat-cheeked baby standing in an old-fashioned round wooden walker shaped like a miniature hoopskirt. The child is wearing a dress, quite rumpled, and all you can see of the face is chubby cheeks, a button nose, and short flaxen hair. It could be a girl, it could be anybody, but on the back is written "JMM 1906." He is holding on to the rim of the walker with one hand, and reaching out to pat the dog's nose with the other. He is not afraid of the dog, and the dog sniffs his hand with interest. Perhaps there is, or was, a cookie in it. Perhaps they are just friends. Throughout his life, all dogs anywhere in his proximity will always love him; will always belong to him in fact if not in name regardless of whom they were intended for.

Other photographs of him as a small child show him mostly with his sisters Ruth and Katharine, who bracketed him in the family, Ruth five years older (there was another girl who died before his birth), Kathy two years younger. They pose stiffly, solemnly arranged, tight little smiles on their faces, in dresses and hair ribbons, looking over there. In due course he will appear in a dark middy blouse, tie, and knickers, one hand on his little sister's chair, one foot crossed casually over the other at the ankle, smiling slightly at the photographer, possibly looking bored, possibly mischievous. In later pictures, he is often the only one looking directly at the camera, not always smiling, but always with an indefinably wry, perhaps ironic expression that seems to say, "Well, here I am."

He was the son of a stern, upright, strictly disciplinarian father and a secretly humorous, possibly subversive mother—when we grandchildren were all gathered around the solemn Sunday dinner table bored out of our minds with grown-up talk but not allowed to be excused, when no other adult was watching, eyes twinkling, she would quietly detach her upper bridge and roll it out on her tongue with the three tiny false teeth riding on it, and as our eyes bugged out, we could hear her characteristic deep delighted chuckle as a barely discernible rumbling in her throat. And though good-natured and generally tractable, my father too was known on occasion to misbehave. There is a story about how when he was three, at their wits' end with his constant activity, his exhausted parents tied a long rope around his waist, gave him a garbage-can lid to bang on with a wooden spoon, and hitched him to a tree in the backyard of their home in the small Pennsylvania town where my grandfather was the Presbyterian minister. Before they even took in the fact that it had grown oddly quiet, the call came from the general store a half mile away: "Reverend McIlvaine, your little boy is here," and so he was, rope, lid, spoon, and all.

There are a few photographs from his boyhood, mostly with his father. Here are two taken when he was about nine years old. He and his father are on top of a high grassy hill overlooking a valley with a lake, and my father is wearing the quasi-military Rough Riders' hat and uniform of the early Boy Scouts. My brother tells me this is Ridgway, Pennsylvania, where my grandfather founded a Boy Scout troop in 1914. In the first picture they are both standing, my tall, slender grandfather with some sort of staff or long stake in his hand, my father shoulder-high and sturdy, reaching tentatively toward the stake as he squints in the direction of the camera, the sun in his eyes in spite of the wide-brimmed hat, a vaguely quizzical expression on his face as though he's not quite sure what's expected of him. In the other, taken just a few moments later, my grandfather is sitting in the tall grass holding the stake in his lap, and my father is kneeling, leaning forward toward the photographer, one shoulder raised, hands on his knees, still squinting, the sun still in his eyes, but now he is grinning broadly, his chubby boy's cheeks thrown into relief, shining.

About this period of his life I know virtually nothing else, except the brief glimpses contained in letters from his grandmother Clara. "I send James the picture of an Indian whom I had the pleasure of meeting. He held a reception and is very much alive at 103." perhaps he was interested in wild Indians; perhaps he also was one. Was he called James, Jimmie, Jim, or Jamie? I don't really know; later, when I knew him, he was always Jimmie or Jim, but on the day he died, my grandfather beat his breast and cried, "Lord, O Lord, why couldn't you have taken these old bones, and not my dear boy Jamie?"

One more photograph, one of the few in which he is not smiling, cut somewhat raggedly around the edges, probably to fit in someone's wallet. The date penciled on the back in my mother's handwriting says Meadville, 1920, and I suppose he could be about fifteen, though he looks somewhat older. He is dressed in a thick wool suit and white shirt with a tab collar, his striped tie slightly askew, the knot twisted toward his right shoulder. His collar looks uncomfortably tight; perhaps that is why is he is not smiling. Or maybe he's been told to look serious for once. In fact, his lips are slightly pursed as though in concentration, pushed forward slightly and crimped at the corners in another characteristic expression, as though to say, "Let's get on with it." His hair, clearly blond and wavy, is carefully combed up in a pompadour, artfully parted in the middle, almost as though sculpted. He stares levelly at the camera, the irises of his eyes so light-colored they are barely visible, and he is not smiling, not at all, but his right eyebrow is cocked, slightly raised, one corner of his mouth is twitching, and right after this photograph is taken, he will (yes, as always) make some wry, witty remark, and break into a grin.

———

Here is a college transcript, which for some reason I have never seen before, although it must have always been here in the candy box along with everything else, contained in a packet returned to him by the War Office with his application to the Flying Cadet School of the Air Corps in 1928. Among other things, it tells me that he entered Washington and Jefferson College (from which both his father and his grandfather Morrow had graduated) on September 19, 1923, after attending Meadville High School. Distinguished, even honors level his first year, his grades declined over the four years to "approved" and "passed," the proverbial gentleman's C. One of the honors was in physical education, but in his third year he was excused from the four-year requirement and took no more gym. He was graduated with the degree of A.B. on June 8, 1927; the entry in his college yearbook, *Pandora,* next to a picture of a handsome, slicked-down, mild-mannered-looking young man gazing off into the distance, reads:

James Morrow McIlvaine   Delta Tau Delta
  Meadville, Pa.

  Meadville High School: Junior Week Committee

  Picture a chubby-faced youth, cheeks fresh and shining from recent applications of soap and water, wearing the well-known immaculate collar and impeachable tie (pardon, cravat), and the popular Society Brand Chiltnum ulster (double-breasted) crowned by the dark laughing hair and curly eyes, and you have "Jimmie" on his way to the movies. But picture a stalwart youth with his shirt open at the throat, striding across the campus, with his head erect and a fanatic glow in his steel-blue eyes, and you have McIlvaine on his way to a class. Take your choice; they're both good.

I remember poring over this entry again and again after he died, so fascinated by these words, the image they conjured, that I practically memorized the whole description, trying to relate it to the impression I had of the way he was so much later on. At some point the yearbook was lost, but I had the page copied and sent to me by a kind librarian at W. and J. Along with it she sent something else I had never seen, my father's actual graduation picture, published the next year. There he is in cap and gown, staring out of the page with a detached, even slightly jaded "Ha, I'm out of here" expression, the lips pursed, unsmiling, but there, see, the cocked eyebrow, the quirk at the corner of the lip. (He may also be hung over: here's another story I know about him: The Reverend McIlvaine, a stern teetotaler, promised his children a reward if they would not drink or smoke until they were twenty-one. James reached the age of twenty-one, collected the prize, promptly lit up, got drunk, and continued to smoke Camels and drink manhattans with great enjoyment for the rest of his life. He never, however, swore or took the name of the Lord in vain.) No blurb this time, just the photograph and the motto he must have chosen for himself from William Lloyd Garrison's *The Liberator:* "I am in earnest; I will not retreat a single step."

But, earnest and determined as he was, there were after all some things he couldn't do. One more document. Among the recommendations returned with his application to Flying Cadet School is this one, typed, with hand corrections, from the former president of Allegheny College:

> I have known Mr. McIlvaine since he was a boy. He is all right in every way. He is a man of good mentality—keen, alert and with initiative and force. He is also a man of fine character, and is well thought of by his associates. He comes from one of our very best families. I hope he may have the appointment.

Yet for all his "earnest purpose, high ideals, and sterling integrity," he didn't get the appointment; he flunked the physical. Years after his death, which had fallen upon my younger sister and brother and me like a huge cataclysm, so sudden, so unexpected, my mother, perhaps in response to my own husband's life-threatening illness, my complaint that I was always expecting something awful to happen, announced out of the blue that my father had had a heart defect, and that all those years they "knew he could go anytime." The story was that he had had rheumatic fever in college, and it had damaged his mitral valve. We didn't believe her at first: the idea that they might have known, could have expected, even have done something, seemed too horrible to contemplate. But here is the excuse from gym, the failed physical, the remark my brother remembers him making that he never played sports because he was afraid he'd "hurt somebody," now possibly to be understood as "hurt himself." Although he was also a fine swimmer (and in fact taught me to swim during our summer visits to Skaneateles: but I now recall his telling me that he took it up to expand his lungs after he had been "sick"), the only physical activity he indulged in with any regularity from this point on was golf, an interest he had shared from boyhood with his stalwart, highly athletic father, and practiced every weekend he was home, weather permitting, as long as I knew him.

Photographs from his college days and some years after show a fairly tall, somewhat burly young man with a fleshy face and large, straight, rather imposing Roman nose, invariably dressed to the nines in white knickers and hose, blazers, sweaters, cravats, his dark blond (he called it "muddy") hair now clearly wavy, rippling, often tousled, his forehead prematurely creased (he needed glasses for farsightedness but wouldn't wear them). No longer baby-faced, he continues to look older than his age, but obviously good-natured and genial. In these pictures, he is usually accompanied either by dogs or women gazing admiringly at him, or surrounded by his family, equally admiring.

In one, clearly earlier than the rest, he is sitting on a stump in his white knickers and silk hose, blazer and cravat, reaching down absently to scratch the ears of a little dog who is sniffing at his foot. He looks very handsome, sitting there in the sun, his mouth open slightly as though he's about to say something to the photographer. In another, he is standing against the rail of a ship with his arms folded, a good-looking young woman on either side of him, looking out at the camera with that same enigmatic, not-quite smile. Perhaps he is on his way to South America to buy the patent involving an early form of vinyl he and a friend were planning to parlay into a multimillion-dollar business called the Pyrostamp Corporation, which they formed in 1936, with an office in the Graybar Building in New York. Or perhaps he is simply taking a ride on the Staten Island Ferry. Though during these years he still lived with his parents in Tenafly, New Jersey, he spent a lot of time in the city, going to the opera and concerts—he was a lover of classical music, and was known to have played the violin himself, not terribly well but persistently; after he died I took it up for a while, but was even worse. With his ever-ready tuxedo, shiny shoes, top hat (I remember playing with this as a child—it collapsed into a pancake—but it's long since vanished), and opera cape, his law degree from NYU, and his own corporation, he must have been quite the eligible young man-about-town.

Here he is again, sitting on a stone wall in a bathing suit that reveals well-muscled arms and shoulders, slightly flabby middle, rather skinny legs and ankles, feet clad in rumpled socks and shoes, a cigarette dangling from his fingers, caught in the act of saying something wry and clever to the pretty young woman who sits next to him, gazing at him with an adoring smile, amused or besotted or both, leaning toward him so their shoulders are almost touching, her hands resting on her knees, fingers stretched out in appreciation of the joke. Is this Gladys, whom he called, to everyone's shock and horror, Happy Bottom? It is certainly not my mother; he did not meet her until late 1936.

One more from this time, my favorite, the one I call the movie-star shot, taken about the time he met my mother, sitting on the lawn in a folding chair, dapper as the devil, dressed in a double-breasted suit, one leg crossed over the other, pants immaculately creased, socks straight (he must be wearing garters), shoes shined to a metallic luster, tie straight, white handkerchief protruding just so from his breast pocket, and the look, in response to the "Jim, you are a handsome dog" remark one can't help making, the look that says, but always with that little ironic quirk at the corner of his mouth, "That's just the way I am."

He met my mother, Virginia Tucker, at a Thanksgiving house party given by his cousin, whose wife had been at Syracuse University with her. As she tells it, she nearly had heart failure sitting next to him at dinner, he was so handsome and charming. He volunteered to drive her to the Newburgh ferry, and when he got her there, said unceremoniously to the ticket agent, "Where do I get rid of her?" She forlornly supposed that might be the end of it, and went back to her apartment and her job at Burroughs Wellcome in New York City. Not one to give up easily herself, she dropped him a note on some pretext or other, and less than a week later received a note in reply inviting her to lunch. It was the first of a series of letters between them. Perhaps a dozen survive. So here he is, then, in his own words:

> my dear miss tucker
>
> i have delayed answering your kind letter of the 7th ins pending learning to type by the pitmann system as you can see i am not yet very expert but understanding that practice makes perfect i shall keep trying.
>
> i must confess to as much ignorance as before regarding the legend appearing over the burroughs wellcome portal since the translation of the strange languages is not set forth but i thank you nonetheless
>
> i shall approach said portal again friday 18th instat 12:30 approx . . . and if you should happen to be there i would have you to lunch rsvp
>
> vvss [signed]
James M. McIlvaine
>
> vp
>
> n b next lesson is punctuation and capitals.

By February 1937 he was addressing her jokingly as "Virgie" (in these letters he never did get her name right, calling her variously Ginia, Auntie, Jinny, Darling, and finally, just before their marriage, Sweetie; everyone else called her Ginnie) and signing his letters "love and kisses, Jimmie." Most of the letters were written soon after my father and his partner in the ill-fated Pyrostamp Corporation set out in the dead of winter on a month-long trip to Ohio and points west to peddle their patented machinery that had something to do—the details are vague—with bonding vinyl to cloth. The letters are full of jokes and humor, legal references (he wasn't practicing law, but he had his J.D. degree), and, very shortly, allusions to withdrawals from his "account of X's in Mutual Trust" with her. Their letters crossed in the mail, my mother's typewritten, long, newsy, funny, encouraging, his elegantly handwritten on hotel stationery (the neatness, legibility, and beauty of his handwriting is a reproach to me even to this day). Here is how he describes the view out his window at the Allerton Hotel in Chicago on a March evening:

> Helena Rubinstein has a neon sign across the street depicting two female silhouettes in osculatory juxtaposition. . . . And Zenith Radio no doubt generates power for its sample sets with a windmill device set atop its building with lights on the blades, which revolving at night, creates a kaleidoscopic pattern on my bedroom walls, and which when gazed upon at length makes answering patterns in an idle brain. This last paragraph reminds me of some of the language Rex Tugwell tangles himself up with, except that mine is more intelligible, at least to me. I'm really training for a spelling bee. Why do you suppose people get themselves so involved with words?

Why indeed? But these words of his show him to be articulate, observant, and literate (Rex Tugwell was a prolific economic architect of the New Deal, whose principles my father, being a more or less conservative Republican, obviously did not agree with). They also reveal the wit, the humor, certainly the self-irony that one would expect of the man whose face looks out at me from all his photographs. He was not a writer, but he had a way with words. And he could spell.

The weather in the Midwest in late March was terrible, blizzardy and cold, and after lugging 1,000 pounds of machinery from place to place, he and his partner were getting tired. On the road he wrote my mother several generally lighthearted letters full of silly rhymes, jokes about the green-eyed monster (accompanied by a drawing resembling an alligator with warts), deposits in the kissing account, and speculations on the possibilities of their genetic matchup (my mother had told him when they first met that she was looking for a brown-eyed blond as the appropriate opposite to her dark hair and blue eyes, to which he responded: "No gentlemen with Browneyes and the requisite golden curls. I think such a person would be just too pretty and wouldn't have any character anyway. . . . Now a very nice combination, I think, would be striking brunette and blue-eyed, muddy blonde"). But the same letter also contains this somewhat somber meditation:

> Life is not simple, it's very complex, business is complex, I'll tell you someday. Civilization is complex. Politics are and so is the human mind. In the face of such complexity it's no wonder people get selfish. A matter of self-preservation, maybe. People are selfish, most of them, very few gentle maidens, meek and mild. Very few women in my ken with the capacity of being what I call Grande Dames, those rare untouchables who fill one with wonder. You'll be a Grande Dame one day, Jinnie, and live in Peace and dignity. Maybe I'll be able to explain that in a more explicit mood some day. . . . Attempts at humor seem puny tonight for some reason, perhaps because I'm tired and it's past midnight, and it rained all day, and I was very busy.

In fact, it wasn't just the weather that was not going well. "The trip so far has been both successful and disappointing," he wrote. "It was disappointing to have failed to land American Fruit." But then his characteristic optimism reasserted itself: "But in all other cases the spark has been kindled, and if it does not go out due the d— weather, a very hardy blaze should result."

It didn't. The trip was a disaster; they failed to land any significant contracts, returned home early, and soon after, the Pyrostamp Corporation, James Morrow McIlvaine, V.P., folded for good. By the summer of 1937, my father was officially unemployed. Except for a brief stint as a legal researcher with a printing outfit in Garfield, New Jersey (whose later recommendation was distinctly cool), he would remain out of a job until he joined the Sun Oil Company in 1939, where he remained, eventually becoming their land manager, for the rest of his life.

The letters continue, chipper and good-humored. "Dere Miss Tucker—" begins an invitation to a dinner dance "with tails and gowns decollete, and much political chatter since it is the disgruntled young women of the Republican party who are giving the party . . . and I do not think they would miss a chance to convert such virgin non-politicoes as you and I are . . ." When my mother left New York to go home for a rest in the summer of 1937, it was clear that things were serious. She visited him and his family at Martha's Vineyard; he went to Skaneateles to meet her family. "Darling," he writes. "I guess I am a sociable person, essentially, after all, for I find myself at a loss as to just how to put in my free time since I came away from you and Skaneateles . . . Maybe it's on account of I'm in love, hunh?"

In the winter they visited his older sister and her husband in the Connecticut countryside; there are pictures of the two of them ice-skating hand in hand, my father looking somewhat unsteady, my mother, a former member of the women's speed-skating team at Syracuse, showing him a crossover. In photographs taken that summer at my aunt and uncle's place, they are relaxed and happy, grinning all over themselves, she with her knitting, he carrying around a copy of *I Knew Hitler*, caught reading it in the hammock, obviously unable to put it down. The last letter from this time, dated a week before their wedding, is not the least bit sentimental or mushy, but breezy and almost businesslike, full of arrangements, reports on his search for a job (they were married anyway, job or no job, and went to live with his parents); the only reference to the event coming up at the end of "the longest week of my life," the anticipatory expletive, repeated several times: "Mr. and Mrs. James M. McIlvaine. Hot dog!"

They were married on July 31, 1938, at my mother's home in Skaneateles, by my grandfather, the stalwart Reverend McIlvaine. In the story "Facing Front," I described at some length (though with significant alterations; the story is, after all, fiction) the reel of 16mm film showing the happy couple and their family and friends after the ceremony. Though the movie has no sound, I can watch my father walk and talk, looking now at the camera, now away, gesturing, and laughing, his mouth moving in that slightly constricted, tight-upper-lip way he had, as he speaks the silent words. I can almost read his lips, and the odd way they move reminds me of the way my sister's and brother's lips move when they are talking, the way my own mouth feels sometimes when I am suddenly self-conscious about the way I speak. There they are, the two of them, young and smiling, and there they go, ready to begin their life together.

Here is where I come in. In 1939, thanks to the uncharacteristically immodest but very impressive, professional-looking dossier my mother typed (and probably wrote a good bit of; it sounds more like her than my father), my father got the job with the Sun Oil Company, and they moved to Elizabeth, New Jersey. The birth announcement is from Tiffany's, a calling card with "Mr. and Mrs. James Morrow McIlvaine," and a smaller card attached piggyback with a tiny pink bow, that reads: "Susan Fuller McIlvaine, April 28, 1941." A telegram to the grandparents: "Susan arrived 10 A.M. today 7 lb 5 oz. Both fine. Me too. Love Jimmy." A photograph accompanying a newspaper announcement shows my father sitting on a park bench with his back to the camera, me at six weeks peering over his shoulder with hair combed to a point, like a wobbly Kewpie doll.

There are many more photographs that come before the memories: my grandparents and my godparents Aunt Ruth and Uncle Fred at the christening that fall, standing by the screen porch of my grandparents' house in Tenafly, my mother dark, elegant, and smiling in her huge raccoon coat, my father looking jaunty and pleased and proud (I was the first grandchild) in a tailored overcoat and snap-brimmed hat, holding me with one arm around my belly facing toward the camera, legs dangling in my one-piece baby bunting and pointed hat. In a small envelope labeled in my grandmother's hand is a lock of my baby hair, dark brown, the same color it is now; I inherited his steel-blue eyes and chubby cheeks, but not his golden hair.

In one early photograph of the two of us, he is hunkered down holding me squirming between his knees, one leg raised about to take a step, the sun throwing both our chubby cheeks into relief. It's July 1, 1942, the day I learned to walk, and he is grinning broadly, the cocked eyebrow if anything more pronounced, the sun in his face making his expression seem almost saturnine, except that he is so proud and happy, laughing. And here my father and I are together on the shore of Skaneateles Lake in 1943; I am coming out of the water toward him in my droopy-drawered wet bathing suit, round-faced and giggling, shivering perhaps; he stands there in his baggy swim trunks belted up around his thick waist, the still-skinny shanks ankle-deep, and he is laughing as he points toward the camera, saying to me, "Watch the birdie, honey. Look over there."

Now my memories begin and with them the narrative of our life together, too complex to recount. Here is a letter to his parents from when we lived in Toledo, Ohio, actually a carbon of a letter that must have been dictated to his secretary Jean; my mother's name is misspelled, and a word obviously meant to be Tucker is written "tougher," as though misheard. After some remarks about his parents' acquisition of a television set (it was 1950), he has this to say about family life:

Ginny is busy with preparations for Patsy's birthday party February 4. Susie got outstanding in spelling, and above average in everything else except arithmetic, which leads me to believe she favors the Tucker side. She only got average in arithmetic. Andy has had the sniffles but is better now and we have a second coat of snow for the winter.

My sister, Patricia, was going to be three; my brother, Andrew, was eighteen months. I was in third grade; my report card from this period notes my difficulty in arithmetic as "due to errors in the facts. Her knowledge of the processes and reasoning powers are very good." My father, explaining to me about carelessness, with a few asides about paying attention and behaving well, drilled me every night for several months, and the arithmetic grade improved. My next report card, in 1951, documents my difficulty with messy handwriting, the threat of a totally horrifying, unacceptable "below average" grade. Once again my father (his fine, clear, legible hand) showed me what to do: I had to hold the pen just so between my thumb and fingers, and, resting only the tip on the paper, not supported by my wrist, make line after line of rounded, elegant "o's." It was hard, I got a cramp, complained bitterly to him, "But, Daddy, I can't!" And he replied with those words that have stayed with me these many years: "There's no such word as 'can't.' " (Not that I didn't puzzle a little over this statement, taking it quite literally at first, as I did everything my father said to me—if my father said something was so, then that's the way it was, but how could there not be such a word as "can't" if I could hear and see and say it?—though eventually I realized it was another way of saying, "Never give up.")

That and his version of the Golden Rule—"Do unto others as you would have them do unto you"—are the only words I can still hear him speaking in that sometimes squeaky voice so unexpectedly high and light for so stocky a man. The rest of what he said to me, the lecture on how shyness is really a form of selfishness, the importance of patience as a virtue, our many conversations over the years—all these words are lost.

We spent a lot of time together, the two of us (my sister and brother were too young and rambunctious, a team of hellions; we couldn't take them anywhere), going to the movies on rainy weekends (he preferred thrillers, so we didn't tell my mother it was Boston Blackie instead of Disney again), to circuses and rodeo shows. We shared a love of games and puzzles, played checkers and word games; driving in the car with him I learned the capitals of all the states, then all the countries of the world (he, of course, knew them already, and more; any question I asked, it seemed, he knew the answer to). The woodworking, the train layout, my marionette theater and props, the ongoing home-improvement projects in the basement workshop of the house in Toledo, I have written of elsewhere. He let me watch and even help, and we talked and talked. Though by this time I was already writing stories, I don't remember if he knew, or what he thought of them. Did he ever see anything I wrote, did he think I had talent; did he know? "Oh yes," my mother tells me. "We spotted you right away, from those puppet scripts you wrote. Oh yes, he encouraged you, of course he knew." The most important thing about our time together was this: whatever his politics or view of the role of women, he never made me think there was anything I couldn't do.

A few more photographs, these not family but more formal shots with his business associates or golf buddies, lined up in a row. In one shot of the foursome on the links, he appears in side view, chin thrust forward, peering skeptically at the scorecard his friend is toting up. He is wearing a loudly striped tee shirt, baggy pleated pants, and a baseball cap, and he looks quite young for a change, his face seen from the side lean and classic, still drop-dead handsome. And here he is one last time, with other Sun executives in Sarnia, Ontario. The others are somewhat stiffly posed, supposedly perusing an important document, but not my father. He is the only one looking at the camera, and he stands there grinning broadly, one hand casually stuck into his pants pocket, snappily dressed in a three-piece suit and outrageous spotted tie—pardon, cravat—and his cheeks are fresh and shining, his wavy hair slicked back but still rippling, and he is smiling, yes, still smiling in the sun.

June 22, 1951

Dear Mom and Dad

Your check for ten bucks in commemoration of my advanced age of 46 was used to defray in part the expenses of a very pleasant business trip, which to you might not seem much of a birthday present, but it was, though, and the ten bucks afforded me a very fine dinner at a very fine inn on a very fine river in the very fine state of Michigan. It was also a very fine day.

There is one other thing about receiving a check for one's birthday. Money, of course, is a nice thing to have a little bit of, but if the birthchild goes into conference with dependents upon what use the money shall be put to, there are usually many suggestions of a community sort to which the money may well be applied, like curtains for the living room or a new can opener for the kitchen or a cork for the swimming pool drain or a new porch chair. The community uses of money are practically limitless, so you see, employing your kind birthday gift for purely selfish uses was about the only way that I could evolve having my gift and eating, too, which I did.

The day passed more or less uneventful. I must say that I felt neither older or younger than the day before, in fact I felt pretty good. Ginny took me to dinner at a Smorgasbord place in Toledo on Saturday, the day before, to commemorate the event, and it was very pleasant. She also threw a surprise party for me Sunday afternoon, when I was caught in my painting pants after doing a little glazing and touching up of some window frames. Her surprise was so complete that even though, looking back, I could see certain clues: viz., did you shave today; viz. 2, do you think you should cook a whole steak for the children; viz. 3, don't you think you have worked long enough today?; and numerous other "vizzes," I certainly was surprised; in fact I shaved and changed my trousers and finally my shirt in three separate steps between turning the steak for dinner on an outdoor grill which, incidentally, was a gift from my wife, so that about dessert time I was fairly presentable.

We are coming along fine in Toledo. The children are growing and learning, and the dog is getting bigger, and Susie is going to Scout Camp for two weeks next week and everything is in a bustle of preparation. We all send our love, and I, my thanks.

Your favorite son,

I have quoted this letter in its entirety because I think it best shows him the way he was—in words the way he would have spoken them, for this letter was clearly dictated too— thoughtful, articulate, good-natured, lover of dogs and children, puzzles, surprises, jokes, good company and plain fare, as businessman, handyman, husband, father, son. And as always the wry nudge of humor, ever so slightly ironic. "Your favorite son," he signs it. It's just a little joke. Of course he was their favorite son; he was the only one they had.

I have also quoted it because, although certainly not the last letter he wrote, through whatever random process governs the preservation of such things, it is the last there is. Scraps, orts, and fragments; words and pictures, things. That's all; there isn't any more. The rest is silence, the long absence stretching after.

Or is it?

Two photographs of two young men, aged seventeen, set for the moment almost accidentally (we are rearranging family portraits on the bookshelves to include the recent senior picture) side by side. One is my father, James, one is my son, named after him. They do not look at all alike, and never have.

How much I wanted that baby, that first grandchild, to be a boy, so I could name him James McIlvaine, as if this might in some small way replace my father, or anyway, his name. I looked for some physical resemblance as well, but that was too much to hope for; though he has my coloring, dark hair and gray-blue eyes, neither he nor the daughter who came after (also much wanted, and not just to complete the set) resembles me or anyone in my family in the least; they both look just like their father to the point where it's a running joke—forget the Mom, just call me Xerox; hey, Mom, did we adopt you? He has, I like to think, inherited my father's good nature, the evenness of his temperament, perhaps some of the wit, certainly his taste in food, but not a hint of face or build. Even though, my mother now tells me, of the three of us I am the one who most resembles my father (perhaps because this year I am finally his age), my brother hardly at all, it is my brother's young son who looks just like my father as a boy, the same sturdy build, round cheeks, blond hair, quick smile.

Still, there are the pictures, momentarily side by side. A friend of my son's passes by and glances down. "Wow! That's just amazing! They look just alike! Who is that, anyway?" I stare, we all stare at the two photographs. My son is standing in the sun, looking directly at the camera. And there it is, caught in passing, the same arched eyebrow, wryly cocked, the quirk at the corner of the mouth, the slightly pulled-back lips, the not-quite smile, the same carefully combed-back wavy hair (though his is dark, not muddy blond) falling away ever so slightly in exactly the same way from the unwanted center part. They do not look at all alike, they never have, but in these two moments frozen in time nearly seventy years apart, no longer even looked for, thought about, or wished, the resemblance is remarkable, even eerie. It is not the same face, not even close, but in these two dissimilar faces, the way the features fall momentarily into place, the expression—slightly bemused, wry, perhaps ironic, as if to say, "Well, here I am"—the expression is the same.

Later, driving in the car with my daughter (who is at the wheel, just learning), because I have already started writing this I ask her casually if she misses having known my father, minds the fact that he is not around.

"No, not really," she replies. (Why should she, this grandfather she never knew, who died so long ago?) But what she says next is completely unexpected. After a moment's thought, still gazing straight ahead (she is an attentive, careful driver), she adds, "I guess because I feel I really do know him. I have the feeling that he's around a lot."

I stare at her. She has always had this capacity to surprise me, and I am puzzled by what she's said. I don't think she believes in ghosts; I know I don't. Though there have always been photographs of him around the house, I have never talked much about my father to either of my children, never spent any time telling them what he was like, not for any reason really; it just never seemed to come up. So I ask, "What do you mean?"

"I mean," she says, "that I feel like he is here, that he's watching, and he knows all about us. I don't know why I think that, I just do." She shrugs. "So there you are."

"Do you think maybe it's the pictures, or that he's always been in my thoughts so much?"

She considers this a moment. "No, that's not it," she says. "I used to know your thoughts when I was younger, but it's a lot easier when you're small. No, it's just there, the feeling . . ." Then, with a trace of irritation—there is no question of an equable temperament here—"Oh, *I* don't know." End of discussion; shut up and let me drive.

I look at her, this daughter almost grown, and here is what I see: the already classic profile with the prominent though not the least bit chubby cheeks, the almost Roman nose, the wavy, dark blond ("Muddy! Come on, Mom, give me a break!") hair. Here too, oddly enough, in the latest toss of the genetic dice two generations later, are the long ago speculated-upon brown eyes.

Well, there you are, I think.

There you are.

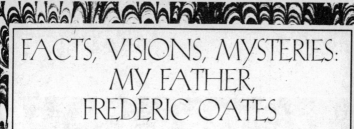

FACTS, VISIONS, MYSTERIES: MY FATHER, FREDERIC OATES

by Joyce Carol Oates

*Joyce Carol Oates, the Roger S. Berlind
Distinguished Professor of the Humanities at
Princeton University, is a National Book Award
winner and the author, most recently, of*
American Appetites, *a novel, and* The Time
Traveler *(poems).*

A November day, 1988, and I am sitting in my study in our house in Princeton, New Jersey, as dusk comes on listening to my father playing the piano in another wing of the house. Flawlessly he's moving through the presto agitato of Schubert's "Erl-King," striking the nightmarish sequence of notes firmly but rapidly, there's a shimmering quality to the sound, and I'm thinking how the mystery of music is a paradigm of the mystery of personality: most of us "know" family members exclusive of statistical information, sometimes in defiance of it, in the way that we "know" familiar pieces of music without having the slightest comprehension of their thematic or structural composition. We recognize them after a few notes, that's all. We can't explain why we know, what astonishing circuits the brain has closed for us in a split second, a species of knowledge that seems almost instinctual. The powerful appeal of music is inexplicable, forever mysterious, like the subterranean urgings of the soul, and so too the powerful appeal of certain personalities in our lives. We are rarely aware of the gravitational forces we embody for others but we are keenly aware of the gravitational forces certain others embody for us. To say "My father," "my mother," is for me to name but in no way to approach one of the central mysteries of my life.

How did the malnourished circumstances of my parents' early lives allow them to grow, to blossom, into the exemplary people they have become?—is there no inevitable relationship between the personal history and personality?—*is* character, bred in the bone, absolute fate? destiny? excluding if not in active defiance of the "environment"? of "family"?

And what are facts, that we should imagine they have the power to explain the world to us? On the contrary, it is facts that must be explained.

Here are facts:

My father's father, Joseph Carlton Oates, left his wife and son when my father, an only child, was two or three years old. Abandoned them, to be specific: they were very poor. Twenty-eight years later, unannounced, Joseph Carlton reappeared to seek out his son Frederic . . . arrived at a country tavern in Millersport, New York, one night in 1944, not to ask forgiveness of his son for his selfishness as a father, not even to be reconciled with him, or to explain himself: he'd come, Joseph Carlton said, to beat Frederic up.

It seems that Joseph Carlton had been hearing rumors that Frederic had long held a grudge against him and wanted to fight him, thus Joseph Carlton sought him out to bring the fight to him, so to speak. (Joseph Carlton Oates had been living not far away from his ex-wife, my grandmother, but in those years twenty miles was far away, or could be; they'd been out of contact completely.) But when the drunken, belligerent Joseph Carlton confronted Frederic, the one in his early fifties, the other a young married man of thirty, it turned out that the younger man had in fact no special grudge against the older and did not, though challenged, care to fight him.

Says my father, now in his seventies, "I couldn't bring myself to hit someone that old."

Joseph Carlton and Frederic Oates are said to have resembled each other dramatically. But though I resemble my father, so too my long-deceased grandfather, I never saw this grandfather's face, not even in a photograph. Joseph Carlton, of whom my grandmother would say, simply, whenever she was asked of him, "The man was no good," became one of those phantom beings, no doubt common in family histories, who did not exist.

My father was born in 1914 in Lockport, New York, a small city approximately twenty-five miles north of Buffalo and fifteen miles south of Lake Ontario, in Niagara County; its distinctive feature then and now, and a haunting feature of the landscape, is the steep rock-sided Erie Canal that runs literally through its core. Because they were poor my grandmother (the former Blanche Morgenstern) frequently moved with her son from one low-priced rental to another, but after he grew up and married my mother (the former Carolina Bush) my father came to live in my mother's adoptive parents' farmhouse in Millersport; and has remained on that land ever since.

My mother has lived on this attractive rural property at the northern edge of Erie County, by the Tonawanda Creek, in the old farmhouse (built 1888) and then in the newer, smaller house in which my parents now live (wood frame, white aluminum siding and brown trim, built 1961 largely by way of my father's efforts), virtually all her life. This is over seventy years: Carolina Bush was born November 8, 1917, the youngest of a large farm family, given out for local adoption as an infant when her father suddenly died and left the family impoverished.

(Is "die" too circumspect a term? In fact, my maternal grand-father was killed in a tavern brawl.)

In time, Frederic and Carolina had three children: I was born in 1938 (on Bloomsday: June 16), my brother, Fred ("Robin" for most of our childhood, thus to me "Robin" forever), was born in 1943, my sister, Lynn (who has been institutionalized as autistic since early adolescence), in 1956.

The generation that preceded my parents' is vanished of course. First-generation Americans, many of them; or immi-grants from Hungary, Ireland, Germany. My father's mother, Blanche, whom I knew as "Grandmother Woodside" (she remarried after her early, dissolved marriage), the person whom all the world I loved most after my parents, died in 1970 after a lengthy illness.

Facts: The property my parents shared with my Bush grandparents was a small farm with a fruit orchard, some cherry trees, some apple trees, primarily Bartlett pears. My memories are of chickens, Rhode Island Reds, pecking obses-sively in the dirt . . . for what is a chicken's life but pecking obsessively in the dirt? Chicken duties (feeding, egg gathering) seem to have fallen within a specifically female province, meaning my grandmother Bush, my mother, and me; fruit picking, especially the harvest of hundreds of bushel baskets of pears, fell to my father, when he was not working in Lockport at Harrison Radiator. For a brief fevered interim there were pigs . . . pigs that broke free of their enclosure in the barn and were desperately chased by my father . . . pigs that sickened and died . . . or, worse yet, were successfully slaughtered but somehow imperfectly cured, so that their meat, the point after all of so much comical despair, was inedible.

Now, decades later, nothing remains of the Bush farm. My childhood seems to have been plowed under, gone subter-ranean as a dream. The old house was razed years ago when the county highway was widened, the old barn was dismantled, most of the fruit orchard is vanished. *My* lilac tree near the back door, *my* apple tree at the side of the house, *my* cherry tree . . . long uprooted, gone. Fields once planted in corn, in potatoes, in tomatoes, in strawberries . . . gone. Looking at the property now from the road, you would not be able to guess that it was once a farm.

My father maintains an enormous grassy lawn with a suburban style to it, evergreens, a weeping willow, ornamental shrubs; my mother, a lifelong gardener, maintains flower beds. My parents are happy, sometimes, it seems, idyllically happy, now that my father is retired, now that life is so clearly not going to turn tragic after all, and I am happy that they are happy, for how can I not be happy in that some degree of their happiness seems a consequence of my own career as "Joyce Carol Oates" . . . ? Yet I contemplate that suburban house, an attractive house certainly, and the property, the carefully maintained lawn, and I know that, had I been born in that house, had I grown up on that property, I would not be the person I am. Had my mother been born there, yes and above all my father . . .

But it's unimaginable. It's that category of possibility you dare not imagine.

Though frequently denounced and often misunderstood by a somewhat genteel literary community, my writing is, at least in part, an attempt to memorialize my parents' vanished world; my parents' lives. Sometimes directly, sometimes in metaphor. Of recent novels *Marya: A Life* (1986) is an admixture of my mother's early life, some of my own adolescent and young-adult experience, and fiction: reading *Marya,* as my parents read everything I write, they immediately recognized the setting . . . For of course it is *the* setting . . . that rural edge of Erie County just across the Tonawanda Creek from Niagara County, not far from the Erie Canal (and the Canal Road where Marya lives). The quintessential world of my fiction. *You Must Remember This* (1987) is set in a mythical western New York city that is an amalgam of Buffalo and

Lockport, but primarily Lockport: the novel could not have been imaginatively launched without the Erie Canal, vertiginously steep-walled, cutting through its core. And though my father is not present in the fictional world of *You Must Remember This* his shadow falls over it; it's a work in which I tried consciously to synthesize my father's and my own "visions" of an era now vanished. Felix Stevick is not my father except in his lifelong fascination with boxing and with what I consider the romance of violence, which excludes women; that conviction that there is a mysterious and terrible brotherhood of men by way of violence.

But it is in an early novel, *Wonderland* (1971), that my parents actually make an appearance. My beleaguered young hero, Jesse, stops his car in Millersport, wanders about my parents' property, happens to see, with a stab of envy, my young mother and me (a child of three or four) swinging in our old wooden swing; and when my father notices Jesse watching he stares at him with a look of hostility. So I envisioned my father as a young man of twenty-seven—tall, husky, with black hair, intent upon protecting his family against possible intrusion. "In such a way," thinks my fatherless hero, "does a man, a normal man, exclude the rest of the world."

Memory is a transcendental function. Its objects may be physical bodies, faces, "characteristic" expressions of faces, but these are shot with luminosity; an interior radiance that transfixes the imagination like the radiance in medieval and Renaissance religious paintings . . . that signal that Time has been stopped and Eternity prevails. So though we can't perceive "soul" or "spirit" firsthand it seems to me that this is precisely the phenomenon we summon back by way of an exercise of memory.

And why the exercise of memory at certain times in our lives is almost too powerful to be borne.

F̃rom a letter of my father's, 10/8/88:

Your postcard asking about my history came the day after I phoned so I don't quite know how to give you what you want because I have no school records like you and Fred—all I can do is guess.

Born in Lockport 3/30/14. Parents separated when I was two or three years old. Started violin lessons in sixth grade (class instruction) then began private lessons with money earned peddling newspapers. My mother bought my violin for me otherwise I would have had to quit because the one I used in class belonged to the school. I played in the high school symphony orchestra as a freshman. My mechanical drawing teacher got me a job with Schine theaters in Lockport in the sign shop working after school. At summer vacation I worked full time at the job and quit school in my second year. Worked at the theater until I was about 17 when the sign shop closed and I went into production advertising.

Got a job in local commercial sign shop when I was about 18 and bought a car. After about 4 years of this work I got a job at Harrison Radiator in the punch press department and, thinking I had a steady job, I learned to fly, got married, then found myself laid off for extended periods so I had to continue working at the sign shop until the second world war began when I was able to get transferred into the engineering tool room and learned the tool and die making trade, later on was able, after going to night school to learn trig and related subjects, started tool and die design. At about fifty years of age, I took piano lessons for about four years at which time I was operated on to remove herniated disc material and was out of commission for six months then worked about ten more years and retired. Took a course in stained glass as a hobby, a class in painting, then four years ago I started classes in English Literature and music at S.U.N.Y. (State University of New York at Buffalo) which I hope to continue for a few more years.

F̃rom my journal, 5/20/86:

Last week, my parents' visit. And it was splendid. And it went by with painful swiftness. They arrived on Wednesday, left on Saturday afternoon, immediately the house is too large, empty, quiet, un-used. . . . My mother brought me a dress she'd sewed for me, blue print, quite feminine one might say; long-sleeved, full-skirted. "Demure"—to suit my image.

(Another family secret revealed, with a disarming casualness. Perhaps because of their ages my parents don't want to keep secrets? Not that they are *old* at seventy or seventy-one. My father told of how his grandfather Morgenstern tried to kill his grandmother in a fit of rage, then killed himself—gun barrel placed under his chin, trigger pulled, with my grandmother Blanche close by. My father was about fifteen at the time. They were all living in a single household evidently . . . A sordid tale. Yet grimly comical: I asked what occupation my great-grandfather had, was told he was a gravedigger.)

(Family secrets! So many! Or, no, not so very many, I suppose; but unnerving. And I think of my sweet grandmother Woodside who nearly witnessed her own father's violent suicide. . . . She had come home to find the house locked. Her father was beating her mother upstairs in their bedroom. Hearing her at the door, he came downstairs with his gun, and for some reason (frustration, drunk-enness, madness?) he went into the basement and shot himself. Several times I said to my father, dazed, But you never told me any of this! and my father said, with that air of utter placidity, Didn't I?—I'm sure I did. This is a countertheme of sorts. The secret is at last revealed, after decades; but it's revealed with the accompanying claim that it had been revealed a long time ago and isn't therefore a secret. . . .)

One of my most deeply imprinted memories of childhood is being taken up in a small plane by my father: tightly buckled in the front seat of a two-seater Piper Cub as my father in the cockpit behind me taxis us along the bumpy runway of a small country airport outside Lockport . . . and suddenly the rattling plane leaves the ground, lifts above a line of trees at the end of the runway . . . climbing, banking, miraculously riding the air currents . . . until the roaring noise of the engine seems to subside, and we're airborne, and below is a familiar landscape made increasingly exotic as we climb.

Transit Road and its traffic . . . farmland, wooded land, hedgerows . . . houses, barns, pastureland, intersecting roads . . . creeks and streams . . . and the sky opening above us oceanic, unfathomable.

My father has always been a happy, energetic, imaginative man, but never more so than when airborne, riding the waves of invisible currents of air. For what is flying your own plane but defying the laws of nature and of logic? transcending space and time and the contours of the familiar world in which you work a minimum of forty hours a week, own property in constant need of repair, have a family for whom you are the sole breadwinner? What is flying but the control of an alien, mysterious element that can at any moment turn killer: the air?

My father began flying lessons in 1935, when he was twenty-one years old, made his first solo flight in 1937, and, over the decades, logged approximately 200 hours of flying time. It was during the 1940s, especially after the end of World War II when Air Force training planes came into private ownership, that he flew most frequently, on weekends, out of small country airports near our home. What a romance of the air! He took members of the family, including his very young daughter Joyce, up in Piper Cubs, Cessnas, Stinsons; he flew a sporty Waco biplane; the most powerful aircraft in his experience was a Vultee basic trainer, 450 horsepower, an ex-Air Force trainer with a canopied open cockpit that flew at a height of 12,000 feet. Intense excitement—unless it was something beyond excitement—has blurred my precise memory of the flight we once made, my father and me, in a Fairchild primary trainer, 175 horsepower, another open-cockpit plane with a canopy. I wore a helmet and goggles, but no parachute, for the very good reason that I wouldn't have known how to use a parachute.

Flying is safer than driving a car, my father has always insisted.

In these planes my father and his flying buddies performed loops . . . turns . . . split S's . . . slow rolls . . . spins. Possessed of a brash sense of humor, as it might have been called, my father sometimes flew low to buzz friends' and neighbors' houses. Upon a number of daring occasions he flew gliders— if "flew" is the correct expression—borne up to a height of 1,500 feet by a plane, then released. A few years ago when a West German film crew came to interview him and my mother in preparing a film on "Joyce Carol Oates" for German public television, the program director arranged for him to fly the director and a cameraman (in a Cessna 182 single-propeller plane) over the terrain of my childhood: and it's as if, eerily, seeing this footage, I have come full circle . . . seeing again these exotic-familiar sights, my father in the cockpit.

I have been speaking of my father's avocational life, his "personal" life, but most of the actual hours of his (waking) life were spent at work. For forty years he was an employee of Harrison Radiator of Lockport, New York; since the early 1940s he was a dues-paying member of the United Automobile Workers of America. It has always seemed that Frederic Oates's temperament and intelligence might have better suited him for some sort of artistic or theoretical or even teacherly career but, born in the circumstances in which he was, and coming of age during the Depression, he shared the collective fate of so many. Schooling even through high school was not an option.

(So when it is said of me that I am the first member of my family to graduate from high school, still less college, this is another misleading fact: only chance saved me and others of my generation from the work-oriented lives of our parents. At the time of this writing my father is a student at SUNY-Buffalo—the kind of deeply engaged "older" student whom professors, and I speak as one, dearly appreciate in their classes.)

In the old days at Harrison Radiator, as at all un-unionized factories, plants, mills, shops, "sweatshops," it was not uncommon that workers might arrive for work in the morning only to be told cursorily that they weren't needed that day, and that there was no promise of when, or if, they might be needed again. Management owed nothing to labor; not even simple courtesy. A few weeks after I was born in 1938 my father reported to work and was told there was no work, the entire press room was laid off indefinitely . . . and I have to wonder what a young husband tells his wife when he returns home so early in the day . . . what the words are, what the tone of voice. About all my father will say of such episodes is: "They were hard." He has never been a person given to self-pity, nor yet to a nostalgic reinvention of the past.

If there was anger it's long since buried, plowed under, to be resurrected in his daughter's writing, as fuel and ballast. *How to evoke that world, that America, rapidly passing from memory?*

One definite advantage of my father's shaky economic situation was that he developed a second career of sorts—i.e., sign painting, at which he was very good. (For decades my father's signs were immediately recognizable in the area. I can "see" the distinctive style of their lettering even now.) And he acquired a habitude of busyness, a predilection for work, for using his hands and his brain, not so much in gainful employment as in useful employment; a trait everyone in my family shares. This is not puritanism but something less abstract, perhaps even visceral: we love to work because work gives us genuine happiness, the positing and solving of problems, the joyful exercise of the imagination.

I spoke of anger, and, yes, it's a "class" anger as well, but I want to make clear that this is a personal anger, not one I have inherited from my family.

A few days ago my husband and I took my parents for lunch on the Delaware River (they are visiting us here in Princeton for a week), to one of those "historic" inns for which the region is famous, and while we sat contemplating the antique furnishings of the Black Bass Inn—the tables in the dining room are made of old sewing machines—the subject turned to Harrison's, to the old days, in the 1930s. And after a while my mother said, as so often she sums up an era, and a theme, in a single succinct remark, "I guess we were poor but it didn't seem that way at the time . . . somehow we always managed."

The old farmhouse in Millersport was razed in 1960 yet there is a dream of mine in which I wake yet again to find myself there, in my old room . . . the first of the countless rooms of my life. I open my eyes in astonishment to see the square half-window overhead . . . the child's bureau at the foot of my bed and the child's desk facing it . . . and, through the doorway (no door, only a curtain), in the farthest right-hand corner of the living room the upright piano my father played and on which in time I would practice my piano lessons. A musical instrument is a mysterious thing, inhabiting a complex sort of space: it is both an ordinary three-dimensional object and a portal to another world; it exists as a physical entity solely so that it, and, indeed, physicality, can be transcended. Thus my father's old upright in that long-vanished living room inhabits its luminous space in my memory.

For nearly his entire life my father has played, and loved playing, the piano: classical music, popular music, Scott Joplin, jazz. He is a precise sight reader of music but he can also play by ear and improvise, neither of which I can do; he is far more naturally musical than I, though I have inherited from him a temperament thoroughly imbued in music. That is, people like us are always involved in music no matter what it appears we are doing.

If we aren't actually sitting at the piano and playing, our fingers are going through the phantom motions of playing; if we aren't singing or humming out loud, we are singing or humming silently. We are captivated by Mozart, Schubert, Beethoven, Bach . . . but just as readily by "St. James Infirmary,"

"As Times Goes By," one or another old Hoagy Carmichael tune. For people like us music is a matter of a pulsebeat, melody and rhythm and occasional lyrics, a constant interior beat in a counterpoint of sorts to the world's exterior beat. It must be a way of defining ourselves to ourselves, or perhaps it's purely pleasure, to no purpose. If from my father, Frederic Oates, I'd inherited nothing more palpable than a habit of singing to myself, I'd say this was more than enough.

So I sit listening to my father playing piano in another wing of the house . . . now he's playing Satie's elegant "Gnossiennes" . . . and I think these things. How to write a memoir of him? How even to begin? I spoke of mystery, and it's primarily mystery I feel when I contemplate my father; indeed, both my father and my mother. The quality of personality they embody, their unfailing magnanimity of spirit, is so oddly matched with their origins and with the harsh and unsentimental world out of which they emerged. I can only bear a prolonged consideration of that world in my writing, and there it is transmogrified as writing—as fiction. To consider it head-on, not as art but as historical reality, leaves me weak and bewildered.

If there is one general trait I seem to have inherited from both my parents it's their instinct for rejoicing in the life in which they have found themselves. They remain models for me, they go far beyond me, I can only hope to continue to learn from them. "Happiness is a kind of genius," Colette shrewdly observed, and in this genius my parents abound.

WILD WOMEN OUT OF CONTROL

by Sara Paretsky

*Sara Paretsky grew up in rural Kansas and now
lives in Chicago. She is the author of a series of
popular mystery novels featuring V. I.
Warshawski, the most recent being* Blood Shot.

A̲t four the little girl's hair is a frizzy mass, a
knot of tight curls around her head instead of the fine straight
silk of other girls her age. Her mother makes one forlorn
attempt to set it right, to put it in pin curls and smooth it out.
But when the bobby pins come off, instead of the glossy curls
the mother hoped for the daughter's frizz now stands up wildly
all over her head.

"Witch! You're a witch!" Her older brother dances in a
circle around her, pointing and doubling up in laughter.

The little girl scowls fiercely. "I *am* a witch," she says
menacingly. "And witches know everything."

The brother's laughter collapses. He races to the kitchen
calling to his mother. "Sara says she's a witch and witches
know everything. She doesn't really know everything, does
she?"

The mother soothes him and tells him of course not, that
his sister was just making it up. That was my first story.

The Witch of the Seahouse lived in a beautiful stone house
on a deserted beach. The water shimmered as if under moonlight

even during the day. The Witch of the Seahouse used to come to me when I was very little, but afterward she was replaced by the evil Witch of the Moon, who lived only in the dark, including the darkest part of my brain. After the day of my hair the Witch of the Seahouse never came back to me.

Soon after that my mother, weary of my unruly frizz and the tears at shampoo time, cut my hair close to my head. If I tried letting it grow out my father would mock me at dinner, telling me I looked like a sheepdog and to get it cut. I wore it short for many years, like my four brothers, like a fifth son.

In the stories I told in my head my hair was long and straight and glossy. In real life I was the Witch of the Moon, a monster. I struggled unsuccessfully for years to overcome the differences of appearance, of personality, of sex, that seemed to mark me as a monster both at home and in the world beyond.

It was only as I got older and began to absorb the example of my mother's cousin Agnes that I came to see myself differently. It took a long time to realize you could be independent, have a strong will, be a woman—and be human, not an evil witch. (And it wasn't until I read Woolf's "Professions for Women" two years ago that I realized how universal the conflict between being angel and monster is for women who write.)

When I was little Agnes frightened me: she embodied too many strange qualities anathema to the world I lived in. I grew up in Kansas in the golden age of America, in a society where everyone had a defined place, where everyone knew right from wrong—and what happened when you forgot.

We had mandatory prayer (Protestant) in our public schools. The same schools barred blacks from college-track courses. In those golden days they knew better than to agitate about it. Abortion was a crime. Only bad girls had sex outside marriage—whereupon they reaped their inevitable punishment since such contraceptives as existed weren't available to unmarried women.

Best of all, we little girls knew we were destined to be mommies. We didn't worry about careers. Except for some married teachers the only women who worked were those too strange or too unfortunate to get husbands. And they were secretaries or waited tables in the coffee shops.

Our dreams were of our weddings. When Roxanne Farrell "had to get married" in our sophomore year of high school, to us the most tawdry part was that she bought her trousseau at Woolworth's. Good girls who waited until they graduated from high school or college bought fancy bridal wear at the Plaza in Kansas City.

Agnes—unmarried, traveling where and when she wanted (as I write this she's seventy-one and trekking in Nepal), living not with a husband but with a woman friend—was an embarrassment to be hidden from the neighbors.

Everything about her was labeled in red, danger, especially the fact that she was unmarried by choice. "Who would want her?" my father demanded. "She's too bossy—what man wants to be pushed around?"

With her friend Isabel she ran a girls' school, the first time I ever heard of a woman running her own business. Something about that made my father guffaw in a nasty way. "Girls, of course she surrounds herself with girls. If she could get herself a real man she wouldn't be afraid of a few boys."

My father had a way of saying things like that that made you feel you were an imbecile if you didn't know what he was talking about. We would whisper our questions—in case he treated them with contempt we could pretend we hadn't said anything.

"Why not?" I whispered now.

"The girls are irremediable," said my mother, as if that was an answer. "No one else can make them behave except Agnes."

I still didn't understand, but knew better than to probe further.

When Agnes dropped in out of the blue—as she did from

time to time on all her relatives—my father treated her with a nervous deference. It made me think she had great power—not only could she make irremediable girls behave but she even controlled him. My father terrified all of us, but in a way, her power over him frightened me even more: he would mock her behind her back but to her face, against his will, he was forced to obsequiousness.

Male writers such as Sartre and Bellow have recorded knowing early in life that their destiny lay in literature. Bellow knew he was "born to be a performing and interpretive creature," Sartre that he was born for words.

I call myself a writer, but feebly, without conviction. Where did they get this sense? I wonder. Were their childhoods spent like mine? I wrote from an early age, but I knew that, as with all fields, literature belonged to men. The history and biography we studied in school told tales of the deeds of men. We learned to speak of the aspirations of mankind and of "man's inhumanity to man"—his inhumanity to woman not being worth recording.

And the literature we studied was all written by men. If they were like me Bellow and Sartre may not even have known that women wrote in a serious way, that the first novelist to treat psychology as a significant force in human lives was a woman. Sartre's boyhood was spent with Flaubert, Cornelius, Homer, Shakespeare. Bellow went to Anderson, Dreiser, Edgar Lee Masters, Vachel Lindsay.

The books Sartre's grandmother read were feminine, he says, and he was taught by his grandfather to deem them inferior. By an odd chance I was taught the same lesson. We studied only one novel by a woman in my school—and her first name was George. Although I wept over *Little Women,* the moral of Jo March's life is that little girls must put aside the dream of literature to perform the higher duty of looking after their families.

Did their childhoods resemble mine in other ways? Was Jean-Paul or Saul's first responsibility to look after the little children—to spend summer vacation and evenings after school taking them for walks, changing their diapers, feeding them, reading them their stories? Did their fathers tell them their works were derivative, that they lacked the genius necessary for originality? Did their mothers assure them that the work their sisters did was superior to anything they could ever do, that the future lies with girls, not boys? Can destiny swim in such waters?

All my childhood dreams were directed to the present, specifically to escaping it, until I learned escape wasn't possible. My older brother and I would look at a picture of a ship at sea or a beautiful island, some strange wonderful place we wished to be. We would hold hands and run toward the picture, and by wishing hard enough be transported into it. More often we climbed onto the two hitching posts in front of our house—remnants of the days when visitors had horses to tie up. After turning around three times we jumped, landing in a magic world where we fought dragons and loving elves came to our rescue.

The walls of my bedroom were papered with cabbage roses and behind the roses lay a corridor, a long hall whose windows looked on perpetual sunlight. After going to bed I could get into this corridor and live a life of total secrecy.

When I was eight my mother had a baby. While she was pregnant I dreamed of having a sister, but she produced another boy to go with the two she already had. She put the baby in my room and told me to look after him.

I had longed for a doll that cried real tears—I'd seen one at Grand Central Station when we moved from New York to Kansas and had always wished for one. They gave me my brother and said I would like him much better than a doll. In fact they gave him my dolls to break, since I was now too grown-up to want them. Getting a baby to look after ended my magic worlds. In my stories I was still a princess but I knew now they were stories and would never come true.

When I was seven my mother stood me on a chair next to the kitchen counter and had me bake a cake and cookies for my father and brothers, beginning a weekly baking stint that lasted until I left their house at seventeen.

Sartre writes he knew his mother existed to serve him. I raised the two babies born when I was eight and thirteen and cleaned the house every Saturday. I would have made somebody a good old-fashioned kind of wife. It wasn't that I fought my destiny—it just somehow sidestepped me.

Maybe my hair saved me, cropped close to my head when everyone else wore hers long—it made me look too strange. Or maybe it was my stories—I wanted a man from one of my stories, not the pimply, self-absorbed ones who came to dorm mixers. Or maybe it was a message absorbed from Agnes—against my will at first, then later with great eagerness.

The summer I turned ten, on one of her abrupt visits, Agnes learned I was writing a story. She asked me to read it to her. She sat in the living room and listened with total attention. It still seems unbelievable to me that a grown woman could really *want* to spend an hour hearing a young girl read a story. She didn't offer any literary criticism. I don't even remember her saying anything. Just that she sat and listened.

Sartre records how his mother used to go into transports over his writing, showing his boyish "novels" to neighbors and to her father, with whom they lived. She would stand over his shoulder while he wrote, in ecstasies over his imagination. It was one of her intimates who named writing as young Jean-Paul's career when he was seven or eight. His cousins were told they would be engineers.

Both of my parents had stories to tell, their sides in an unending feud, and both would make use of my writing to help them make their points—my mother wanting me to write poems describing her entrapment, my father stories proclaiming his unlauded glories. But beyond that my words created so little interest that my mother tells me my father burned all my childhood papers in some housekeeping frenzy or other. I keep hoping she got it wrong. I spend hours feverishly hunting through her attic for some story, some diary, a remnant that will connect me with my past, that may tell me what dreams I used to have. Nothing comes to light. Despite my anguish I'm relieved that the forced bondage of my words to my parents has also vanished.

Agnes's listening to one story was not enough to give me a sense that my future lay in words. It was enough, though, to keep me writing.

After Agnes listened to my story I would lie in bed imagining my parents dead and me adopted by her, taken into her school where there were only girls.

The dream took on new dimensions the following year when we moved to a house in the country five miles from the town of Lawrence. At first I loved it: I finally had my own room and we went to a two-room country school—just like in *Understood Betsy* or *On the Banks of Plum Creek*. Later I came to hate it. My parents' fights intensified and the isolation of the country made it easy to seal me off completely from friends my own age, from any activities but school and housework.

The main line of the Santa Fe crossed the road at the bottom of the hill on the outskirts of Lawrence. There wasn't any crossing gate or bell and every now and then the Kansas City Chief, roaring around a blind curve toward San Francisco, would annihilate a family.

Mary and Dave would be arguing, not paying attention to the road or to the tracks. The crash would be appalling. We'd be at the house, of course, my four brothers and I, lounging around reading or maybe playing softball. We should have been doing a dozen chores—mowing the lawn (my older brother's job), vacuuming (mine), changing the baby's diapers (mine again), or sorting the bottles out of the trash to take to the dump (my brother). I don't need a dishwasher, Mary used to tell visitors—I have two right here. And she would point at my older brother and me.

When we heard the car in the drive we leaped into action, attacking our chores—there was hell to pay if we were found loafing in bourgeois self-indulgence. And then we saw it was the sheriff's car, the red light flashing. We raced over to see what he wanted, me grabbing the baby and carrying him along on my hip.

The sheriff looked at us very kindly. He said maybe we should go sit down. He had something very serious to tell us. There'd been an accident and we were orphans now. Was there someone we could call to look after us? Of course not, we already did any looking after there was to do, but we couldn't tell him that, and anyway, of course we were underage, we needed guardians.

I would go to Agnes, to the school for irremediable girls. Even though she only took girls I would have to bring the two little boys with me, they were mine to look after. (They thought I was their mother. When they started kindergarten they didn't know what "sister" meant—they didn't know that was me: they thought they had two mothers.) I didn't care where the other two went, they could look after themselves.

We looked solemnly at the sheriff, conjuring up tears out of shock, but we couldn't believe it had really happened: we were really orphans. Just like *Anne of Green Gables* or *English Orphans*. Our future changed miraculously.

And then Mary and Dave would come up the drive, still arguing, not dead at all, and we would leap into activity that was never quite frenzied enough. My older brother could never get tasks quite right, or the tasks set for him would change between when they were assigned and when he did them, and most of the yelling went his way. The rest of us slid upstairs.

Agnes didn't come to see us again after the summer she heard me read. Maybe she grew too busy, or maybe the number of fights in our house and their ferocity drove her away. I don't know. Maybe it was simply her paying so much attention to me—it might have frightened my father into telling her she couldn't come again.

He thought she was a lesbian, of course, although I only realized that later. WOMAN ON THE LOOSE! WEIRD WOMAN OUT OF CONTROL! That was the headline on my father's face when he talked about Agnes. It was out of the question for me to live with her—he wasn't going to risk losing control of me.

I've never known if she was a lesbian or not, even when I came to spend more time with her: it's never seemed particularly important. One thing I found out about Agnes was that her mother died when she was ten, died giving birth to a baby that didn't survive long either. Agnes was named for her mother, who gave her her wedding ring as a memento when she knew she was dying. I don't know how that affected Agnes, but it would have frightened me out of marriage. (When I got married she insisted I take her mother's ring. I'm still not sure if that gift portends good or ill; just in case, I never wear it.)

Agnes took a more active role in my life after I moved to Chicago. She appeared to me suddenly, a *dea ex machina*, during my first winter there. Although she didn't stay there long, Chicago is where she ran to when she was twenty, away from the care of a family that took more than they gave. She might have come to see me looking for her younger self.

I was twenty-one then, fat, ungainly. I'd never had a boyfriend and aside from my three roommates I didn't have many women friends in Chicago either. My roommates and I shared a dismal apartment on the South Side—six rooms for a hundred sixty-five dollars a month and all the cockroaches we could eat. We killed two hundred and fifty of them one night, spraying the oven where they nested and stomping on them when they scampered out. You'd have to be twenty-one to want to count the bodies.

It was never warmer than fifty-five in the building and that was a most bitter winter. The city code says it has to be at least sixty-two during the day. We'd get building inspectors out who would solemnly measure the air. Then they'd learn the landlady worked as a precinct captain for the Daley machine and their thermometer miraculously would register fifteen degrees higher than ours.

I had gone to Kansas for the Christmas holidays and was back several days before my roommates. Carrying my heavy suitcase up the stairs to the apartment entrance, I blundered into the doorjamb, knocking the wind out of myself. I dumped my suitcase down and sat on it, not even going inside, so miserable with my fat, my clumsiness, my loneliness that I hoped I might just die right there.

My two youngest brothers would care, of course, as would my friend Kathleen, but my parents wouldn't even come to the funeral. I'd been active in community organizing both in Chicago and in Lawrence; admiring community leaders came to the service to pay me homage. In my coffin I looked like a Botticelli angel, miraculously slender with long, soft golden curls. The picture moved me to tears.

"What's wrong with you?" It was Agnes. I hadn't seen her come into the unlit stairwell.

I was so startled that I lost my balance and fell to the floor with a crash of suitcase and legs. "Nothing," I muttered. "I didn't know you were going to be here."

I was terrified I'd been told and had forgotten—during this very low point in my life people were always telling me things that I didn't seem to hear.

"Neither did I. I called Mary to get your phone number and she told me you were just getting back to town today. Sorry if I frightened you."

I got back to my feet somehow and unlocked the apartment door. Just navigating the strip from the hall to the living room was an agony—I ran into the jamb once more and was so nervous that I tripped over the suitcase. Agnes made no comment then or later on my shambling, awkward gait, or on the freezing apartment which stank of mold and Raid.

She took me out to dinner, just her—Isabel hadn't come

on this particular trip—and made me feel alert, witty, intelligent. She assumed I had an adult understanding of people—from the waiters to the U.S. Congress to my own parents—and I responded with what seemed to me to be enormous sophistication. Late in the evening she told me I had beautiful hands and should plan to do something fine with them, and to this day, in the disgust I can't overcome for my body, I look at my hands with a loverlike admiration.

After that I used to visit her and Isabel. In those days you could fly on student standby for some trivial price and I'd go in the summer and during the Christmas holidays. She didn't run the school anymore. In the wake of Title VII legislation she'd been asked to take a role in shaping education policy. And she thought perhaps the country was changing in some way that would make it easier for little girls, that they wouldn't need special schools anymore. Now she's not so sure, but in that era we all had heady dreams.

I've never stopped walking into doorjambs, but Agnes trained me to do it with my head up, without apologizing. She and Isabel taught me some of the basics that I'd never gotten the hang of, such as how to feel at better ease inside my own body. As a teenager I'd tied down my breasts, ashamed of their betrayal, their announcement that I was a girl. Agnes taught me, if not to love them, at least to live with them. Most of all she and Isabel taught me how to listen when other people talked, by listening to me with interest.

Agnes didn't ask about my stories and I was too uncertain about them to remind her of the day she'd listened ten years before. I kept thinking I should go to medical school, become a surgeon to justify her faith in my hands. Or perhaps a painter, but painting is such a public art. You can write a story and no one will know you've done it, but when you paint a picture it's apparent that you've been doing something, even if you only keep it in the privacy of your home.

A few years later I finally showed Agnes one of my stories because I couldn't explain in any other way the lives of some people I cared about yet who troubled me. She was amazed—she didn't know I still wrote—she thought my academic work had taken that place in my life. She praised my writing and made me feel it might be something fine, like my hands. She urged me to try to publish my tale and told me about the burgeoning feminist magazines that nurtured women's art. I sent my story out and *Women: A Journal of Liberation* accepted it.

I'd published one other story, when I was eleven, in *American Girl*. They had a section called "My Turn" for contributions by readers. My entry was a story but they printed it as nonfiction, an uneasy sign to me that it wouldn't have made the grade if they'd known it was original, creative. Until Agnes urged me I never tried sending any of my other writing to publishers.

After *A Journal of Liberation* published my story, the romance I wove in my head was that I would write a book, a novel, and that it would be published. It took six more years before I was strong enough to make that dream happen. It was then that I started work on my first book, *Indemnity Only*.

I haven't seen Agnes for some time now, since 1982, when she came to celebrate the publication of *Indemnity Only*. Although I still hear from Isabel I find it painful that Agnes thinks I no longer need her.

For me the hardest part of telling stories is crossing the line from private words to public ones. When I write for myself alone the words come freely, but when I know someone else will read them they're like water squeezed from a stone. I think I still need Agnes, to give me more confidence in my voice, but she's spending her time with other irremediable girls whose troubles seem more serious—not running her school again, but seeking them out as she sought me.

Still, I've finally let my hair grow out. I've even learned to like my wild frizz. It gives me some assurance that I too may yet come to be a wild woman, not under anyone's control.

I've written five novels, all of them featuring a woman

named V. I. Warshawski, a detective who lives alone but whose close friend is a doctor some twenty years her senior named Lotty Herschel. People sometimes ask if V.I. is me, if Lotty is based on someone real. They're not: you can't put real people in a book, at least I can't—if I try to describe a real person's idiosyncrasies and make a fictional character act the way that real person would, everything becomes wooden. The action can't flow naturally because my imagination is penned in by how that living person would have acted.

But V.I. and Lotty are real, of course, because the only basis for imagining people is people. Even if V.I. isn't me, Lotty isn't Agnes, their relationship is real. Everyone needs Agnes so that she can find her own voice, so that her stories don't die in her head.

REMEMBERING
UNCLE WILL

by Walker Percy

I remember the first time I saw him. I was thirteen and he had come to visit my mother and me and my brothers in Athens, Georgia, where we were living with my grandmother after my father's death.

We had heard of him, of course. He was the fabled relative, the one you liked to speculate about. His father was a United States senator and he had been a decorated infantry officer in World War I. Besides that, he was a poet. The fact that he was also a lawyer and a planter didn't cut much ice—after all, the South was full of lawyer-planters. But how many people did you know who were war heroes and wrote books of poetry? One had heard of Rupert Brooke and Joyce Kilmer, but they were dead.

The curious fact is that my recollection of him even now, after meeting him, after living in his house for twelve years, and now thirty years after his death, is no less fabled than my earliest imaginings. The image of him that takes form in my mind still owes more to Rupert Brooke and those photographs of young English officers killed in Flanders than to a flesh-and-blood cousin from Greenville, Mississippi.

I can only suppose that he must have been, for me at least, a personage, a presence, radiating that mysterious quality we call charm, for lack of a better word, in such high degree that what comes to mind is not that usual assemblage of features and habits which make up our memories of people but rather a quality, a temper, a set of mouth, a look through the eyes.

For his eyes were most memorable, a piercing gray-blue and strangely light in my memory, as changeable as shadows over water, capable of passing in an instant, we were soon to learn, from merriment—he told the funniest stories we'd ever heard—to a level gray gaze cold with reproof. They were beautiful and terrible eyes, eyes to be careful around. Yet now, when I try to remember them, I cannot see them otherwise than as shadowed by sadness.

What we saw at any rate that sunny morning in Georgia in 1930, and what I still vividly remember, was a strikingly handsome man, slight of build and quick as a youth. He was forty-five then, an advanced age, one would suppose, to a thirteen-year-old, and gray-haired besides, yet the abiding impression was of a youthfulness—and an exoticness. He had in fact just returned from the South Seas—this was before the jet age and I'd never heard of anybody going there but Gauguin and Captain Bligh—where he had lived on the beach at Bora Bora.

He had come to invite us to live with him in Mississippi. We did, and upon my mother's death not long after, he adopted me and my two brothers. At the time what he did did not seem remarkable. What with youth's way of taking life as it comes—how else can you take it when you have no other life to compare it with?—and what with youth's incapacity for astonishment or gratitude, it did not seem in the least extraordinary to find oneself orphaned at fifteen and adopted by a bachelor-poet-lawyer-planter and living in an all-male household visited regularly by other poets, politicians, psychiatrists, sociologists, black preachers, folksingers, itinerant harmonica players. One friend came to seek advice on a book he wanted to write and stayed a year to write it. It was, his house, a standard stopover for all manner of people who were trying to "understand the South," that perennial American avocation, and whether or not they succeeded, it was as valuable to me to try to understand them as to be understood. The observers in this case were at least as curious a phenomenon as the observed.

Now belatedly, I can better assess what he did for us and I even have an inkling what he gave up to do it. For him, to whom the world was open and who felt more at home in Taormina than in Jackson—for though he loved his home country, he had to leave it often to keep loving it—and who in fact could have stayed on at Bora Bora and chucked it all like Gauguin (he told me once he was tempted), for him to have taken on three boys, age fourteen, thirteen, and nine, and raised them, amounted to giving up the freedom of bachelorhood and taking on the burden of parenthood without the consolations of marriage. Gauguin chucked it all, quit, cut out, and went to the islands for the sake of art and became a great painter if not a great human being. Will Percy not only did not chuck anything; he shouldered somebody else's burden. Fortunately for us, he did not subscribe to Faulkner's precept that a good poem is worth any number of old ladies—for if grandmothers are dispensable, why not second cousins? I don't say we did him in (he would laugh at that), but he didn't write much poetry afterward and he died young. At any rate, whatever he lost or gained in the transaction, I know what I gained: a vocation and in a real sense a second self—that is, the work and the self which, for better or worse, would not otherwise have been open to me.

For to have lived in Will Percy's house, with "Uncle Will" as we called him, as a raw youth from age fourteen to twenty-six, a youth whose only talent was a knack for looking and listening, for tuning in and soaking up, was nothing less than to be informed in the deepest sense of the word. What was to be listened to, dwelled on, pondered over for the next thirty years was of course the man himself, the unique human being, and when I say unique I mean it in its most literal sense: he was one of a kind: I never met anyone remotely like him. It was to encounter a complete, articulated view of the world as tragic as it was noble. It was to be introduced to Shakespeare, to Keats, to Brahms, to Beethoven—and unsuccessfully, it turned out, to Wagner, whom I never liked, though I was dragged every year to hear Flagstad sing Isolde—as one seldom if ever meets them in school.

"Now listen to this part," he would say as Gluck's *Orfeo* played—the old 78s not merely dropped from a stack by the monstrous Capehart, as big as a sideboard, but then picked up and turned over by an astounding hooplike arm—and you'd make the altogether unexpected discovery that music, of all things, can convey the deepest and most unnamable human feelings and give great pleasure in doing so.

Or: "Read this," and I'd read or, better still, he'd read aloud, say, Viola's speech to Olivia in *Twelfth Night*:

> *Make me a willow cabin at your gate,*
> *And call upon my soul within the house;*
> . . . .
> *And make the babbling gossip of the air*
> *Cry out "Olivia!"*

You see? he'd as good as say, and what I'd begin to see, catch on to, was the great happy reach and play of the poet at the top of his form.

For most of us, the communication of beauty takes two, the teacher and the hearer, the pointer and the looker. The rare soul, the Wolfe or Faulkner, can assault the entire body of literature single-handedly. I couldn't or wouldn't. I had a great teacher. The teacher points and says *Look*, the response is *Yes, I see*.

But he was more than a teacher. What he was to me was a fixed point in a confusing world. This is not to say I always took him for my true north and set my course accordingly. I did not. Indeed my final assessment of *Lanterns on the Levee* must register resevations as well as admiration. The views on race relations, for example, diverge from my own and have not been helpful, having, in my experience, played into the hands of those whose own interest in these matters is deeply suspect. But even when I did not follow him, it was usually in *relation* to him, whether with him or against him, that I defined myself and my own direction. Perhaps he would not have had it differently. Surely it is the highest tribute to the best people we know to use them as best we can, to become, not their disciples, but ourselves.

I used him as best I could, sometimes even against him. I was as unheeding and as selfish as any youth, but I had sense enough to see what he was and to take what I could. What he was was a true aristocrat. But his aristocracy was meritocracy of character, talent, performance, courage, and quality of life.

About him I will say no more than that he was the most extraordinary man I have ever known and that I owe him a debt which cannot be paid.

LOOKING BACK AT MY FATHER

by May Sarton

May Sarton was born in Belgium. She is the
daughter of the eminent historian of science
George Sarton and the English artist Mabel
Elwes Sarton. The family came to America as
refugees from World War I. Ms. Sarton is
seventy-seven and has recently published her
nineteenth novel, The Education of Harriet
Hatfield. She is also a poet, memoirist, and
journal keeper.

I never say my father old;
I never saw my father cold.
His stride, staccato vital,
His talk struck from pure metal
Simple as gold, and all his learning
Only to light a passion's burning.
So, beaming like a lesser god,
He bounced upon the earth he trod,
And people marveled on the street
At this stout man's impetuous feet.

Loved donkeys, children, awkward ducks,
Loved to retell old simple jokes;
Lived in a world of innocence
Where loneliness could be intense;
Wrote letters until very late,
Found comfort in an orange cat—

Rufus and George exchanged no word,
But while George worked his Rufus purred
And neighbors looked up at his light,
Warmed by the scholar working late.

These are the first two stanzas of "A Celebration for George Sarton," an elegy I wrote shortly after my father died suddenly of a heart attack on his way to give a lecture in Montreal. That was thirty-two years ago. He was seventy-two and I have outlived him, a strange and sometimes disturbing thought. For both my parents old age was unknown territory. I embark upon it very much alone and, as their elder now, feel it is time I came to terms with my feelings about these two remarkable beings who, to a large extent, made me what I am.

My mother and I were always intimate. Her letters to me, recently published by the Puckerbrush Press, make this abundantly clear. But I could not get over the wall to George Sarton himself. Now it is possible at last, and for two major reasons.

The first reason is that I recognize my father in myself more than I ever have till now, and in a hundred ways. We are kin. I stem from that root: the fierce dedication to work, the irrational rages, the compulsion to answer letters, the hatred and fear of worldliness, the love of animal pets, the absurd resentment of anything that interrupts the adamant routine that makes work possible.

From the time I was a small child I learned the sacredness of work. I had to be very quiet because when we first came to Cambridge as refugees from Belgium during World War I, we lived in a three-room apartment and the living room was his study. I spent a lot of time lying on the floor surrounded by newspapers and a bowl of water, soaking the stamps off letters (they came from all over the world) for my collection, but I had to be absolutely silent—how silent is made clear by the fact that when my mother gave me goldfish in a bowl that stood on a cupboard in that studious room, my father said after a day or so that they must be removed. He could not stand the noise they made! That "noise" was the faint bubbly sound when they came up for air. Before I was eight I had absorbed that if you worked very hard it justified a great deal. I had that conviction bred in my bones.

George Sarton spent his life translating his vision of the history of science as a discipline that must help to humanize and humble an increasingly technological culture into the six huge volumes called *An Introduction to the History of Science*. These end with the fourteenth century. His Harvard lectures on Greek science make two more. All of them have been translated widely into Arabic, Greek, Turkish, Japanese, etc.

When we arrived in the U.S.A. in 1916 the history of science hardly existed as a field in itself, was taught, if at all, by specialists in separate fields, such as the history of medicine or mathematics. By the time George Sarton died there were chairs in the history of science all over the country and at least part of his dream had come true.

I celebrated my fiftieth birthday by going around the world alone, starting in Japan and moving westward via India to meet in Greece what seemed the youngest of civilizations. Everywhere I was astonished and moved by the welcome I received as George Sarton's daughter. I felt like the ambassador of a great power.

Although not an international star like my father, I have done good work in literature in four genres and am at last beginning to be recognized. What we share and shared while he was alive was, in part, the loneliness of the long-distance runner and, in part, the traumas and disappointments of solitary work outside the mainstream. For George Sarton as for me it was a long uphill road. I remember well the day he came home after an interview with Vannevar Bush, then, during World War II, head of the Carnegie Institution, of which my father was a fellow, and which paid him a yearly stipend without which we could not have managed. My father was so pale when he came home and said so little about this interview that my mother and I were alarmed. He was silent for more than a week, silent and ill, and finally told my mother what Bush had said: "As far as I can see, Sarton, your work is irrelevant."

When *Cloud, Stone, Sun, Vine* came out, a selection from four of my published volumes, Karl Shapiro opened his review in the Sunday *Times* with the words: "May Sarton is a bad poet." Every time I get this kind of blow, am slapped in the face and unable to defend myself, I think of my father and feel a real communion with and pride in the breed I come from. We take such blows, may never get over them (who could?), but keep on running.

When I was a small child there was, of course, no such connection. He had no idea how to be fatherly with a small child except to tease, by throwing me as an infant into the air and shouting, "Wah, wah!"—a terrifying experience; or taking me on his knees and then abruptly opening them so I fell through. At that time I think I saw him as a kind of natural force like a thunderstorm but hardly as a loving father. But as soon as I was old enough to understand, my mother told me about his extremely deprived childhood. That did not help much while I was growing up, but when I reimagine it now, it opens the door into compassionate love.

George's mother, Léonie Van Halmé before she married Alfred Sarton, a man twenty years older than she was, died of a hemorrhage when she was twenty-one, too frightened or shy to ask for help. Her son George was just a year old, abandoned in that tall somber house in Ghent to the tender mercies of an eccentric father and the primitive Flemish maids who taught him neither manners nor tenderness but when he was ill did swallow his medicine if it had a bad taste!

Only recently have I come to fantasize what George Sarton might have been like had his father brought in an English nanny. As head of the Belgian railroad he could have well afforded this. Instead of that kind of care, the little boy was brought into dinner in his high chair and placed opposite his father at the end of the long table. His father was absorbed in the evening paper and if little George made the slightest sound, tapped a bell, and when the servant arrived said, *"Enlevez-le."* (Take him away.)

I ask myself now how did that neglected child survive, to marry an adorable woman, bring up a daughter, do significant scholarly work, become a legend in his time and after? What I see now is an acutely lonely child, of course, but also willful, very much aware of being the master except where his father was concerned. No one taught him to think of others. No one taught him anything about loving-kindness until he married Mabel Elwes. But loneliness is not a wholly negative state. It forced little George at any rate to make himself what he wanted to be with almost no help from the outside. As he grew up and went to school, he was known as a joker, a tease, and hardly bothered to work. He sat in the back of the classroom and was once addressed by the furious teacher: *"Sarton, tu pues la paresse jusqu'ici!"* (Your laziness stinks across the room.)

In looking back George Sarton himself always told these stories with great enjoyment and no bitterness. That is quite amazing. Does one come to enjoy even the hardships that help make one the person one is? Or is it that the past becomes a legend to be remembered with laughter? At any rate, at some point the lazy student began to work furiously and received a doctorate both in chemistry and in celestial mechanics at the University of Ghent, where several years ago I attended a moving celebration of his hundredth birthday. But was he to become a professor in one of the sciences? Apparently he went through a year of self-doubt, wandering the cafés of Ghent, writing a romantic imaginary autobiography, *Vie d'un Poète*, which he had privately printed. I am sometimes aware that I am living one of his imaginary lives. Slowly, through hours of solitary walks and solitary pipes in the cafés, his dream began to come into focus, the huge dream he would spend the rest of his life realizing.

I was a witness of part of that life of course. As I think it over now, I am touched by all kinds of little things in which I recognize his influence, absorbed by osmosis. Every January, "Daddy," as I called him, noted in his pocket calendar the birthdays of friends and colleagues throughout the year. He kept a fine collection of museum cards to send off when a birthday was imminent and people, sometimes far away in distant countries, were very touched. I realize suddenly that is exactly what I do myself and learned from him. My compulsion to answer letters is an inheritance which I sometimes regret, and then I remember how faithful he was to what he called "the charity of the scholar" and feel ashamed.

I began to smoke cigarettes when I was in high school and of course Daddy was upset, but I think he realized he was not going to win that battle, especially as he was a smoker himself. So one evening at Symphony Hall, during the intermission, he took a little box out of his pocket and saying, "Be nonchalant," offered me a Murad. At that time the fashionable Turkish cigarette was advertised by the slogan "Be nonchalant. Smoke Murad!" That way of yielding was George Sarton at his most charming.

He often decided to stop smoking himself, but stopping was his idea of stopping, for, as he said: "My rule now is one a day, one cigarette after breakfast, one cigarillo after lunch, one cigar after dinner, and one pipe before retiring." If that is not exactly giving up smoking, he proved that he could do it when Mother was dying. She hated smoke, and especially cigar smoke, which filtered down from his study. He had smoked a cigar only up there or out in the garden, but when she was dying he gave it up altogether for her sake.

If we had a small skirmish over my smoking, it became a battle royal when at about that time I decided not to go to Vassar, where I would have been given a scholarship, but instead to join Eva Le Gallienne's Civic Repertory Theatre in New York as an apprentice. My father had taken Mother and me to see three plays offered by the company in Boston. I was entranced by the atmosphere, the dedication, the purity of Miss Le Gallienne's vision of theater as not "a machinery for getting but an instrument for giving." I went backstage later alone and talked with her. She was persuasive. If acting was what I wanted I should start immediately!

There were loud and bitter arguments at home, and I begin to understand only now how hard it was for my father to conceive of his daughter rejecting an education for a profession as ephemeral and risky as the theater. The more remarkable, then, that he did finally agree that I might go to New York and that he would give me a hundred-a-month allowance. My mother, no doubt, had helped to make him see that I must be allowed the freedom of choice. Although theater did not end by becoming my life, I did have a rich five years, first as an apprentice and, after the Civic failed, directing a small company of my own. I have no regrets about college.

For many years I was always introduced when I gave a lecture or read poems as "George Sarton's daughter." I was proud of being the daughter of such an illustrious scholar but also a little irritated, for I wanted to be a person in my own right. Then came the time when George Sarton was crossing the Atlantic by boat to deliver in Paris a lecture on Leonardo da Vinci and a young man approached him to ask, "Are you by any chance May Sarton's father?" Daddy was much amused and after that signed his letters with the Arabic Abu-May, "Father of May."

The truth is that he could be delighted by all sorts of things I told him and my mother by letter as long as they did not disturb or dig into the secret space where he lived for his work. Only recently have I come to understand this and perhaps to accept his refusal to help me when I was in dire need. In 1931–32 the Civic Repertory was closed while Miss Le Gallienne recovered from terrible burns suffered when the furnace in her cellar exploded. My parents had arranged to spend that winter in Beirut so my father could learn Arabic, and they agreed to let me live in Paris and study theater. It was a seminal year for me in many ways, but it ended by being a disastrous one. I had unfortunately become involved with a woman who used me for all she could get and by late spring I was five hundred dollars in debt. My allowance was a hundred a month. I had finally to tell my parents. Daddy's response was a terrible letter of recrimination which ended by saying that he could do nothing to help me, that it was my problem. I was just nineteen! I was saved by an acquaintance who saw that I was close to breakdown and wrote a check for five hundred dollars when I told her the story. Little by little I managed to pay her back. My father never asked me how I managed or what had happened. It was easier to close the door. At the time I found his reaction not so much unforgivable as unbelievable.

I have to contrast this "washing of the hands" with the charming way he handled another disaster. I was staying with our old friends the Limbosches outside Brussels and bought directly from its owner an ancient black sedan for two hundred dollars. I named her La Vieille Caroline. After two weeks the dear thing stopped in the middle of the great beech woods and nothing could make her go, for the simple reason that I found out then from a mechanic, that she had been a taxi all through World War II and was on her deathbed when I bought her. To this misadventure which did not stem from emotional problems my father responded with humor and generosity. On June 13, 1949, he wrote me:

Dearest May,

I sympathize with you in your predicament. As Shakespeare said, "O woeful sympathy, piteous predicament," yet we must not exaggerate: worse things might happen and do happen. I shall do what I can to help you. To wit—the two hundred dollars which I send you, I now give and I am willing to lend you another two hundred. The car might still be salvaged. I would entrust it to an *old* mechanic, one old enough to be acquainted with the anatomy and physiology of ancient cars, and kind enough to bother with them. *Young* mechanics don't understand the ways of old cars, or are too impatient and supercilious.

Cheer up!

Tata

He loved cats so much partly because they asked nothing of him that he could not give, nothing that might trouble his mind. So he can speak feelingly of Gus, one of the great Cloudy's sons:

> Gus died last Thursday after a long illness. He came to us but a few days before his final departure, sat down on a chair in the dining room—and stayed there the whole night. Though he was very feeble he tried to show his appreciation by catching a mouse. Next morning Mother took the mouse away from him, and he was nonplussed and demoralised. I was one of the few people who understood him. I knew that he suffered a good deal—and that was the main cause of his being melancholy and saturnine.

Daddy wrote me about another cat, Oliver:

> Oliver celebrated his first birthday, but he was so triste and so tram that I felt obliged to give him a new name, to wit, *Tristram*. It seemed inescapable.

Writing such a letter was pure amusement for him, a way of playing.

And always the great work went on:

> I have restarted work, on the first volume of my Harvard lectures, and that will oblige me to spend a year in Athens in the Fifth Century B.C. I had got so used to the fourteenth century of our own era, and now I must go down nineteen centuries and far away. Of course I'll continue to spend part of my time in Cambridge.

George Sarton's humor, his charm, his innocent smile all made it hard to see through to the mischievous boy who managed to get what he wanted even as a grown-up person. When he was very young, for instance, and went over to see his first cousin Marguerite, at teatime each was given a piece of cake. George gobbled his down (he was always a lightning absorber of food) and then asked Marguerite to give him half of hers, which she did of course. He swallowed that and demanded the half of the half she still had! So it ended by her having next to nothing.

After his death when I was going through his library I came on a magnificent French-English, English-French dictionary in two thick volumes. On the flyleaf of the first was inscribed: "May Sarton received this book from Daddy on her birthday, Cambridge, Massachusetts, May 3rd 1940." I have no memory of receiving it and expect it disappeared almost at once into George Sarton's library, where it must have proved extremely useful—as it was to me when I uncovered it after his death, when I was engaged in translating poems of Valéry with Louise Bogan!

I see my father vividly as I write, a short, stocky man with broad shoulders and a noble head, a high, domed forehead, sparkling brown eyes behind thick glasses, and a beautiful generous mouth. He had an irresistible smile. Anyone seeing it might guess that here was a man who enjoyed being himself.

The second reason why I feel closer to my father than ever before is that I am lonely, and more so every year, for the values by which he and my mother lived. How I would love to walk over to Channing Place around four some afternoon in June and find them in the garden having tea. My father has on a battered straw hat and is smoking a cigar and my mother, a white Chinese shawl wrapped around her shoulders, pours the tea from the chaise where she lies, with a cat on her lap. And what are they talking about? If it were now it would be El Salvador perhaps, or Nicaragua, my mother aflame with indignation at our policy in Central America, which seems motivated exclusively by the fear of communism. Before World War I these two were socialists and met through a group they both belonged to, a group of intellectuals who wanted to be in touch with the working class and organized lectures and walks they shared with blue-collar friends. George Sarton was a feminist who addressed women in those prewar days by their last names. It has to be admitted that although theoretically a feminist it never occurred to him to help my mother with housework!

In the garden I see my mother drinking in the iris and columbine she had planted, resting her eyes on flowers even as she argues passionately about politics. My father too could be and was aroused to fury by injustice, by narrowness of mind, by racism in any form.

But art was as important to them as anything they shared. My father spent most Saturday afternoons at the Museum of Fine Arts in Boston poring over Chinese paintings which the curators unrolled for him. If people asked, "Who is that scholar so absorbed in Chinese painting?" the answer would be, with a smile, "Oh, that's George Sarton, the historian of science, giving himself a holiday." My mother, who had been first a painter of miniature portraits on ivory and a designer of furniture before they were married, was as involved in the arts and as articulate as he was.

How many museums they visited together in their separate ways! For my father insisted on seeing everything, moving tirelessly from room to room and absorbing it all into his encyclopedic mind. My mother, on the other hand, looked at a few things for a long time, feeling her way into the work of art, making it part of her. In a letter she says:

> I cast duty to the winds and went to the Museum (Boston)— looked at the benevolent, mercy-full Chinese Kwannons (large figures only four or five in a room). I was all alone, utterly quiet— the room was dimly lighted so I felt literally in a sort of "twilight of the gods," where a dim and utterly peaceful smile seemed to reign—a kindly certitude, like sunshine which soaks into one and effaces pains and ills or at least transforms them into something that does not matter.

As dusk came, after tea in the garden, they often, especially at the end of their lives when there was no cook, went upstairs to Daddy's study to listen to music together. He had a remarkable collection of records and might have planned a "concert" for her, the celebration of Mozart's birthday, perhaps, or simply hearing for the first time a record he had ordered and was eager to hear. It meant that she still had to cook their supper, but it was worth it.

Music, paintings, all the arts were a constant in their lives together, but then there were also books. Since George Sarton had been brought up in Belgium he came upon the English classics only after we came to the United States, and I can remember his excitement when he first discovered Sarah Orne Jewett, for example. I have to remind myself that before dinner he usually read for pleasure and as a way of relaxing, either *The Arabian Nights* in Arabic or the New Testament in Greek. But late at night, smoking a pipe, sitting in a comfortable armchair, his feet up, he allowed himself to explore English literature. By then Mother was asleep, for she often got up at four to make herself a cup of tea and hope to keep at bay a migraine headache.

It is easy to forget that my father had to learn a new language and both lecture and write in it when he was in his thirties . . . what an uprooting! As a young man he had taken a Berlitz course in English and after the first twenty lessons went to buy a ticket for twenty more, only to be told by the professor, "I do not advise you to go on, Monsieur Sarton, you will never learn English!" But once in the U.S.A., of course he had to, and he did, speaking with a slight accent, his writing style pungent, admirably clear, and in fact quite marvelous. The leopard learned to change his spots!

Of course my mother was an immense help, by correcting his essays, and also of course because we always spoke English, not French, at home.

Certain books they read became real events. I can remember the excitement when Mother discovered Freya Stark and passed her books on to my father, who loved them so much that he came to believe that it was he who discovered Stark and passed her along to my mother—a typical Sartonian piece of childish egotism. For once my mother was quite cross about this.

How can I not miss the richness of their lives together? I do not see any people now who have such passionate interest in the arts, music, gardening, literature, as well as politics. The only real luxury in their lives was travel. What I miss, what fills me with nostalgia these days, is how small the frame of reference is in many Americans and how large it was in my parents' lives. I miss real conversation, even that which dares to be passionate and adversarial. I miss tea in the garden or by the fire on dark winter afternoons, and the intensity of the life my parents lived to the end, in all its richness and diversity.

It is one of the real blessings of my old age that I have at last conjured up, to admire wholeheartedly and to love, George Sarton, my dear, maddening, noble father.

> *And when he died, he died so swift*
> *His death was like a final gift.*
> *He went out when the tide was full,*
> *Still undiminished, bountiful;*
> *The scholar and the gentle soul,*
> *The passion and the life were whole.*
> *And now death's wake is only praise,*
> *As when a neighbor writes and says:*
> *"I did not know your father, but*
> *His light was there. I miss the light."**

I miss the light.

---

* "A Celebration for George Sarton" may be found in its entirety in *Collected Poems* (*1930–1973*), by May Sarton (New York: W. W. Norton, 1974).

BATHSHEBA:
A SACRED MEMORY

by Isaac Bashevis Singer

Isaac Bashevis Singer is a recipient of the Nobel Prize for Literature and author of many books, including Gimpel the Fool, The Family Moskat, and The Magician of Lublin.

It happened, from what my mother told me, in Poland in the year 1904. On a Wednesday during the Jewish month of Cheshvan I was born to Bathsheba, the daughter of the rabbi of Bilgoray. My father, Pinchos Menachem, was the rabbi of a small Jewish village called Leoncin. After twelve years of marriage, my mother had given birth to five children: my oldest sister, Hindele Esther; my older brother, Joshua; two girls who had died in an epidemic of scarlet fever before I was born; and myself. A few years later, my younger brother, Moishe, was born.

I remember how I learned that my mother was pregnant with another child. One day I walked into the kitchen and discovered my mother had a big belly. When I asked her why her belly was so big, she laughed and said there was a child in this belly. That a human being was in my mother's belly seemed terribly strange and unbelievable. What does a child do there? Does it eat? Does it drink? Does it sleep? It was actually the first time that the problem of sex was told to me.

Over the years, my mother related to me a number of details about my birth. There was no Jewish midwife in Leoncin, only a Polish one. As far as my mother recalled, I was born crying. I remember her saying to me, "Why you cried so much I'll never know. My other children seldom cried. You were a crybaby who gave me a lot of trouble."

Because my mother was ill during her pregnancy the healer of Leoncin was afraid that I would not live long, and advised my mother not to suckle this particular baby. Instead, he told her to hire a professional wet nurse. There were a number of German wet nurses living in Leoncin but no Jewish ones since most Jewish women would never take up this profession. So, although it was considered a bad practice to hire a non-Jewish wet nurse and an ominous sign for the future of the child, my parents had no choice in the matter.

It was my lot to be suckled by a German woman—her name I don't remember. Sometime in later years, when my mother spoke about my childhood, she joked that I had drunk the milk of a goy and that this accounted for why I cried so much and why I didn't have any real kosher blood in my veins.

From my mother, Bathsheba, I inherited even more traits than from my father, Pinchos Menachem. Like my mother, I was a redhead with blue eyes. In the years to come I remember that the color of my hair and eyes created a sensation the first time anyone saw me. In the market I heard women remark, "Look at him, he looks like a little *sheigitz!*" and shrug their shoulders and laugh.

My mother's own red hair was always covered by a wig, unlike most of the other Jewish wives, who covered their heads with bonnets. As a child I wondered why she had to wear a wig. When I asked her, she said "It is forbidden"—her answer to most of my ceaseless questions about why certain things are not permitted. Once in a while she took the wig off and I could see her real hair, which was considered a sin, but immediately she put the wig back on and secured it with hairpins.

When I was barely four years old, my parents moved from Leoncin to the town of Radzymin, where my father had taken a post in a yeshiva. In later years I related to my mother a number of incidents that had taken place in Leoncin before we left. She was astonished by my memory and questioned me about details: which family lived in this house, who wore this dress or that hat, and each time I answered correctly. My mother would say to me, "What a memory! Let no evil eye befall you." My mother's blessing stuck with me for life. If it were not for my memory of such details I most probably would not have become a writer, for it is such details that make up the backbone of many of my stories.

As young as I was in Leoncin and Radzymin, I had the feeling that my family was different from other families. My father had a style of dressing that most Jewish men did not follow. He wore a round velvet hat instead of a cap and a long black coat with half shoes. He studied large volumes and wrote day and night in a notebook instead of selling food, wares, and trinkets in a store like other children's fathers. Once I told my mother that I was in love with a little girl because her father was a merchant. She rebuked me, "This is no reason to love a girl. You love her because she is clever and kind, not because her father sells chocolates in a store."

My father, when he was home, spent most of his time in his study poring over books. I was always curious about what my father was reading and writing. When I asked him, he said, "The Torah is bottomless. No matter how much one studies it, there is always more to learn."

As the wife of a rabbi, my mother was extremely pious. She always wore a long skirt down to her ankles and blouses that completely covered her arms. My sister, Hindele, on the other hand, longed to wear modern clothes. From our window she saw girls with hats on their heads and purses slung over their shoulders. She begged my mother to buy her a scarf, a purse, or a short-sleeved blouse, but my mother was scandalized by the idea and would not allow Hindele to dress according to the modern fashion. Hindele cried and pulled her hair out; she accused my mother of favoring her sons. But my mother would not permit Hindele to dress in such a disgraceful manner.

In her own way, though, my mother was enlightened. Even at that time, she was a suffragist, as they called certain women's libbers in those days. Her answer to war was that all women should unite and resolve not to live with their husbands until they had made peace. Only women, she would say, could end war forever. Often, I heard my mother argue with my brother Joshua about this idea. Joshua, who had left the path of righteousness, answered her, "It is not in man's nature to make peace. Neither men nor women will ever unite. Darwin says life will always fight for its existence." My mother's eyes would become moist, and she would say, "If this is the way it is, then there will never be peace in the world."

Not only war but even the smallest act of violence against another human being made my mother cringe. Whenever she read about an outbreak of fighting, a robbery, or a murder in the Yiddish newspapers, she would wince in despair. "Will it never end?" I often heard her say to herself, shaking her head and clicking her tongue. She had great compassion for those she read about in the newspapers who were run over, robbed, raped, beaten. She suffered not only her own afflictions but also those of all mankind.

Perhaps my own compassion for those who suffer and my embrace of nonviolence (I am a vegetarian) stem from my mother's great love for peace. Even as a small child, I was inclined to be afraid of even the slightest violence, whether it was the slaughter of a chicken or the capture of a mouse in a trap.

One morning I ran into my parents' bedroom with a great cry. They asked me what had happened, and I told them that a pig was squealing. "Why are you crying?" they questioned me. "Because a peasant is hitting it with a stick." I was crying so bitterly that it might as well have been me that was being beaten. I suffered from great pity when animals were beaten, whether a dog or a mouse. The suffering of all living creatures made me desperate.

Even today, at eighty-four years old, any act of violence, small or large, still disturbs me immensely. I have never found a reason for the murdering of another human being, the rape of a woman, the beating of a helpless animal. Not a few times I thought I heard my mother, as she read the Yiddish newspapers, rail against the Creator who could see all this misery but remained silent. As a child and as an adult I have wondered the same thing. Still, my mother told me that men must love life and be thankful to God for giving it to people. The bad people, she said, did not love life and did not cherish it. For that reason, many of them became killers and thieves. I often heard my mother tell Joshua that many of the world's misfortunes were a result of human boredom. She told Joshua that the reason for war is that people inevitably tire of peace and cause conflicts to create excitement. Especially after a couple came to our house asking for a divorce, she would say that people quarreled because they were bored with family life.

In our house small arguments were not uncommon, between my mother and father, my sister and Joshua or me. But they were always kept in check and never allowed to explode like bombs. My parents often blamed demons for any kind of discord, from a scuffle to the disappearance of a shoe. The Evil One tempted you at every turn. There was much talk about evil passions and the ruin they could cause when not controlled. I was guilty of many of them myself, even at such a young age. For instance, I could not get enough of watching the acrobats who performed tricks near Krochmalna Street in Warsaw though my parents had forbidden me to do so. One of the worst sins was not to listen to my parents, and what God had told them to tell me. I believed that God always told them what was right and wrong, and they in turn would let me know.

One of the worst temptations was sex. My father told my brothers and me to stay away from salacious women. Sex was something wrong, something not to be spoken about, even evil.

Still, I could not help myself. Love affairs, real or imaginary, fascinated me. I especially loved the story in the Bible of the Queen of Sheba and her love affair with King Solomon. As a writer I have often felt that the only worthwhile stories contain a love affair or two, and even as a child I realized this. It seemed to me as I read about the Queen of Sheba, or sat in my father's courtroom absorbed in the problems of couples, that grown-ups were as hungry for excitement in their own way as I was in mine.

In my father's courtroom I learned that discord and disenchantment sometimes accompany love. It was there that I studied the whims, desires, and conflicts of the human soul. Many people came to my father and mother with various complaints, from the ridiculous to the serious. I never saw my parents turn anyone away and everyone who came was treated with kindness. Sometimes my mother served tea to these guests in the courtroom. She always made everyone feel welcome. Very often people cried, carried on, fought, and screamed, and my parents always listened patiently and tried to resolve these problems. Once when a couple wanted a divorce because of a silly argument I heard my mother say, "Human stupidity has no limit."

Above all, my parents were honest and charitable people. However, it seemed to me that that was where the similarity ended. Though my father, a man with a long beard and stooped shoulders, bred fear in young children, he was always good-natured and rarely became angry. He never questioned the existence of God and had faith in almost all people. My mother, on the other hand, was impatient with the human race and resented life's tribulations. I once heard her say, "I hate the human species."

While my father accepted what most people told him, my mother had the eyes of an eagle, sharp and piercing. No one could fool her. She saw through a person's masks when my father didn't. Often she could be sarcastic and biting. Unlike my father, who never seemed to have any doubts, my mother had to search for comfort in morality books. She was deeply religious, yet a few times I heard her question God's love for mankind, especially after she read a news story about the murder of some victim or the death of a child from a sickness. "Why did it happen?" she would ask. "There is no reason for it."

The source of my parents' compassion was their faith. In our house Jewishness was no mere formality. Religion was the core of our lives. Both my mother and my father descended from generations of rabbis, and I was expected to become a rabbi too. The coming of the Messiah was not a topic one took lightly. My parents never doubted that the Messiah would come. It was just a matter of time, they told me. The fact that I questioned the truth of the Messiah a few times caused my parents great consternation. Even as a child I remember asking my parents, "Is it true the Messiah will come?" I was never completely satisfied with the proof they gave me in the holy books, which promised it would be so.

Worse than my childish doubts, the fact that my brother Joshua, who was eleven years older than me, had all but renounced Judaism caused my parents a lot of pain. Joshua often discussed his modern ideas with my mother. He told her that people did not come from Adam, but from apes. God hadn't created the world in six days; it had exploded from the sun and was billions of years old. God had played no part in creation; it was nature's mighty powers that had breathed life into the world. My mother often spoke of God and the Evil One in order to counter Joshua's arguments, but for Joshua neither the devil nor God existed. My mother's pleas were archaic and meaningless in the face of scientific discoveries.

Such discussions almost always took place in the kitchen when my father was not listening. The kitchen was warm and cozy and usually a fire was burning in the oven and soup was boiling on the stove. Besides books by Darwin and Spinoza, Joshua brought home novels, Yiddish translations of Tolstoy, Dostoyevsky, Turgenev, Knut Hamsun, Mark Twain. He urged my mother to read them. Joshua himself wanted to be a writer. He told my mother that to be a writer like Dostoyevsky or Tolstoy one must have talent and great knowledge of the human soul. My mother, who had read mostly books of religion and morality, scolded Joshua for reading such worldly books, but once in a while we caught her looking into them.

A naturally good reader, my mother often expressed her opinions to Joshua about the books. She would say, "People don't speak this way. This talk is wooden." Or: "This writer really doesn't know how people act." Joshua was amazed by my mother's insights even though her knowledge of literature was limited. He exclaimed, "Mama, you understand literature better than most critics!"

These conversations made a great impression on me. I decided to become a writer, and listened with great attention to what my brother and mother said. I tried to remember each word. I told Shosha, the little girl with whom I played, every detail that I could remember. My brother told my mother that literature was not only concerned with plots and twists, but more importantly it dealt with the characters of people—their emotions, their way of talking, and their behavior. My mother was never disinterested in Joshua's opinions. It seemed to me, even then, that my mother was a highly intelligent reader and appreciated good literature, though she could not admit it, especially to my father, who read almost nothing but religious works and who did not approve of secular literature.

Many times I came into the kitchen after playing and found my mother sitting at the table reading a book. I would ask, "Mama, what are you reading?"

She would say, "Can't you see? It's a book."

"What is the book about?"

"It says that people should not fight with each other but should be kind to one another."

I would relate some tale about a boy slapping another boy and ask if this was good.

"No, this isn't right."

"Will he be punished in Gehenna for hitting the boy?"

"Maybe. But children should not be allowed to behave badly anyhow. If you do something wrong you should apologize."

"Can I read your book, Mama?"

"When you grow up you will read many books. For the time being, go outside and play."

As she predicted, I read many books when I grew older. My mind was constantly plagued with questions about life, God, the soul, and I read with a hunger that could not be satisfied. Even in the first years of my life my mind was busy with questions. Where was God? Why did He create men and animals? Why was one born male, another female, some Jewish and others Gentiles? Why did some animals eat up other animals? When my mother wearied of my questions she would say to me, "Don't bother me with so many questions," and push me away.

The question of suffering especially bewildered me. At home my father taught me the Gemara and my mother taught me the Bible. One day my mother and I were reading the Book of Leviticus. I was horrified to learn that sacrifice played such a big part in the Judaism of the Old Testament. The priests burned animals on the altar as a sacrifice to God: sheep, rams, goats, doves. The idea that God, who created all things, enjoyed these horrors shocked me. I asked myself: What kind of a God orders men to do violence on other living creatures?

Especially when I passed a slaughterhouse, the question of why the strong ones had the strength to hurt the weak ones never left me. It has been for me a question forever and a part of my writings. I was told that chickens are sooner or later all slaughtered by a man called a *shochet* or a slaughterer. Once I asked my father if a *shochet* was punished in Gehenna, and he said, "No, he's not punished in Gehenna, because to slaughter is considered a *mitzvah,* not a sin."

The problem of killing animals for sport especially made me sick. Not far from Radzymin there were forests where the squire was heard shooting, and when I asked my mother what made this noise, she said that the squire was hunting animals. I was faced with the problem of whether this man, the squire, was a good or bad man. My mother told me that according to Jewish law, hunting was a sin. At the same time I knew that slaughter was considered a religious act, almost like praying. This has been the question of my life; it has never really left me: How can one kind of killing be sacred while another is a sin? I realized, even then, that there was no answer to these questions either in the holy books or in the explanations of my mother. I still cannot accept the ruthlessness of God, or whatever these high powers may be.

Though the slaughter of animals did not distress my mother in the way that it did me, she could not bear to hear about the sufferings of human beings, especially those of her own people. She once complained that the Jews had more than their share of afflictions. In a land called Russia the Jews were driven out from the villages where they lived because of their Jewishness. I heard her discuss such words as "pogrom," and in the time of a pogrom strong people attacked weak people, drove them out from their houses, and even beat up little children, sometimes crippling them. Some people became so worried that their children or relatives might be hurt in a pogrom that they lost their minds from fear.

"What will happen to us Jews?" my mother asked my brother Joshua. "Must we always live in fear of our lives?"

Joshua talked about the Jewish nation that a Dr. Herzl had wanted to create before he died. Dr. Herzl, he said, believed that the Jews should form a nation like all the other nations and have their own country.

"This is nothing but an idle dream," my mother would say.

During the Hitler years my mother, old and frail, and my younger brother, Moishe, a rabbi, were taken by train from Galicia, Poland, to Kazakhstan, Russia, packed into a cattle car by the Russians, who were supposedly "saving" them from the Nazis. The cars were so crowded that the people could not move and were forced to relieve themselves like animals.

I can see my mother and brother months later trying to chop trees in the forest in the midst of frosts and snowstorms in order to build a hut for themselves. They finally died from the cold, from starvation, or possibly from fright of being denounced as anti-Stalinists, religious reactionaries, Zionists. People were sent to dig gold in the north for such accusations and perished.

Many years ago I was surprised by a visit from a man who was on the same train as my mother and brother. He had survived the war years in Soviet Russia and come to America. He told me a story I will never forget. Despite the fact that Poland was occupied and divided by the Nazis and the Bolsheviks, the Polish zloty still had some value at the time of this tragic journey. One could still buy hot water or a slice of bread when the train made its stops. The man told me that my mother had received money from my brother Joshua who was living in the United States, and she shared the little she had with those who traveled without a penny. The man said to me, "She was a saint."

My house was a house of charity. My father, bless his memory, once took in a man who looked to me like a corpse. He was dying of an illness and had no money. My father gave him a bed and my mother took care of him. He died a pauper, but he was taken care of until his last days. Another time my father gave a man sixty rubles so that he could marry off his daughter. "God is merciful and compassionate and it is the duty of the human race to follow His example," my father would say.

My mother knew, when she gave her last zloty away, that the smallest act of mercy, even an encouraging word, can save a life. From my mother I learned that to tolerate cruelty is cruelty itself. Neglect of any kind of life is actually a neglect of God. To love and respect, and even in a way worship, all living things is truly to love, respect, and worship God, the Creator of all things.

REVISITING TEOC

by Elizabeth Spencer

Elizabeth Spencer grew up in Mississippi and has written eight novels, three volumes of short stories, and a play, For Lease or Sale, *produced recently by Playmakers Repertory Company in Chapel Hill, North Carolina, where she now lives. Her most recent collection of stories is* Jack of Diamonds.

ake two anxious young parents living in a snobbish little Mississippi town during the hard times of the twenties and thirties, hoping to please the fine families they had always known, hoping to do the right thing in every way, hoping their children would excel in school, succeed socially, be praised for good looks, dress well, never say the wrong thing, never be criticized, be friendly to all. Furthermore, and most important, those children were rigidly expected to attend church and Sunday school and young people's meetings and read the Bible every day and say their prayers every night and grow up to be good Presbyterians.

Take two lively children with inquiring minds who were not overly anxious to please and who had scant concern about what anybody thought.

Help!

Something, obviously, had to come to the rescue.

The something that did come for my brother and me was what an attentive guardian angel or, more likely, a wise and witty fairy godmother might have had made to order. He was not a something but a someone, and was there all the time: our uncle, our mother's youngest brother.

Joseph Pinckney McCain was charming and funny, full of jokes, songs, and teasing. But he listened with care to what people said, and people to him did include children. He was irreverent, tolerant of sins and friendly with sinners, was happily married to a pretty woman who loved him completely, and by some inexplicable curse, which was for us like a final touch of miracle, he was childless.

The outline is enough to let you see it all.

But wait. There are wonderful things to tell.

The McCain family since the early 1800s had owned a plantation, some two thousand acres in all, in Carroll County, Mississippi, thirteen miles by winding gravel roads from Carrollton, our hometown in the hills. The land lay largely in "the Delta," that flat farming area along the Mississippi River south of Memphis, but the old family home, which burned about the time of my mother's birth, was on a hill overlooking it. The new family home, a pleasant one-story house surrounded by verandas, stood in a grove of live oaks near the foot of the last hills which skirt the plain. This was Teoc.

It was not to be seen from a distance. In blistering July heat, the oaks spread a depth of cool shade; their great shallow roots crawled and sprawled, breaking through the surface of the sandy soil between the cattle gap and the front gate, pushing up close to the broad front steps. In the still of night, an occasional oak ball banged on the tin roof like a fist. In winter, too, the oaks made an evergreen shelter in a swept landscape.

Coming there in a car from town over those crooked roads heavy with dust or sloppy with mud, you took a final sharp turn at the plantation store, a plain brick building with gas pumps out front. A scant half mile beyond, past a hillslope with a cemetery among the trees on the right and a long spread of infinite flat fields on the left, you would see the grove. Just over a small bridge, you would enter it. You would have telephoned ahead.

Uncle Joe would be waiting. He would have seen the cloud of dust the car made from the time it passed the store, watched it advance, heard the rumble of the cattle gap, and come out to stand on the veranda, waiting, one foot on the porch railing, wearing seersucker trousers and rolled-up shirt sleeves, ready.

Squeezing past our parents, my brother and I were the first ones out; the way I remember it, we couldn't wait. Cars stopped habitually in the wide sandy space between the cattle gap and the front fence. In my memory we were through the gate before the motor died. What joy in that sand beneath our shoes, or maybe we were even barefoot, though Aunt Esther would not be too happy about it.

"Come on in! Come on in!" my uncle would call. I always had bandages. "How'd you skin yourself this time? Lord have mercy. Can't you learn to stand up?" And hair to pull straight over too large ears. "A little more and you could use 'em to fly." And new tennis shoes in an ever bigger size. "How firm a foundation, ye saints of the Lord." All this for me, with another store for my brother. Whatever he said, we were happy to hear it. Though it couldn't be called complimentary, we would stand there anyway, grinning in mindless delight at his ragging and railing. He picked us over like a hound with puppies; he carried us in his teeth like cubs.

Our parents would have come in, standing back and admiring us, glad to be there, my mother especially—her home, after all. Her brother, her children. I think, too, that, like us, what they felt there was freedom. Away from it all. A long sigh.

Aunt Esther was coming. Out through the shadowy hallway with its comfortable chairs and sofas and gleaming tables, or in from the screened-in half of the veranda with its rugs and ferns and rocking chairs, and the "glider," so nice to nap on in the afternoon. The oak boughs lifted in the breeze.

"That was quite a storm last night," says my uncle. "I thought it struck one of the oaks."

"Which one?" asks my mother, proprietary.

"Don't think it did. Just sounded like it."

"I was scared," my aunt says.

"She was callin' on the Lord to save her," he says. He lifts one finger in a mock sermon. "The day of repentance was at hand." We all laugh. It is nice to be friendly about the Lord.

Maybe we were all just there for the day, but maybe one of us would be staying on. "I can't let them both go at once," my mother would say, so we had our separate lengthy visits. Perhaps it was better that way, we were so different.

"Joe Pink," he sometimes called himself, for Joseph Pinkney, his full name. He was of medium height, with rather broad shoulders, one held higher than the other, a family trait, and the lean limbs of all the McCains. The hands were large-knuckled, the joints all over were big, something we attributed to Scottish ancestry; we had all come from Scotland, way back when. His hair was sandy brown, getting a little thinner and grayer with the years, though he never got bald; and his face was florid, burnt and scaled from exposure, and maybe from the occasional bouts of drinking Aunt Esther frowned on, holding him down. His expression was changeable, serious and inward to the point of somber meditation in repose, but more often broken into a dozen planes with foolishness and affection. He loved to rag people, observe them carefully for what he could draw out as material for his stories about them, lie in wait for their more embarrassing moments to occur (sometimes prearranged little traps they were bound to blunder into). Then he was off, relentless. Cries of protest. General aggravation. Yet no real anger. How did he do it? I don't know. It was said that everybody loved Joe McCain.

But he did not love everybody. He liked attractive women, but he often disliked "ladies." He disliked properness and put-on, pretense. There was a good bit of that sort of thing around, especially in Carrollton, and a number of my mother's models of fine behavior bored him. He would sit in their company with his hat in his lap, saying the right things, but you knew the small boy in him was counting the minutes till they left. He hated hypocrisy, and these mincing ways smacked of it to him.

He loved his friends in the Teoc community: "Teoc Tillila," "Tall Pines" in Choctaw, was actually the Indian name for the whole area. It had then a rural delivery service, a church four or five miles distant from the McCain place; and a number of farming families, who came to the store to get gasoline and groceries, were in lively touch with one another.

Aunt Esther was social in the fashion of the times. She was by general consensus very pretty, with rich dark brown hair drawn into a chignon, large brown eyes to match, and delicate features. She loved pretty things and often drove to Greenwood, a Delta town about ten miles away, to shop for materials, sewing supplies, spices, gloves, and many other items on her list. She often left time to go to the picture show. She worked hard. She crocheted spreads and afghans, embroidered linens, briar-stitched throws in velvet and satin. She canned and pickled and preserved in late summer, raised abundant flowers in beds outlined in native rock, reached by winding sandy paths. Here in this garden beside the house she gave evening parties with Japanese lanterns hung from the oak branches. The ladies wore their fragile dresses; their husbands or bachelor friends, dressed in shirts and ties and summer-weight coats, standing around, eating and talking; a fine evening. At her bridge parties, she set tables out in the open hallway. Organized, and a bit sharp-tongued, with so much to do, she bossed us around. "She thinks my children belong to her," my mother used to say, but without resentment at first—a little, maybe, later on.

As for Uncle Joe, there was no debate. He knew in what ways we belonged to him, knew it all along, knew what a difference he could make and was making. Occupied with business, my father spent a lot of time worrying.

There were four brothers and two sisters in my mother's family, plus my grandfather, who lived throughout my childhood, and numerous cousins, aunts and uncles, and "connections." A part of my uncle's love for my brother and me was rooted deep in his clannish family feeling. He could and did get mad at you for hypocrisy, or churlishness, or what he called "welshing," failing to do what you'd promised. You had to measure up. But he never rejected you. Thirteen miles away, along twisted roads almost but never quite impassable, he was always there, through the years, foot on the porch railing, looking out, waiting.

Though both my brother and I spent long periods "on Teoc," I must separate us now, for my brother was seven years older than I, and the education Uncle Joe obliged himself to give us took, I think, different forms. Even when we were very young he met us on our own ground, my brother's ground being always very different from my own.

I loved to read and I loved to ride. In Carrollton we lived on a forty-acre property, so there were barns and pasture enough first for ponies, then for a riding horse or two. When school let out in the spring, the day would come when I would put on a long-sleeved shirt and a straw hat, pants or even overalls (not jeans but real bib overalls), and catch my horse, brush him down, saddle him carefully, and set out to ride to Teoc. My suitcase with dresses, pajamas, comb, and toothbrush would probably be in the mail carrier's car for leaving at the store.

Thirteen miles to go: out past the outskirts where known families lived, then four miles or so to the crossroads, then left. Another five miles through bare country nobody knew much about. There were gullies, washed red from erosion, pines among low hills, some small fields. I was scarcely twelve. "If anybody stops you," my instructions ran, "you say, 'I'm Mr. Spencer's daughter from Carrollton, and my uncle is Joe McCain.' " I don't remember ever seeing anyone. It was strange, vacant land.

On to a right turn where a brown-painted house stood in a heavy surrounding hedge, and then there was safe territory, homes of people we all knew—the Longs, the Meeks, the Balls. A sound feeling. Finally to reach the long descent down the last hill before the Delta stretched out, glimmering green and distant in the midmorning sun. Teoc Creek was just ahead, where the horse shied, balked, and worried his way over the iron overhead bridge, clanking from his hooves, with a wooden floor so often patched it was layered in various-colored wood, and the brown creek showed through the planks and holes from far below.

Just ahead was the store. On either side of the road, the cotton plants, in long rows wobbly as a child's line on a page, ran outward, broken by patches of new corn. There were willows near the store.

My uncle might be there. If not, somebody I knew would see me go by. Sam Long, the storekeeper, old Dr. Maybry stopping in to play cards or have a Coke, or Miss Lucy Wollard Ball, waiting in her car for the mail. Somebody would wave. The Negroes all knew me—"Miss 'Lizbet . . . done come down . . . Yes, ma'am!" Inside, whether I saw them or not, somebody would be calling ahead, turning the crank on the dusty store phone in that midmorning still hour, with most labor out in the field, to say I had arrived.

Left turn for the last lap then, with the oak grove ahead and the house and him on the front porch in shirt sleeves, foot on the railing. "Get on down, just hitch him there. Hurry up, you limb of Satan. It's close to dinnertime." Later than I thought. Soon from out in the backyard the huge plantation bell would ring, calling the wage hands to come in from the fields, time to eat.

He rode the place in those days. I had brought my horse to ride with him. Those were pre-jeep times, and no car could maneuver the plantation roads. They were swampy in places, broken by drainage ditches, or heavy with dried mud from the winter.

Uncle Joe would get up before day, while I was still asleep. My mother, complimenting my aunt, often said of her, "She gets up and dresses at four in the morning to eat with Joe. She'll never let him eat alone." Harvey Hoskins, the overseer at the barns, would bring up my uncle's mare in the dim light and he was off to the fields. Later, when I woke and ate, I would walk down to the barns for my horse. I would ask along the way, riding out through the huge wooden gates of barns and lots, out onto the land, "Where's he got to? Where is he by now?" and whoever I passed would tell me, or guess at it. I would find him not long after. A little at a time, out in the dazzle of full sun, we covered the great fields, stopping where a tractor might be broken down for a while, or to pass the time of day with the cotton choppers, who would come close to talk about the crop stand, or to look in on a cabin where somebody might be sick. Sometimes we got off to pick black-berries from bushes along a drainage ditch, or to drink water that gushed from the iron pipe at one of the artesian wells scattered over the place. We watered the horses from the concrete trough, and drank right from the pipe, letting the water run over face and neck to wash the sweat away. The water tasted of iron, was clear and bright and so iron-cold it hurt your teeth to drink it. The Negroes came to these wells, usually in the late evening after work, riding a mule-drawn slide with a barrel on it to fill for daily water at home.

In late morning we would wind up at the store. The mail, a Coke or Nehi if not too near dinnertime, a quick hand of cards with Sam, or Rosewell Long, or Dr. Maybry, or Arnie

Meeks (the men sitting on the smooth bare oak counter, dealing from a deck worn to rags). The loser paid for the drinks. Then back to the house, maybe hearing the great bang and bong of the dinner bell along the way.

I've tried to think back, tried earnestly to remember if there were evidences of bad feeling between my uncle and the many black people, descendants of the original slaves for the most part, who worked his land, lived on it year round, and were furnished out of the store. As I remember it, they were exceptionally good-humored around him in a way that seemed to make their dependency a reassurance to them rather than a burden. I can't to this day believe I would not have noticed any deep-seated animosity.

It was slightly different as regards my aunt. I knew the house Negroes often felt themselves ordered around, and I knew that some of them resented her. She railed at them for laziness, for forgetting, for doing what she wanted less than perfectly.

Her story is interesting just for itself. She was married quite young, at eighteen, and at that a year older than my uncle. She had come from being a small-town teacher (French and elocution), and found herself, a "town girl," cast up in the midst of a plantation with an entirely black population for miles around to see daily and call on for everything she couldn't do herself. In addition, she had the running of what amounted not just to a house, a home, but a whole system of providing year-round food and civilized living, from the raw material of sheep shearing and hog slaughtering, milking, separating butter and cream, cutting and hauling wood for fires, to keeping well, or nursing the illnesses of, all and sundry around her. As if that were not enough, she also, in the first days, felt it her duty to "educate" the blacks and so called them into classes and gave them, among other subjects, "moral instruction." Very soon she gave it up. There were episodes later to be laughed at, of her running in from the garden in tears, apron flung over her head, of stormy vexation and despair. But she turned her corner. "She had grit," my uncle often said, adoring her, though there had been a lot of quarrels too, and still were, for they were two spirited fighters. And lovers too: we never doubted that.

By the time I came along she was very much the chatelaine, a demanding mistress, quick, with a no-nonsense way of making sure she was listened to, obeyed, obeyed on time. She kept the keys tied with rawhide thongs to small cedar boards, labeled "smokehouse" or "pantry" or "woodhouse" or "tools." These had to be returned my nightfall. From a country house, hastily built after the old home burned, added to in haphazard wings and tacked-on porches, she fused and embellished a gracious welcoming plantation dwelling, never a mansion, but beautiful to look at, serene to stay in. For this she had to have help in plenty, and her help admired, obeyed, but sometimes resented her. They did not cling to her the way they clung to him.

Out on the place, riding with my uncle, I noted how Negroes came to find him, sometimes in pairs, trouble on their minds. "You go on ahead, Lizzie," he would say. So it was a marriage dispute. He wouldn't think it suitable for me to hear. Nor would they have told it before me. I would ride ahead and wait. He would sit his mare, leg up perhaps, with loose reins, and they would stand near her head or at the stirrup and he would listen, take off his cork helmet at times, scratch his brow, nod, following everything. Something would be, if not settled, advanced by the time they left, what I don't know, but they would look more at peace, would have agreed maybe to come back and talk again. At other times, some scrawny black woman would come up, or rather grow up, right out of high weeds, the pernicious Johnson grass that cursed that particular region, and complain that she didn't have enough food to get through the month. He would stop his horse. "Lord have mercy, I done furnished you twice already," he would say, but then the story would come up, rising up in all its detail. "Well, go on up to the store, then. Side meat and cornmeal . . . put it on the books."

It was an ugly system, of course, enslaving, grown up after slavery and not possible, apparently, ever to lose. But in that childhood time of enchantment and love, it never seemed to me anything but part of the eternal. Might as well question why the live oaks were there, or the flowers in Aunt Esther's garden, or the stars in the sky, as to say that Teoc could be run any way but the way it was, always had been, always would be. I myself was a slave more willing than any.

Once or twice, when invited, my aunt and I attended Negro services at the plantation church. We were solemnly made welcome. Later, during the thirties, the blacks on the place collected enough money among themselves to build a new church. It was neat, of wooden construction, with a modest white steeple and sturdy front steps. They named it "St. Joseph's Chapel" for my uncle. Some left, but wherever they went to, they were apt to write him, either for money or about some problem. I remember one well, a field hand named Joe Willie, who left and went to Memphis. I saw him a year or so later, back at the place. "I thought you'd left us, Joe Willie," I said. My uncle told me later that he had got into some scrape and got hit in the head. "Yes'm," was Joe Willie's version, "I went up yonder, but they tried to keel me, so I done come on back home."

We would ride all summer, often as much as twenty or thirty miles a day. Sometimes in late afternoon, when the shadows grew long, we would race our horses along the levee road near the creek, and often my uncle would suddenly turn his mare and drive her straight up the levee to the very crest, where he would halt, take off his hat, and catch the evening breeze, looking out all around him, while I came trotting up behind to join him.

All the time, the life of that land and those people was going on all around me. There is nothing like it I know of today, and not as much resembling it as there seemed to us to be, even then. I came later to see that my memories have more in common with country life as described by Chekhov, Tolstoy, and Turgenev than with the America of that time as we read about it in Dreiser or Sinclair Lewis. Enlightened as to its ills, as one would have to come to be, I could never deny that I loved it, or cease to look back on it with the greatest affection. I still claim joy as a good portion of its quality, and I love it still.

I have said I liked to read. Here Uncle Joe could also be a real companion, for the McCains were brought up around books, always had books, talked about books, took characters from books into their lives. They enjoyed fiction mainly, though they had studied history in the schools and academies they attended, and everyone had taken Latin. Also mathematics, said "to improve your mind." My aunt Katie Lou McCain, the elder sister, even taught Latin, in a town to the south.

Books at Teoc and at home in Carrollton stood two deep in the bookshelves, and most of them were good ones, would be thought so to this day. It's true that my uncle liked adventure tales, Rafael Sabatini, for instance; just as my mother confessed to liking such books as *V.V.'s Eyes* and *Queenie's Whim,* but for the most part the shelves were solid in their Dickens and Thackeray and Jane Austen and Hawthorne. My brother's favorite book, read many times over, was *Moby-Dick.* He persists in believing it is about a whale hunt. I agree.

My uncle saw to it that I read every word of his favorite book, *Les Misérables.* As early as age twelve he sent me plodding though this tome, well over 700 pages long, I recall, in the edition he had on Teoc. His own enthusiasm spurred me on. He kept me at it. Fantine and Cosette, Marius and most of all Jean Valjean himself were objects of his comment. He had thought of them a lot. He admired Valjean for his courage, his endurance, his masculinity, and his ability to grow, become greater than he was at first. He dwelt with some amusement on the love of Marius for Cosette. "He couldn't eat or sleep. He grew thin and pale. Look what love will do. That's how it is, Lizzie." "Poor things," my mother would chide. "It's such a cruel book. They were all so poor. It can't be good for her to read all that." "It's life," he would say. "She ought to learn about it."

He also admired Dickens, especially *A Tale of Two Cities;* the St. Evrémonde story was a fascination to him. Where did all this Frenchness come from? I've no idea. My grandmother, whom I did not remember, she having died about the time I was born, read Walter Scott, but Uncle Joe confessed that Scott bored him with long descriptions. Perhaps Hugo by comparison was more interesting, and the same went for Dickens when he didn't try "to put in too many characters."

During rainy days we sat and talked about these things. He liked Mr. Darcy in *Pride and Prejudice* and thought that Becky Sharp in *Vanity Fair* was "a mean little devil." He smoked Target cigarettes and let me roll them for him on a little orange-colored machine. The tobacco was spread in a small canvas trough, the fine paper set in place, and when I pressed the lever, one rolled around the other. I made them for him fifty at a time, and he kept them in a humidor on the hall table.

Nothing gold can stay.

I grew, entered awkward adolescence, suffered through growing pains, made everybody as miserable as possible, including myself.

Aunt Esther developed a malignancy. Incurable. She died during my first year away at college.

For a long while Uncle Joe was blindly depressed. There were the drinking, the late nights, the gambling, the women.

But a discovery emerged.

Still in his early forties, he was not only charming but desirable. He was a "planter." Prestigious: a McCain. Slowly, he reawakened to life, but this time that life was himself, a new revelation.

Things were never like before, but they were similar enough still to be clung to, and many times to be enjoyed. He would take me out to his favorite restaurants at times, showing me off as a prank as his "latest girlfriend." The owner of one came out to peek at me. Back in the kitchen she scolded him. "Just rocking the cradle now. Shame on you."

He had some questionable acquaintances. My mother got wind of one and reproached him at some length. He checkmated her easily. "She's a good woman," he said. What he meant by that phrase was not at all what she meant. But she couldn't go further with it. There was a family meaning he had put to use—"a good woman" would certainly be approved. My mother gave up.

He took trips to New Orleans. He had sometimes gone before in the company of an older brother, Uncle Sidney, a Navy officer, whenever he was home. Together they had created for me the vision of a glowing myth-city long before I had ever had a chance to see it for myself. When I first went there, early in my college years, I fully expected magnolia-scented air, walls draped in perpetually blooming bougainvillea, violet orchids opening by the light of scarlet moons. It was almost true. Uncle Joe often named his favorite restaurants and what he liked to order. Pompano *en papillote* at Antoine's, shrimp Arnaud at Arnaud's, and trout Marguéry at Gallatoire's. Don't neglect Tujaques's for lunch.

He still danced about at bedtime in his old pongee dressing gown, his "deshables," as he said. Sang the old foolish songs. Enjoyed movies, books, pretty women.

And married again.

Had two boys, his pride and joy. General happiness.

Then, the accident.

How did it happen? His second wife, Rebecca, afraid of the fierce storms, had got him to build a storm pit for refuge. There was water in it and some snakes. Alone, he had gone out with the gun to shoot them. She had driven up to meet the school bus bringing the boys home. Midafternoon in winter, no one around, even the kitchen empty. He evidently slipped on some broken steps. A shot rang out over winter-quiet fields. A bloody period.

Teoc was never to revive. He had recovered its life once, along with his own; but without him there was no new life possible. Rebecca left, moved to Greenwood with the boys. I'm told the house was rented first to one family, overseers, then to others. The oaks were cut down. I never went there again.

My brother, bolder, or maybe more nostalgic, drove there once with his wife, just to see. In the old days, on a happy afternoon, he and my uncle had buried a small store of articles inside the concrete support to a water tower—coins of that year, stamps, some newspaper clippings, statements they had written about themselves, all to reconstruct that time and place for whoever might come after, like capsule testaments shot out into space if time, say, is the space shot into.

But the house had fallen to ruins, and growth had come up so thick my brother could not force his way through to reach that spot and reclaim what they had so hopefully put there for the future to find and know them by. He came away with nothing.

A year or so ago cousins of my father's family held a reunion at a weekend country house in that area. Being in the state, I came. One after another, they fell to recalling Teoc, remembered having met my uncle, how grand and courteous he treated you. They spoke of Aunt Esther, how lovely she was, what a table she set, how welcome she made them. In the past, one or two my brother's age had come as weekend guests and marveled at the house, the gardens, the fun they remembered having.

A little at a time, they came to a decision. "It couldn't be far from here! Let's go there!" Two cars were filled on the spot.

Some came to find me. "You aren't going? But you used to nearly live down there! Don't you want to go?" I shook my head. "No, I don't. No, thanks." Then the final question, bound to come: "Don't you care?"

"Yes, I care too much," I answered, but I'm not sure they heard me. My father's side of the family are all busy people, doing something all the time. They went there and came back, immediately got interested in the fact that certain children had strung a slant wire and a trolley over a pond and were riding it across with shouts of glee. Either I didn't hear or I don't remember what they said they found on Teoc.

LETTER—MUCH TOO LATE

by Wallace Stegner

*Wallace Stegner was on the faculty of Stanford
University for many years and was the founder
and director of the Stanford Writing Program.
Among his novels are* Angle of Repose, *awarded
the Pulitzer Prize for Fiction, and* The Spectator
Bird, *fiction winner of the National Book Award
in 1977.*

Mom, listen.

In three months I will be eighty years old, thirty years older than you were when you died, twenty years older than my father was when he died, fifty-seven years older than my brother was when *he* died. I got the genes and the luck. The rest of you have been gone a long time.

Except when I have to tie my shoelaces, I don't feel eighty years old. I, the sickly child, have outlasted you all. But if I don't feel decrepit, neither do I feel wise or confident. Age and experience have not made me a Nestor qualified to tell others about how to live their lives. I feel more like Theodore Dreiser, who confessed that he would depart from life more bewildered than he had arrived in it. Instead of being embittered, or stoical, or calm, or resigned, or any of the standard things that a long life might have made me, I confess that I am often simply lost,

as much in need of comfort, understanding, forgiveness, un-
critical love—the things you used to give me—as I ever was at
five, or ten, or fifteen.

Fifty-five years ago, sitting up with you after midnight
while the nurse rested, I watched you take your last breath. A
few minutes before you died you half raised your head and
said, "Which . . . way?" I understood that: you were at a dark,
unmarked crossing. Then a minute later you said, "You're a
good . . . boy . . . Wallace," and died.

My name was the last word you spoke, your faith in me
and love for me were your last thoughts. I could bear them no
better than I could bear your death, and I went blindly out
into the November dark and walked for hours with my mind
clenched like a fist.

I knew how far from true your last words were. There
had been plenty of times when I had not been a good boy, or
a thoughtful one. I knew you could no longer see my face, that
you spoke from a clouded, drugged dream, that I had already
faded to a memory that you clung to even while you waned
from life. I knew that it was love speaking, not you, that you
had already gone, that your love lasted longer than you yourself
did. And I had some dim awareness that as you went away
you laid on me an immense and unavoidable obligation. I
would never get over trying, however badly or sadly or
confusedly, to be what you thought I was.

Obviously you did not die. Death is a convention, a
certification to the end of pain, something for the vital statistics
book, not binding upon anyone but the keepers of graveyard
records. For as I sit here at the desk, trying to tell you something
fifty-five years too late, I have a clear mental image of your
pursed lips and your crinkling eyes, and I know that nothing I
can say will persuade you that I was ever less than you thought
me. Your kind of love, once given, is never lost. You are alive
and luminous in my head. Except when I fail to listen, you still
speak through me when I face some crisis of feeling or sympathy
or consideration for others. You are a curb on my natural

impatience and competitiveness and arrogance. When I have been less than myself, you make me ashamed even as you forgive me. You're a good . . . boy . . . Wallace.

In the more than fifty years that I have been writing books and stories, I have tried several times to do you justice, and have never been satisfied with what I did. The character who represents you in *The Big Rock Candy Mountain* and *Recapitulation,* two novels of a semi-autobiographical kind, is a sort of passive victim. I am afraid I let your selfish and violent husband, my father, steal the scene from you and push you into the background in the novels as he did in life. Somehow I should have been able to say how strong and resilient you were, what a patient and abiding and bonding force, the softness that proved in the long run stronger than what it seemed to yield to.

But you must understand that you are the hardest sort of human character to make credible on paper. We are skeptical of kindness so unfailing, sympathy so instant and constant, trouble so patiently borne, forgiveness so wholehearted. Writing about you, I felt always on the edge of the unbelievable, as if I were writing a saint's life, or the legend of some Patient Griselda. I felt that I should warp you a little, give you some human failing or selfish motive; for saintly qualities, besides looking sentimental on the page, are a rebuke to those—and they are most of us—who have failed at them. What is more, saintly and long-suffering women tend to infuriate the current partisans of women's liberation, who look upon them as a masculine invention, the too submissive and too much praised victims of male dominance.

Well, you were seldom aggressive, not by the time I knew you, and you were an authentic victim. How truly submissive, that is another matter. Some, I suppose, are born unselfish, some achieve unselfishness, and some have unselfishness thrust upon them. You used to tell me that you were born with a redheaded temper, and had to learn to control it. I think you were also born with a normal complement of dreams and hopes and desires and a great capacity for intellectual and cultural growth, and had to learn to suppress them.

Your life gave you plenty of practice in both controlling and suppressing. You were robbed of your childhood, and as a young, inexperienced woman you made a fatal love choice. But you blamed no one but yourself. You lay in the bed you had made, partly because as a woman, and without much education, you had few options, and partly because your morality counseled responsibility for what you did, but mostly because love told you your highest obligation was to look after your two boys and the feckless husband who needed you more even than they did. Your reward, all too often, was to be taken for granted.

Just now, thinking about you, I got out *The Big Rock Candy Mountain* and found the passage in which I wrote of your death. I couldn't bear to read it. It broke me down in tears to read the words that I wrote in tears nearly a half century ago. You are at once a lasting presence and an unhealed wound.

I was twenty-four, still a schoolboy, when you died, but I have lived with you more than three times twenty-four years. Self-obsessed, sports crazy or book crazy or girl crazy or otherwise preoccupied, I never got around to telling you during your lifetime how much you meant. Except in those moments when your life bore down on you with particular weight, as when my brother Cece died, and you turned to me because you had no one else, I don't suppose I realized how much you meant. Now I feel mainly regret, regret that I took you for granted as the others did, regret that you were dead by the time my life began to expand, so that I was unable to take you along and compensate you a little for your first fifty years. Cinderella should end happily, released from the dark unwholesome house of her servitude.

One of my friends in that later life that you did not live to share was the Irish writer Frank O'Connor, who was born Michael O'Donovan in a shabby cottage in Cork. His father was a drunk; his mother, he firmly believed, was a saint. He put her into many of his short stories, and he wrote her a book of tribute called *An Only Child*. Though he was not much of a Catholic, he expected to meet her in heaven, garbed in glory. From what he told me, she was much like you: she was incomparably herself, and yet she always thought of herself last. I can't believe that he is with her now in heaven, though I wish I could. I can't believe that eventually, pretty soon in fact, I will meet you there either. But what a reunion that would be! It would be worth conversation to assure it—the four of us enjoying whatever it is that immortals enjoy, and enjoying it together. I admired Frank O'Connor for his great gifts; but I loved Michael O'Donovan for the way he felt about his mother, and envied him for the chance he got, as a mature man, to show it. If the man-dominated world, with all its injustices, now and then produces women like his mother and mine, it can't be all bad.

I began this rumination in a dark mood, remembering the anniversary of your death. Already you have cheered me up. I have said that you didn't die, and you didn't. I can still hear you being cheerful on the slightest provocation, or no provocation at all, singing as you work and shedding your cheerfulness on others. So let us remember your life, such a life as many women of your generation shared to some extent, though not always with your special trials and rarely with your stoicism and grace.

I have heard enough about your childhood and youth to know how life went on that Iowa farm and in the town where everybody spoke Norwegian, read Norwegian, did business in Norwegian, heard Norwegian in church. The family Bible that somehow descended to me is in Norwegian, and in Gothic type at that. Next to it on my shelf is the preposterous five-pound book that they gave you on your fifth birthday: *Sandheden i Kristus,* Truths in Christ, a compendium of instructions and meditations geared to the religious year. You would have had to be as old as I am, and as rigid a Lutheran as your father, to tolerate five minutes of it.

Though your father was born in this country, you did not learn English until you started school. You learned it eagerly. Some of our mutual relatives, after five generations in the United States, still speak with an accent, but you never did. You loved reading, and you sang all the time: you knew the words to a thousand songs. When I was in college I was astonished to discover that some songs I had heard you sing as you worked around the house were lyrics from Tennyson's *The Princess*. Maybe you got the words from *McGuffey's Reader*. Where you got the tunes, God knows. You always made the most of what little was offered you, and you kept hold of it.

School was your happy time, with friends, games, parties, the delight of learning. You had it for only six years. When you were twelve, your mother died of tuberculosis and you became an instant adult: housekeeper to your father, mother to your two younger brothers and sister, farmhand when not otherwise employed. All through the years when you should have had the chance to be bright, girlish, even frivolous, you had responsibilities that would have broken down most adults.

Many farm wives had a "hired girl." You did not. You were It, you did it all. At twelve, thirteen, fourteen, you made beds, cleaned, cooked, sewed, mended, for a family of five. You baked the bread, biscuits, cakes, pies, in a cranky coal range. You made the *lefse* and *faiitgmand* and prepared the *lutefisk* without which a Norwegian Christmas is not Christmas. You washed all the clothes, and I don't mean you put lightly soiled clothes into a washing machine. I mean you boiled and scrubbed dirty farm clothes with only the copper boiler, tin tub, brass washboard, harsh soap, and hand wringer of the 1890s—one long backbreaking day every week.

At harvest time you often worked in the field most of the morning and then came in to cook dinner for the crew. You were over a hot stove in a suffocating kitchen for hours at a time, canning peas, beans, corn, tomatoes, making jams and jellies, putting up cucumber and watermelon pickles or piccalilli. When a hog was slaughtered, you swallowed your nausea and caught the blood for the blood pudding your father relished. You pickled pigs' feet and made headcheese. You fried and put down in crocks of their own lard the sausage patties that would last all winter. Morning and evening you helped with the milking. You skimmed the cream and churned the butter in the dasher churn, you hung cheesecloth bags of curd on the clothesline to drip and become cottage cheese. Maybe you got a little help from your brothers and sister, especially as they got older; but they were in school all day, and whined about having homework at night.

I am sure there were times when you bitterly resented your bond-servant life, when you thumped your lazy and evasive brothers, or sent hot glances at your father where he sat reading *Scandinaven* in the parlor, totally unaware of you as you staggered in with a scuttle of coal and set it down loudly by the heater, and opened the heater door and lifted the scuttle and fed the fire and set the scuttle down again and slammed the heater door with a bang. Those were the years when you had unselfishness thrust upon you; you had not yet got through the difficult process of achieving it.

But however you might rebel, there was no shedding them. They were your responsibility and there was no one to relieve you of them. They called you Sis. All your life people called you Sis, because that was what you were, or what you became—big sister, helpful sister, the one upon whom everyone depended, the one they all came to for everything from help with homework to a sliver under the fingernail.

Six years of that, at the end of which your father announced that he was going to marry a school friend of yours, a girl barely older than yourself. I wonder if it was outrage that drove you from his house, or if your anger was not lightened by the perception that here at last was freedom and opportunity. You were eighteen, a tall, strong, direct-eyed girl with a pile of gorgeous red hair. In the tintypes of the time you look determined. You do not yet have the sad mouth your last photographs show. Maybe the world then seemed all before you, your imprisonment over.

But nobody had prepared you for opportunity and freedom. Nobody had taught you to dream big. You couldn't have imagined going to Chicago or New York and winning your way, you could never have dreamed of becoming an actress or the editor of a women's magazine. They had only taught you, and most of that you had learned on your own, to keep house and to look after others. You were very good at both. So when you were displaced as your father's housekeeper, you could think of nothing better to do with your freedom than to go to North Dakota and keep house for a bachelor uncle.

There you met something else they had not prepared you for, a man unlike any you had ever seen, a husky, laughing, reckless, irreverent, storytelling charmer, a ballplayer, a fancy skater, a trapshooting champion, a pursuer of the main chance, a true believer in the American dream of something for nothing, a rolling stone who confidently expected to be eventually covered with moss. He was marking time between get-rich-quick schemes by running a blind pig. He offended every piety your father stood for. Perhaps that was why you married him, against loud protests from home. Perhaps your father was as much to blame as anyone for the mistake you made.

You had a stillborn child. Later you had a living one, my brother Cecil. Later still, on a peacemaking visit back to Iowa, you had me. Then, as you told me once, you discovered how not to have any more, and didn't. You had enough to be responsible for with two.

To run through your life would be lugubrious if it were not you we were talking about. You made it something else by your total competence, your cheerfulness under most uncheerful conditions, your resilience after every defeat. "Better luck next time!" I have heard you say as we fled from some disaster, and after a minute, with your special mixture of endurance, hope, and irony, "Well, if it didn't kill us, I guess it must have been good for us."

Dakota I don't remember. My memories begin in the woods of Washington, where we lived in a tent and ran a lunchroom in the logging town of Redmond. By getting scarlet fever, I had balked my father's dream of going to Alaska and digging up baseball-sized nuggets. Then there was a bad time. You left my father, or he you; nobody ever told me. But Cece and I found ourselves in a Seattle orphans' home, stashed there while you worked at the Bon Marché. In 1913 you didn't have a chance as a husbandless woman with two children. When you found how miserable we were in that home, you took us out and brought us back to the only safety available, your father's house in Iowa.

I can imagine what that cost you in humiliation. I can imagine the letters that must have passed between you and my father. I can imagine his promises, your concessions. At any rate, in June 1914 we were on our way to join him in the valley of the Whitemud River in Saskatchewan. Perhaps it sounded romantic and adventurous to you, perhaps you let yourself listen to his come-all-ye enthusiasm, perhaps you thought that on a real frontier he might be happy and do well. Very probably you hoped that in a raw village five hundred miles from anywhere we could make a new start and be a family, something for which you had both a yearning and a gift. If you went in resignation, this time your resignation was not forced on you. It was a choice. By 1914, at the age of thirty-one, you had finally achieved unselfishness.

Saskatchewan is the richest page in my memory, for that was where I first began to understand some things, and that was where, for a half dozen years, we had what you had always wanted: a house of our own, a united family, and a living, however hard.

I remember good days for the shared pleasure we took in them—family expeditions to pick berries in the Cypress Hills, when we picnicked on the edge of Chimney Coulee and watched great fleets of clouds sail eastward over the prairie. Raising a sandwich to your mouth, you exclaimed, "Oh! Smell your hands!" and we did, inhaling the fragrance of the saskatoons, gooseberries, chokecherries, pin cherries, and highbush cranberries we had been working in. I remember that on our way home from one of those expeditions the democrat wagon tipped over on a steep hillside and spilled us and our overflowing pans and pails of berries out onto the grass. You took one quick look to see if anyone was hurt, and then began to laugh, pointing to the embarrassed and bewildered team standing among the twisted tugs. We sat in the sudden grass and laughed ourselves silly before we got up and scraped together the spilled berries and straightened out the buggy and relieved the team and drove home. Singing, naturally. You never lost an opportunity to sing. You sang, too, among the rich smells in the kitchen as you made those wild berries into pies and jams and sauce and jellies and put a lot of them up in jars and glasses to be stored on the cellar shelves.

Do you remember a day on the homestead when Pa came back from Chinook with a big watermelon, and we cooled it as well as we could in the reservoir and then sat down in the shade of the shack and ate it all? How simple and memorable a good day can be when expectation is low! You made us save the rinds for pickles. Your training had been thorough, you never wasted anything. One of our neighbors, years later, wrote me about how amazed he was to see you, after you had peeled a lot of apples and made pies of them, boil up the peelings and turn them into jelly.

I think you loved that little burg in spite of its limitations. You loved having neighbors, visiting with neighbors, helping neighbors. When it was our turn to host the monthly Sunday-school party, you had more fun than the kids, playing crocinole or beanbag like the child you had never been allowed to be. You loved the times when the river froze without wind or snow, and the whole channel was clean, skatable ice, and the town gathered around big night fires, and skaters in red mackinaws and bright scarfs moved like Breughel figures across the light, and firelight glinted off eyeballs and teeth, and the breath of the community went up in white plumes.

You loved having your children in a steady school, and doing well in it. You read all the books you could lay hands on. When your North Dakota uncle died and left you a thousand dollars you didn't let my father take it, though I am sure he would have found a use for it. Instead, you bought a Sears, Roebuck piano and you set my brother and me to learn to play it under the instruction of the French doctor's wife. Alas, we disappointed you, resisted practice, dawdled and fooled around. Eventually you gave up. But you could no more let that piano sit there unused than you could throw perfectly good apple peelings out to the pig. You learned to play it yourself, painstakingly working things out chord by chord from the sheet music of popular songs. How hungry you were! How you would have responded to the opportunities ignored by so many who have them!

Many good days. Also, increasingly, bad ones. Hard times. While you lived your way deeper into the remote and limited place where my father's enthusiasms had brought you, he felt more and more trapped in what he called "this dirty little dung-heeled sagebrush town." On the homestead where we spent our summers, he had made one good and one average crop out of five. One summer he grew hundreds of bushels of potatoes on rented bottomland near town, and stored them in the basement of the hotel waiting for the right price, and the hotel burned down. That winter he supported us playing poker. By the summer of 1920 he was raging to get out, do something, find some way of making a real living.

Eventually he got his way, and we abandoned what little you had been able to get together as a life. During the next fourteen years you lived in much greater comfort, and you saw a lot of the western United States. You continued to make a home for your boys and your husband, but it was a cheerless home for you. We lived in a dozen towns and cities, three dozen neighborhoods, half a hundred houses. My brother and I kept some continuity through school and the friends we made there, but your continuity was cut every few months, you lost friends and never saw them again, or got the chance to make new ones, or have a kitchen where women could drop in and have a cup of coffee and a chat. Too much of your time, in Great Falls, Salt Lake, Reno, Los Angeles, Long Beach, you were alone.

You believed in all the beauties and strengths and human associations of place; my father believed only in movement. You believed in a life of giving, he in a life of getting. When Cecil died at the age of twenty-three, you did not have a single woman friend to whom you could talk, not a single family of neighbors or friends to help you bear the loss of half your loving life.

You're a good . . . boy . . . Wallace. That shames me. You had little in your life to judge goodness by. I was not as dense or as selfish as my father, and I got more credit than I deserved. But I was not bright enough to comprehend the kind of example you had been setting me, until it was too late to do anything but hold your hand while you died. And here I am nearly eighty years old, too old to be capable of any significant improvement but not too old for regret.

"All you can do is try," you used to tell me when I was scared of undertaking something. You got me to undertake many things I would not have dared undertake without your encouragement. You also taught me how to take defeat when it came, and it was bound to now and then. You taught me that if it hadn't killed me it was probably good for me.

I can hear you laugh while you say it. Any minute now I will hear you singing.

RUTH'S SONG
(BECAUSE SHE COULD
NOT SING IT)

by Gloria Steinem

Gloria Steinem, a founding editor of Ms.
magazine, is the author of numerous articles,
essays, and books.

Happy or unhappy, families are all mysterious.
We have only to imagine how differently we would be described—and will be, after our deaths—by each of the family members who believe they know us. The only question is, Why are some mysteries more important than others?

The fate of my Uncle Ed was a mystery of importance in our family. We lavished years of speculation on his transformation from a brilliant young electrical engineer to the town handyman. What could have changed this elegant, Lincolnesque student voted "Best Dressed" by his classmates to the gaunt, unshaven man I remember? Why did he leave a young son and a first wife of the "proper" class and religion, marry a much less educated woman of the "wrong" religion, and raise a second family in a house near an abandoned airstrip; a house whose walls were patched with metal signs to stop the wind? Why did he never talk about his transformation?

For years, I assumed that some secret and dramatic events of a year he spent in Alaska had made the difference. Then I discovered that the trip had come after his change and probably been made because of it. Strangers he worked for as a much-loved handyman talked about him as one more tragedy of the Depression, and it was true that Uncle Ed's father, my paternal grandfather, had lost his money in the stockmarket crash and died of (depending on who was telling the story) pneumonia or a broken heart. But the crash of 1929 also had come long after Uncle Ed's transformation. Another theory was that he was afflicted with a mental problem that lasted most of his life, yet he was supremely competent at his work, led an independent life, and asked for help from no one.

Perhaps he had fallen under the spell of a radical professor in the early days of the century, the height of this country's romance with socialism and anarchism. That was the theory of another uncle on my mother's side. I do remember that no matter how much Uncle Ed needed money, he would charge no more for his work than materials plus 10 percent, and I never saw him in anything other than ancient boots and overalls held up with strategic safety pins. Was he really trying to replace socialism-in-one-country with socialism-in-one-man? If so, why did my grandmother, a woman who herself had run for the school board in coalition with anarchists and socialists, mistrust his judgment so much that she left his share of her estate in trust, even though he was over fifty when she died? And why did Uncle Ed seem uninterested in all other political words and acts? Was it true instead that, as another relative insisted, Uncle Ed had chosen poverty to disprove the myths of Jews and money?

Years after my uncle's death, I asked a son in his second family if he had the key to this family mystery. No, he said. He had never known his father any other way. For that cousin, there had been no question. For the rest of us, there was to be no answer.

For many years I also never imagined my mother any way other than the person she had become before I was born. She was just a fact of life when I was growing up; someone to be worried about and cared for; an invalid who lay in bed with eyes closed and lips moving in occasional response to voices only she could hear; a woman to whom I brought an endless stream of toast and coffee, bologna sandwiches and dime pies, in a child's version of what meals should be. She was a loving, intelligent, terrorized woman who tried hard to clean our littered house whenever she emerged from her private world, but who could rarely be counted on to finish one task. In many ways, our roles were reversed: I was the mother and she was the child. Yet that didn't help her, for she still worried about me with all the intensity of a frightened mother, plus the special fears of her own world full of threats and hostile voices.

Even then I suppose I must have known that, years before she was thirty-five and I was born, she had been a spirited, adventurous young woman who struggled out of a working-class family and into college, who found work she loved and continued to do, even after she was married and my older sister was there to be cared for. Certainly, our immediate family and nearby relatives, of whom I was by far the youngest, must have remembered her life as a whole and functioning person. She was thirty before she gave up her own career to help my father run the Michigan summer resort that was the most practical of his many dreams, and she worked hard there as everything from bookkeeper to bar manager. The family must have watched this energetic, fun-loving, book-loving woman turn into someone who was afraid to be alone, who could not hang on to reality long enough to hold a job, and who could rarely concentrate enough to read a book.

Yet I don't remember any family speculation about the mystery of my mother's transformation. To the kind ones and those who liked her, this new Ruth was simply a sad event, perhaps a mental case, a family problem to be accepted and cared for until some natural process made her better. To the less kind or those who had resented her earlier independence, she was a willful failure, someone who lived in a filthy house, a woman who simply would not pull herself together.

Unlike the case of my Uncle Ed, exterior events were never suggested as reason enough for her problems. Giving up her own career was never cited as her personal parallel of the Depression. (Nor was there discussion of the Depression itself, though my mother, like millions of others, had made potato soup and cut up blankets to make my sister's winter clothes.) Her fears of dependence and poverty were no match for my uncle's possible political beliefs. The real influence of newspaper editors who had praised her reporting was not taken as seriously as the possible influence of one radical professor.

Even the explanation of mental illness seemed to contain more personal fault when applied to my mother. She had suffered her first "nervous breakdown," as she and everyone else called it, before I was born and when my sister was about five. It followed years of trying to take care of a baby, be the wife of a kind but financially irresponsible man with show-business dreams, and still keep her much-loved job as reporter and newspaper editor. After many months in a sanatorium, she was pronounced recovered. That is, she was able to take care of my sister again, to move away from the city and the job she loved, and to work with my father at the isolated rural lake in Michigan he was trying to transform into a resort worthy of the big dance bands of the 1930s.

But she was never again completely without the spells of depression, anxiety, and visions into some other world that eventually were to turn her into the nonperson I remember. And she was never again without a bottle of dark, acrid-smelling liquid she called "Doc Howard's medicine": a solution of chloral hydrate that I later learned was the main ingredient of "Mickey Finns" or "knockout drops," and that probably made my mother and her doctor the pioneers of modern tranquilizers. Though friends and relatives saw this medicine as one more evidence of weakness and indulgence, to me it always seemed an embarrassing but necessary evil. It slurred her speech and slowed her coordination, making our neighbors and my school friends believe she was a drunk. But without it, she would not sleep for days, even a week at a time, and her feverish eyes began to see only that private world in which wars and hostile voices threatened the people she loved.

Because my parents had divorced and my sister was working in a faraway city, my mother and I were alone together then, living off the meager fixed income that my mother got from leasing her share of the remaining land in Michigan. I remember a long Thanksgiving weekend spent hanging on to her with one hand and holding my eighth-grade assignment of *A Tale of Two Cities* in the other, because the war outside our house was so real to my mother that she had plunged her hand through a window, badly cutting her arm, in an effort to help us escape. Only when she finally agreed to swallow the medicine could she sleep, and only then could I end the terrible calm that comes with crisis and admit to myself how afraid I had been.

No wonder that no relative in my memory challenged the doctor who prescribed this medicine, asked if some of her suffering and hallucinating might be due to overdose or withdrawal, or even consulted another doctor about its use. It was our relief as well as hers.

But why was she never returned even to that first sanatorium? Or to help that might come from other doctors? It's hard to say. Partly, it was her own fear of returning. Partly, it was too little money, and a family's not unusual assumption that mental illness is an inevitable part of someone's personality. Or perhaps other family members had feared something like my experience when, one hot and desperate summer between the sixth and seventh grade, I finally persuaded her to let me take her to the only doctor from those sanatorium days whom she remembered without fear.

Yes, this brusque old man told me after talking to my abstracted, timid mother for twenty minutes: She definitely belongs in a state hospital. I should put her there right away.

But even at that age, *Life* magazine and newspaper exposés had told me what horrors went on inside those hospitals. Assuming there to be no other alternative, I took her home and never tried again.

In retrospect, perhaps the biggest reason my mother was cared for but not helped for twenty years was the simplest: her functioning was not that necessary to the world. Like women alcoholics who drink in their kitchens while costly programs are constructed for executives who drink, or like the homemakers subdued with tranquilizers while male patients get therapy and personal attention instead, my mother was not an important worker. She was not even the caretaker of a very young child, as she had been when she was hospitalized the first time. My father had patiently brought home the groceries and kept our odd household going until I was eight or so and my sister went away to college. Two years later when wartime gas rationing closed his summer resort and he had to travel to buy and sell in summer as well as winter, he said: How can I travel and take care of your mother? How can I make a living? He was right. It was impossible to do both. I did not blame him for leaving once I was old enough to be the bringer of meals and answerer of my mother's questions. ("Has your sister been killed in a car crash?" "Are there German soldiers outside?") I replaced my father, my mother was left with one more way of maintaining a sad status quo, and the world went on undisturbed.

That's why our lives, my mother's from forty-six to fifty-three, and my own from ten to seventeen, were spent alone together. There was one sane winter in a house we rented to be near my sister's college in Massachusetts, then one bad summer spent house-sitting in suburbia while my mother hallucinated and my sister struggled to hold down a summer job in New York. But the rest of those years were lived in Toledo, where both my mother and my father had been born, and on whose city newspapers an earlier Ruth had worked.

First we moved into a basement apartment in a good neighborhood. In those rooms behind a furnace, I made one last stab at being a child. By pretending to be much sicker with a cold than I really was, I hoped my mother would suddenly turn into a sane and cheerful woman bringing me chicken soup à la Hollywood. Of course, she could not. It only made her feel worse that she could not. I stopped pretending.

But for most of those years, we lived in the upstairs of the house my mother had grown up in and that her parents left her—a deteriorating farmhouse engulfed by the city, with poor but newer houses stacked against it and a major highway a few feet from its sagging front porch. For a while, we could rent the two downstairs apartments to a newlywed factory worker and a local butcher's family. Then the health department condemned our ancient furnace for the final time, sealing it so tight that even my resourceful Uncle Ed couldn't produce illegal heat.

In that house, I remember:

. . . lying in the bed my mother and I shared for warmth, listening on the early morning radio to the royal wedding of Princess Elizabeth and Prince Philip being broadcast live, while we tried to ignore and thus protect each other from the unmistakable sounds of the factory worker downstairs beating up and locking out his pregnant wife.

. . . hanging paper drapes I had bought in the dime store; stacking books and papers in the shape of two armchairs and covering them with blankets; evolving my own dishwashing system (I waited until all the dishes were dirty, then put them in the bathtub); and listening to my mother's high praise for these housekeeping efforts to bring order from chaos, though in retrospect I think they probably depressed her further.

. . . coming back from one of the Eagles' Club shows where I and other veterans of a local tap-dancing school made ten dollars a night for two shows, and finding my mother waiting with a flashlight and no coat in the dark cold of the bus stop, worried about my safety walking home.

. . . in a good period, when my mother's native adventurousness came through, answering a classified ad together for an amateur acting troupe that performed biblical dramas in churches, and doing several very corny performances of *Noah's Ark* while my proud mother shook metal sheets backstage to make thunder.

. . . on a hot summer night, being bitten by one of the rats that shared our house and its back alley. It was a terrifying night that turned into a touching one when my mother, summoning courage from some unknown reservoir of love, became a calm, comforting parent who took me to a hospital emergency room despite her terror at leaving home.

. . . coming home from a library with the three books a week into which I regularly escaped, and discovering that for once there was no need to escape. My mother was calmly planting hollyhocks in the vacant lot next door.

But there were also times when she woke in the early winter dark, too frightened and disoriented to remember that I was at my usual after-school job, and so called the police to find me. Humiliated in front of my friends by sirens and policemen, I would yell at her—and she would bow her head in fear and say, "I'm sorry, I'm sorry, I'm sorry," just as she had done so often when my otherwise kindhearted father had yelled at her in frustration. Perhaps the worst thing about suffering is that it finally hardens the hearts of those around it.

And there were many, many times when I badgered her until her shaking hands had written a small check to cash at the corner grocery and I could leave her alone while I escaped to the comfort of well-heated dime stores that smelled of fresh doughnuts, or to air-conditioned Saturday-afternoon movies that were windows on a very different world.

But my ultimate protection was this: I was just passing through, a guest in the house; perhaps this wasn't my mother at all. Though I knew very well that I was her daughter, I sometimes imagined that I had been adopted and that my real parents would find me, a fantasy I've since discovered is common. (If children wrote more and grown-ups less, being adopted might be seen not only as a fear but also as a hope.)

Certainly, I didn't mourn the wasted life of this woman who was scarcely older than I am now. I worried only about the times when she got worse.

Pity takes distance and a certainty of surviving. It was only after our house was bought for demolition by the church next door, and after my sister had performed the miracle of persuading my father to give me a carefree time before college by taking my mother with him to California for a year, that I could afford to think about the sadness of her life. Suddenly, I was far away in Washington, living with my sister and sharing a house with several of her friends. While I finished high school and discovered to my surprise that my classmates felt sorry for me because my mother *wasn't* there, I also realized that my sister, at least in her early childhood, had known a very different person who lived inside our mother, an earlier Ruth.

She was a woman I met for the first time in a mental hospital near Baltimore, a humane place with gardens and trees where I visited her each weekend of the summer after my first year away in college. Fortunately, my sister hadn't been able to work and be our mother's caretaker, too. After my father's year was up, my sister had carefully researched hospitals and found the courage to break the family chain.

At first, this Ruth was the same abstracted, frightened woman I had lived with all those years; though now all the sadder for being approached through long hospital corridors and many locked doors. But gradually she began to talk about her past life, memories that doctors there must have been awakening. I began to meet a Ruth I had never known.

. . . A tall, spirited, auburn-haired high school girl who loved basketball and reading; who tried to drive her uncle's Stanley Steamer when it was the first car in the neighborhood; who had a gift for gardening and who sometimes, in defiance of convention, wore her father's overalls; a girl with the courage to go to dances even though her church told her that music itself was sinful, and whose sense of adventure almost made up for feeling gawky and unpretty next to her daintier, dark-haired sister.

. . . A very little girl, just learning to walk, discovering the body places where touching was pleasurable, and being punished by her mother, who slapped her hard across the kitchen floor.

. . . A daughter of a handsome railroad engineer and a schoolteacher who felt she had married "beneath her"; the mother who took her two daughters on Christmas trips to faraway New York on an engineer's free railroad pass and showed them the restaurants and theaters they should aspire to—even though they could only stand outside them in the snow.

. . . A good student at Oberlin College, whose freethinking traditions she loved, where friends nicknamed her "Billy"; a student with a talent for both mathematics and poetry, who was not above putting an invisible film of Karo syrup on all the john seats in her dormitory the night of a big prom; a daughter who had to return to Toledo, live with her family, and go to a local university when her ambitious mother—who had scrimped and saved, ghostwritten a minister's sermons, and made her daughters' clothes in order to get them to college at all—ran out of money. At home, this Ruth became a part-time bookkeeper in a lingerie shop for the very rich, commuting to classes and listening to her mother's harsh lectures on the security of becoming a teacher; but also a young woman who was still rebellious enough to fall in love with my father, the editor of her university newspaper, a funny and charming young man who was a terrible student, had no intention of graduating, put on all the campus dances, and was unacceptably Jewish.

I knew from family lore that my mother had married my father twice: once secretly, after he invited her to become the literary editor of his campus newspaper, and once a year later in a public ceremony, which some members of both families refused to attend as the "mixed marriage" of its day.

And I knew that my mother had gone on to earn a teaching certificate. She had used it to scare away truant officers during the winters when, after my father closed the summer resort for the season, we lived in a house trailer and worked our way to Florida or California and back by buying and selling antiques.

But only during those increasingly adventurous weekend outings from the hospital—going shopping, to lunch, to the movies—did I realize that she had taught college calculus for a year in deference to her mother's insistence that she have teaching "to fall back on." And only then did I realize she had fallen in love with newspapers along with my father. After graduating from the university paper, she wrote a gossip column for a local tabloid, under the name "Duncan MacKenzie," since women weren't supposed to do such things, and soon had earned a job as society reporter on one of Toledo's two big dailies. By the time my sister was four or so, she had worked her way up to the coveted position of Sunday editor.

It was a strange experience to look into those brown eyes I had seen so often and realize suddenly how much they were like my own. For the first time, I realized that she might really be my mother.

I began to think about the many pressures that might have led up to that first nervous breakdown: leaving my sister, whom she loved very much, with a grandmother whose values my mother didn't share; trying to hold on to a job she loved but was being asked to leave by her husband; wanting very much to go with a woman friend to pursue their own dreams in New York; falling in love with a co-worker at the newspaper who frightened her by being more sexually attractive, more supportive of her work than my father, and perhaps the man she should have married; and finally, nearly bleeding to death with a miscarriage because her own mother had little faith in doctors and refused to get help.

Did those months in the sanatorium brainwash her in some Freudian or very traditional way into making what were, for her, probably the wrong choices? I don't know. It almost doesn't matter. Without extraordinary support to the contrary, she was already convinced that divorce was unthinkable. A husband could not be left for another man, and certainly not for a reason as selfish as a career. A daughter could not be deprived of her father and certainly not be uprooted and taken off to an uncertain future in New York. A bride was supposed to be virginal (not "shopworn," as my euphemistic mother would have said), and if your husband turned out to be kind, but innocent of the possibility of a woman's pleasure, then just be thankful for kindness.

Of course, other women have torn themselves away from work and love and still survived. But a story my mother told me years later has always symbolized for me the formidable forces arrayed against her.

It was early spring, nothing was open yet. There was nobody for miles around. We had stayed at the lake that winter, so I was alone a lot while your father took the car and traveled around on business. You were a baby. Your sister was in school, and there was no phone. The last straw was that the radio broke. Suddenly it seemed like forever since I'd been able to talk with anyone—or even hear the sound of another voice.

I bundled you up, took the dog, and walked out to the Brooklyn road. I thought I'd walk the four or five miles to the grocery store, talk to some people, and find somebody to drive me back. I was walking along with Fritzie running up ahead in the empty road—when suddenly a car came out of nowhere and down the hill. It hit Fritzie head-on and threw him over to the side of the road. I yelled and screamed at the driver, but he never slowed down. He never looked at us. He never even turned his head.

Poor Fritzie was all broken and bleeding, but he was still alive. I carried him and sat down in the middle of the road, with his head cradled in my arms. I was going to *make* the next car stop and help.

But no car ever came. I sat there for hours, I don't know how long, with you in my lap and holding Fritzie, who was whimpering and looking up at me for help. It was dark by the time he finally died. I pulled him over to the side of the road and walked back home with you and washed the blood out of my clothes.

I don't know what it was about that one day—it was like a breaking point. When your father came home, I said, "From now on, I'm going with you. I won't bother you. I'll just sit in the car. But I can't bear to be alone again."

I think she told me that story to show she had tried to save herself, or perhaps she wanted to exorcise a painful memory by saying it out loud. But hearing it made me understand what could have turned her into the woman I remember: a solitary figure sitting in the car, perspiring through the summer, bundled up in winter, waiting for my father to come out of this or that antique shop, grateful just not to be alone. I was there, too, because I was too young to be left at home, and I loved helping my father wrap and unwrap the newspaper around the china and small objects he had bought at auctions and was selling to dealers. It made me feel necessary and grown-up. But sometimes it was hours before we came back to the car again and to my mother, who was always patiently, silently waiting.

At the hospital and later when Ruth told me stories of her past, I used to say, "But why didn't you leave? Why didn't you take the job? Why didn't you marry the other man?" She would always insist it didn't matter, she was lucky to have my sister and me. If I pressed hard enough, she would add, "If I'd left you never would have been born."

I always thought but never had the courage to say: *But you might have been born instead.*

I'd like to tell you that this story has a happy ending. The best I can do is one that is happier than its beginning.

After many months in that Baltimore hospital, my mother lived on her own in a small apartment for two years while I was in college and my sister married and lived nearby. When she felt the old terrors coming back, she returned to the hospital at her own request. She was approaching sixty by the time she emerged from there and from a Quaker farm that served as a halfway house, but she confounded her psychiatrists' predictions that she would be able to live outside for shorter and shorter periods. In fact, she never returned. She lived more than another twenty years, and for six of them she was well enough to stay in a rooming house that provided both privacy and company. Even after my sister and her husband moved to a larger house and generously made two rooms into an apartment for her, she continued to have some independent life and many friends. She worked part-time as a "salesgirl" in a china shop; went away with me on yearly vacations and took one trip to Europe with relatives; went to women's club meetings; found a multiracial church that she loved; took meditation courses; and enjoyed many books. She still could not bear to see a sad movie, to stay alone with any of her six grandchildren while they were babies, to live without many tranquilizers, or to talk about those bad years in Toledo. The old terrors were still in the back of her mind, and each day was a fight to keep them down.

It was the length of her illness that had made doctors pessimistic. In fact, they could not identify any serious mental problem and diagnosed her only as having "an anxiety neurosis": low self-esteem, a fear of being dependent, a terror of being alone, a constant worry about money. She also had spells of what now would be called agoraphobia, a problem almost entirely confined to dependent women: fear of going outside the house, and incapacitating anxiety attacks in unfamiliar or public places.

Would you say, I asked one of her doctors, that her spirit had been broken? "I guess that's as good a diagnosis as any," he said. "And it's hard to mend anything that's been broken for twenty years."

But once out of the hospital for good, she continued to show flashes of the different woman inside; one with a wry kind of humor, a sense of adventure, and a love of learning. Books on math, physics, and mysticism occupied a lot of her time. ("Religion," she used to say firmly, "begins in the laboratory.") When she visited me in New York during her sixties and seventies, she always told taxi drivers that she was eighty years old ("so they will tell me how young I look"), and convinced theater ticket sellers that she was deaf long before she really was ("so they'll give us seats in the front row"). She made friends easily, with the vulnerability and charm of a person who feels entirely dependent on the approval of others. After one of her visits, every shopkeeper within blocks of my apartment would say, "Oh yes, I know your mother!" At home, she complained that people her own age were too old and stodgy for her. Many of her friends were far younger than she. It was as if she were making up for her own lost years.

She was also overly appreciative of any presents given to her—and that made giving them irresistible. I loved to send her clothes, jewelry, exotic soaps, and additions to her collection of tarot cards. She loved receiving them, though we both knew they would end up stored in boxes and drawers. She carried on a correspondence in German with our European relatives, and exchanges with many other friends, all written in her painfully slow, shaky handwriting. She also loved giving gifts. Even as she worried about money and figured out how to save pennies, she would buy or make carefully chosen presents for grandchildren and friends.

Part of the price she paid for this much health was forgetting. A single reminder of those bad years in Toledo was enough to plunge her into days of depression. There were times when this fact created loneliness for me, too. Only two of us had lived most of my childhood. Now, only one of us remembered. But there were also times in later years when, no matter how much I pled with reporters *not* to interview our friends and neighbors in Toledo, *not* to say that my mother had been hospitalized, they published things that hurt her very much and sent her into a downhill slide.

On the other hand, she was also her mother's daughter, a person with a certain amount of social pride and pretension, and some of her objections had less to do with depression than false pride. She complained bitterly about one report that we had lived in a house trailer. She finally asked angrily, "Couldn't they at least say 'vacation mobile home'?" Divorce was still a shame to her. She might cheerfully tell friends, "I don't know *why* Gloria says her father and I were divorced—we never were." I think she justified this to herself with the idea that they had gone through two marriage ceremonies, one in secret and one in public, but been divorced only once. In fact, they were definitely divorced, and my father had briefly married someone else.

She was very proud of my being a published writer, and we generally shared the same values. After her death, I found a mother-daughter morals quiz I once had written for a women's magazine. In her unmistakably shaky writing, she had recorded her own answers, her entirely accurate imagination of what my answers would be, and a score that concluded our differences were less than those "normal for women separated by twenty-odd years." Nonetheless, she was quite capable of putting a made-up name on her name tag when going to a conservative women's club where she feared our shared identity would bring controversy or even just questions. When I finally got up the nerve to tell her I was signing a 1972 petition of women who publicly said we had had abortions and were demanding the repeal of laws that made them illegal and dangerous, her only reply was sharp and aimed to hurt back. "Every starlet says she's had an abortion," she said. "It's just a way of getting publicity." I knew she agreed that abortion should be a legal choice, but I also knew she would never forgive me for embarrassing her in public.

In fact, her anger and a fairly imaginative ability to wound with words increased in her last years when she was most dependent, most focused on herself, and most likely to need the total attention of others. When my sister made a courageous decision to go to law school at the age of fifty, leaving my mother in a house that not only had many loving teenage grandchildren in it but a kindly older woman as a paid companion besides, my mother reduced her to frequent tears by insisting that this was a family with no love in it, no home-cooked food in the refrigerator; not a real family at all. Since arguments about home cooking wouldn't work on me, my punishment was creative and different. She was going to call up *The New York Times,* she said, and tell them that this was what feminism did: it left old sick women all alone.

Some of this bitterness brought on by failing faculties was eventually solved by a nursing home near my sister's house where my mother got not only the twenty-four-hour help her weakening body demanded but the attention of affectionate nurses besides. She charmed them, they loved her, and she could still get out for an occasional family wedding. If I ever had any doubts about the debt we owe to nurses, those last months laid them to rest.

When my mother died just before her eighty-second birthday in a hospital room where my sister and I were alternating the hours in which her heart wound slowly down to its last sounds, we were alone together for a few hours while my sister slept. My mother seemed bewildered by her surroundings and the tubes that invaded her body, but her consciousness cleared long enough for her to say, "I want to go home. Please take me home." Lying to her one last time, I said I would. "Okay, honey," she said. "I trust you." Those were her last understandable words.

The nurses let my sister and me stay in the room long after there was no more breath. She had asked us to do that. One of her many fears came from a story she had been told as a child about a man whose coma was mistaken for death. She also had made out a living will requesting that no extraordinary measures be used to keep her alive, and that her ashes be sprinkled in the same stream as my father's.

Her memorial service was in the Episcopalian church that she loved because it fed the poor, let the homeless sleep in its pews, had members of almost every race, and had been sued by the Episcopalian hierarchy for having a woman priest. Most of all, she loved the affection with which its members had welcomed her, visited her at home, and driven her to services. I think she would have liked the Quaker-style informality with which people rose to tell their memories of her. I know she would have loved the presence of many friends. It was to this church that she had donated some of her remaining Michigan property in the hope that it could be used as a multiracial camp, thus getting even with those people in the tiny nearby town who had snubbed my father for being Jewish.

I think she also would have been pleased with her obituary. It emphasized her brief career as one of the early women journalists and asked for donations to Oberlin's scholarship fund so others could go to this college she loved so much but had to leave.

I know I will spend the next years figuring out what her life has left in me.

I realize that I've always been more touched by old people than by children. It's the talent and hopes locked up in a failing body that gets to me; a poignant contrast that reminds me of my mother, even when she was strong.

I've always been drawn to any story of a mother and a daughter on their own in the world. I saw *A Taste of Honey* several times as both a play and a film, and never stopped feeling it. Even *Gypsy* I saw over and over again, sneaking in backstage for the musical and going to the movie as well. I told myself that I was learning the tap-dance routines, but actually my eyes were full of tears.

I once fell in love with a man only because we both belonged to that large and secret club of children who had "crazy mothers." We traded stories of the shameful houses to which we could never invite our friends. Before he was born, his mother had gone to jail for her pacifist convictions. Then she married the politically ambitious young lawyer who had defended her, stayed home, and raised many sons. I fell out of love when he confessed that he wished I wouldn't smoke or swear, and he hoped I wouldn't go on working. His mother's plight had taught him self-pity—nothing else.

I'm no longer obsessed, as I was for many years, with the fear that I would end up in a house like that one in Toledo. Now I'm obsessed instead with the things I could have done for my mother while she was alive, or the things I should have said.

I still don't understand why so many, many years passed before I saw my mother as a person and before I understood that many of the forces in her life are patterns women share. Like a lot of daughters, I suppose I couldn't afford to admit that what had happened to my mother was not all personal or accidental, and therefore could happen to me.

One mystery has finally cleared. I could never understand why my mother hadn't been helped by Pauline, her mother-in-law, a woman she seemed to love more than her own mother. This paternal grandmother had died when I was five, before my mother's real problems began but long after that "nervous breakdown," and I knew Pauline was once a suffragist who addressed Congress, marched for the vote, and was the first woman member of a school board in Ohio. She must have been a courageous and independent woman, yet I could find no evidence in my mother's reminiscences that Pauline had encouraged or helped my mother toward a life of her own.

I finally realized that my grandmother never changed the politics of her own life either. She was a feminist who kept a neat house for a husband and four antifeminist sons, a vegetarian among five male meat eaters, and a woman who felt so strongly about the dangers of alcohol that she used only paste vanilla; yet she served both meat and wine to the men of the house and made sure their lives and comforts were continued undisturbed. After the vote was won, Pauline seems to have stopped all feminist activity. My mother greatly admired the fact that her mother-in-law kept a spotless house and prepared a week's meals at a time. Whatever her own internal torments, Pauline was to my mother a woman who seemed able to "do it all." "Whither thou goest, I shall go," my mother used to say to her much-loved mother-in-law, quoting the Ruth of the Bible. In the end, her mother-in-law may have added to my mother's burdens of guilt.

Perhaps like many later suffragists, my grandmother was a public feminist and a private isolationist. That may have been heroic in itself, the most she could be expected to do, but the vote and a legal right to work were not the only kind of help my mother needed.

The world still missed a unique person named Ruth. Though she longed to live in New York and in Europe, she became a woman who was afraid to take a bus across town. Though she drove the first Stanley Steamer, she married a man who never let her drive.

I can only guess what she might have become. The clues are in moments of spirit or humor.

After all the years of fear, she still came to Oberlin with me when I was giving a speech there. She remembered everything about its history as the first college to admit blacks and the first to admit women, and responded to students with the dignity of a professor, the accuracy of a journalist, and a charm that was all her own.

When she could still make trips to Washington's wealth of libraries, she became an expert genealogist, delighting especially in finding the rogues and rebels in our family tree.

Just before I was born, when she had cooked one more enormous meal for all the members of some famous dance band at my father's resort and they failed to clean their plates, she had taken a shotgun down from the kitchen wall and held it over their frightened heads until they had finished the last crumb of strawberry shortcake. Only then did she tell them the gun wasn't loaded. It was a story she told with great satisfaction.

Though sex was a subject she couldn't discuss directly, she had a great appreciation of sensuous men. When a friend I brought home tried to talk to her about cooking, she was furious. ("He came out in the kitchen and talked to me about *stew!*") But she forgave him when we went swimming. She whispered, "He has wonderful legs!"

On her seventy-fifth birthday, she played softball with her grandsons on the beach, and took pride in hitting home runs into the ocean.

Even in the last year of her life, when my sister took her to visit a neighbor's new and luxurious house, she looked at the vertical stripes of a very abstract painting in the hallway and said, tartly, "Is that the price code?"

She worried terribly about being socially accepted herself, but she never withheld her own approval for the wrong reasons. Poverty or style or lack of education couldn't stand between her and a new friend. Though she lived in a mostly white society and worried if I went out with a man of the "wrong" race, just as she had once married a man of the "wrong" religion, she always accepted each person as an individual.

"Is he *very* dark?" she once asked worriedly about a friend. But when she met this very dark person, she only said afterward, "What a kind and nice man!"

My father was the Jewish half of the family, yet it was my mother who taught me to have pride in that tradition. It was she who encouraged me to listen to a radio play about a concentration camp when I was little. "You should know that this can happen," she said. Yet she did it just enough to teach, never enough to frighten.

It was she who introduced me to books and a respect for them, to poetry that she knew by heart, and to the idea that you could never criticize someone unless you "walked miles in their shoes."

It was she who sold that Toledo house, the only home she had, with the determination that the money be used to start me in college. She gave both her daughters the encouragement to leave home for four years of independence that she herself had never had.

After her death, my sister and I found a journal she had kept of her one cherished and belated trip to Europe. It was a trip she had described very little when she came home: she always deplored people who talked boringly about their personal travels and showed slides. Nonetheless, she had written a descriptive essay called "Grandma Goes to Europe." She still must have thought of herself as a writer. Yet she showed this long journal to no one.

I miss her, but perhaps no more in death than I did in life. Dying seems less sad than having lived too little. But at least we're now asking questions about all the Ruths and all our family mysteries.

If her song inspires that, I think she would be the first to say: It was worth the singing.

YELLOW PAGES

by Morley Torgov

Morley Torgov is the author of A Good Place to Come From, The Abramsky Variations, *and* The Outside Chance of Maximilian Glick, *winner of the Leacock Medal for Humor in 1975 and 1983. He has practiced law in Toronto since 1954.*

L‚ooking back on that time, trying to imagine what went on, I have this vision in my mind's eye:

My parents, married only a few months and recently settled in a small northern Ontario town, are in the act of conceiving their first child—me. The setting is anything but romantic: a flat at the rear of their clothing store consisting of a kitchen that doubles as a living room if company drops in, a tiny bedroom, natural light admitted through a single window that overlooks a lane, the whole place furnished in Early Suitcase. Nor is this event the culmination of some starry-eyed decision made jointly by the two of them; more likely, the idea of manufacturing an heir is entirely my father's, given that he's already well into his thirties and not getting any younger.

In my mother's head at this moment, questions chase each other in circles. Why, she wonders for the thousandth time, did she—English-born and English-speaking—ever agree to marry this greenhorn from Kamensk Podolsk whose Russian accent is as heavy as a potato kugel? Where, oh where, did the man learn to make love? In a brothel in Odessa during his student days? In the army of Czar Nicholas during World War I military service? How, in these lean early months of their marriage, will they be able to fill three stomachs when there is scarcely enough on the kitchen table to satisfy two? What will they have to sell off to the junkman to clear space for a crib? Will it be even more inconvenient and embarrassing, once the baby arrives, having to share a bathroom with the family of four in the neighboring flat? When will he finish so she can get some sleep? After all, tomorrow's another day in the store . . .

My father, by contrast, is untroubled by questions of this sort. Working away, his tongue protruding slightly between his lips (a characteristic sign of concentration whenever he expends physical energy, even if only shaving himself), he is totally confident of two things: Firstly, the product of this essentially mechanical exercise will be a son. Secondly, the son will become in due course a medical doctor.

Nine months later, in the middle of a December night, my parents, acting out their own version of the Nativity, manage to make it to the Roman Catholic hospital through cold so intense that spoken words crack into frozen syllables. Before long, my mother lies in the operating room screaming her countless questions aloud now as she gives birth to me. The process of delivering seems to take forever, just as her pregnancy seemed to take forever what with unremitting cramps, weakness, nausea, and frequent visits to doctors who could not make up their minds whether or not she should go through with it.

Free of her body at last, I am surrounded by urgent procedures as the two attending physicians and a team of nursing sisters work to assure that my mother and I will survive the untidy miracle of childbirth. Behind surgical masks their voices are muffled and tense. The sounds of a battery of medical gadgets and appliances bounce off the hard white plaster walls and ceilings.

In the corridor outside the operating room, my father paces anxiously, fulfilling the traditional male role at such critical moments.

A full hour passes. Finally, the physician in charge emerges from the operating room, the swinging doors flapping excitedly behind him. Pulling off his surgical mask, he announces in a weary voice that both mother and child will live. My father's smile is one of relief mixed with triumph. His first objective— a son—has been achieved. He is right on target. Overcome with gratitude, convinced that the man in the stained white apron standing before him is really Jehovah in disguise, my father utters a prayer of thanks, sealing it with a silent resolution: Someday the little kid wailing his lungs out in the operating room will stride through those swinging doors masked, gowned, renowned, revered, and making money hand over fist.

And he will have a title: *Dr. Torgov!*

There is, I confess, something sacrilegious, in the nature of after-the-fact voyeurism, about imagining one's conception and birth. Certainly, children of my generation were always raised in the belief that two classes of human beings were exempt from performing sexual and other natural bodily functions—the royal family and parents. Still, from what I came to know about my father and mother, both from direct observation and from word-of-mouth accounts (including solid facts and questionable gossip), my recollection, albeit sacrilege, is rendered legitimate by strong probability.

In the years immediately following my birth, my mother's various systems failed one by one. Before my ninth birthday she succumbed to an accumulation of ailments and died quietly and hopelessly, just as she had lived. I remember her mostly as a shadow who spoke softly and who, even smiling, seemed sad, as though on every surface around her she caught reflections of the mistakes she had made that brought her to this end-of-the-line mill town.

Not surprisingly, while my mother was growing weaker, my father's determination that their only begotten son would one day become a doctor grew stronger, a determination no doubt fed by the fact that doctors and hospitals and medications had become as much a part of the daily life of this small family as the air we breathed. In a time when my parents and their fellow storekeepers were scraping their livings off the rough sidewalks of the town's main street, doctors pulled up in front of their patients' humble abodes in new Buicks. When the doctor entered, smelling of disinfectant, wearing a starched clean shirt and well-pressed three-piece suit, people in the house fell silent waiting for his words; when he departed, he was spoken of in hushed tones. And when his bill was submitted, one thing was clear: Great Depression or no Great Depression, the wolf that showed up daily at other people's doors would never show up at the doctor's door.

"You see?" my father would lecture me, waving the doctor's bill in the air like a flag. "*That* is how you make a living in this world."

"But I'm not sure I like the idea of cutting people up—"

Motioning contemptuously toward the bolts of tweed and worsted cloth on the countertops of his shop, my father said, "Maybe you'd rather cut jackets and pants for the rest of your life, eh?"

I continued to express doubts about my aptitude. "I don't have a head for all that Latin stuff doctors have to memorize."

Such doubts were quickly discarded. "Never mind your head," said my father. "Look at your *hands*. They're the hands of a born surgeon!"

I studied my fingers, the fingers of a ten-year-old. Whatever dexterity they possessed had been channeled thus far primarily in drawing thin black Clark Gable mustaches on men's faces on the covers of *Time*. Hardly the hands of a born surgeon. "I'd rather be an artist," I said, holding aloft with pride the latest issue of *Time*. Franklin Roosevelt was on the cover. I'd succeeded in making the President of the United States of America look like Clark Gable.

"From this you expect to make a living?" my father asked.

I shrugged. "Who knows?"

"*I* know, that's who. You are going to be a doctor, not some schlepper with a paintbrush."

And that was that.

Soon after this exchange, my father made a second major discovery about his son. "Anybody with half a brain can hear it," he declared. "The kid's got the ear of a born musician." Indeed, my father had a point. Every Saturday I would return home after the matinee at the Algoma Theatre singing word for word, note for note, with unerring syncopation, the latest songs from that afternoon's Fred Astaire–Ginger Rogers or Busby Berkeley extravaganza (I had graduated ages ago from the lollipop tunes and lyrics of Shirley Temple). The decision that I would take music lessons struck me as unappetizing, nevertheless. I was already burdened with ordinary schooling. Added to that was compulsory daily attendance at the local cheder, a stuffy one-room Hebrew school where our elderly chain-smoking rabbi desperately attempted to plant Judaism within a handful of pupils who regarded Christmas and Easter as far more alluring greenery.

"Why can't I just go to the movies? Why do I have to take lessons?" I pleaded. "I won't have time to do my homework."

"Oh no? Look at Irving Cohen. Goes to school like everybody else. Goes to cheder like everybody else. And still manages to practice two hours a day, one hour before school in the morning, one hour after supper, like clockwork!"

"Irving Cohen is a freak," I protested. "Irving Cohen should be in a sideshow in a circus."

"Someday," my father said, wagging an index finger in my face for emphasis, "Irving Cohen will be the talk of this town. And what will *my* son be doing meanwhile? *My* son, the artist, will be up on a ladder, in overalls, painting a mustache on a billboard on Queen Street. In my whole life I never saw a single artist that didn't end up a bum. Listen to what I'm telling you: You got a brilliant ear. You could be a prodigy, like Mozart."

Seldom bogged down by conflicting evidence and lengthy argument, my father wasted no time arriving at a judgment. His final word on the subject thundered down magisterially. "I'll see that you have the best music teacher in town."

Case over.

Salzburg had once had its Mozart. Sault Ste. Marie, Ontario, would now have its own young musical genius. *Maestro Torgov!*

The piano arrived a few days later.

It was an upright, at least twenty-five years old. Purchased for fifty dollars, it required several times that amount to be made playable once more. Its dark mahogany case was deeply scarred and its yellowed ivory keys resembled neglected teeth. Once restored, however, the instrument had remarkable tone and the keys, despite their discolor, were yielding and friendly. By now, we occupied a slightly larger apartment over my father's new clothing store but the only room with sufficient space to accommodate the piano was my bedroom. Awake or asleep, I was seldom out of reach of the keyboard. I could hold the loud pedal depressed and play a C-major chord with all my might, then listen as its tones reverberated, echoing and reechoing and, I imagined, rolling in a steady wave clear around the globe before disappearing into some constellation millions of miles away. It was as though the four walls of my bedroom were melting; suddenly there were no longer any town limits confining me to the dozen or so short blocks on the main street that constituted my physical world. There was instead this simple chord, the simplest chord on the musical scale, piercing the atmosphere, connecting me to whatever lay out there, far beyond the St. Marys River and the scrublands along its northern banks.

I had learned to play the C-major scale on my own. "Wait," my father said, beaming encouragement, "you haven't heard *any*thing yet!"

The man engaged to transform me from raw genius into virtuoso performer was Mr. Blackburn, one of the town's two best piano teachers (the other being Mr. Kunzel, who taught Irving Cohen and was therefore disqualified from coming within a country mile of *my* keyboard). Born and educated in England, Mr. Blackburn was a formal man, with Edwardian manners and a strong preference for the music of Mozart, Handel, and Elgar. Like all teachers in those hard times, he was poorly paid. In my search to describe his appearance, one word immediately springs to mind: undernourished. But he knew how to satisfy the appetites of others, particularly mine. "To understand music," Blackburn insisted, "you must live inside the skin of the man who composed it, smell the cobblestone streets he walked, love what he loved, fear what he feared."

And I did.

Thanks to Mr. Blackburn, I was on the stage when they were obliged to turn poor Beethoven around to face his audience so he could at least see, if not hear, the applause he'd just earned. I shivered in Franz Schubert's unheated loft while the dying young man scribbled themes of incredible sunniness on scraps of used paper. I imagined myself in Schumann's household, watching and listening anxiously as, with one hand, he penned masterpieces and with the other hand sought to destroy himself. In the frigid silence of a winter day, I fixed my eyes on the distant point where the gunmetal sky touched endless stretches of snow, and I was Sibelius conjuring up melodic lines clean and clear and piercing as icicles.

"There's a film I want you to be sure to see," Blackburn said to me one day. "It's called *One Hundred Men and a Girl*. It's at the Algoma Theatre. You should see it this Saturday afternoon. I doubt they'll run it beyond Saturday, not in this town at any rate."

Accustomed to the brand of silly romances that Hollywood fostered as excuses to pair Fred Astaire and Ginger Rogers, or Nelson Eddy and Jeanette MacDonald, in front of a camera, I assumed that *One Hundred Men and a Girl* was yet another such piece of nonsense, only on a gargantuan scale.

"Not at all," Blackburn assured me. "This one's all about a symphony orchestra. You've never seen a symphony orchestra, have you?"

"No, never."

"Then go!"

It was as though I had been given a drug that afternoon at the Algoma Theatre. The plot was pure chicken fat, of course: an unemployed coloratura (Deanna Durbin) goes from door to door with an entourage of similarly hungry symphony musicians seeking work, finally attracting the attention of the great Leopold Stokowski just in time to avoid mass starvation. What made this melodramatic schmaltz digestible was a riveting performance, at the happy conclusion of the movie, of the final movement of Tchaikovsky's Fifth (with Adolphe Menjou and Mischa Auer playing their hearts out in the body of the orchestra during the goose-pimply march theme).

My addiction to this kind of music was instant.

Thereafter, while my playmates busied themselves impersonating their sports heroes on hockey rinks and baseball diamonds, and dreamed of athletic stardom, I was on a podium on Sunday afternoons, center stage at Carnegie Hall, flailing away with my arms, like a mad scarecrow in the wind, radio on full volume, extracting every last ounce out of the New York Philharmonic, signaling with fluttering wrists for more vibrato from the fiddles, frowing at the snare drummer for a sharper beat, demanding that the horn section tone down lest they drown out the woodwinds.

Manhattan—that awesome collection of towers I'd seen in the movies, all grasping possessively for more than their fair share of the sun—Manhattan was mine!

Well, *almost* mine, for I soon began to share that magical skyline with another person . . . Irving Cohen.

It turned out that Irving Cohen was not the circus freak I'd accused him of being. A couple of years older than I, Irving was shy and a slight stammer contributed to his reserve. Yet at the keyboard his style was bold, full of energy, meticulous, and devoid of the fakery indulged in by most young pianists who relied on the loud pedal to cover unresolved technical problems, as I discovered when he and I were featured soloists on the same program for the first time. The venue was the one-room Hebrew school that also served as synagogue and meeting hall for the Jewish congregation. The piano was in its dotage and one couldn't be certain whether it would respond to anything less than a sledgehammer, especially in the bass octaves, where death was beginning to overtake the lowest strings. Tuning it for the occasion must have required super-human effort (perhaps the proximity of the instrument to the Torah, only a few feet away in its ark, made the difference).

I performed first, catering to the audience's taste for surefire material by playing Mozart's Turkish Rondo, followed by Strauss's *Tales from the Vienna Woods,* the latter executed with enough rubato to put any beer-garden band to shame. The audience loved it. My father loved it. I thought I loved it.

Now it was Irving's turn. His opening selection was a Bach prelude and fugue. I had to admit: when Cohen played Bach, it sounded like Bach; when *I* played Bach, it sounded like Johann Sebastian Strauss. The second selection was a piano prelude written by someone whose name I failed to catch, so reticent was Irving's introduction, little more than a few muttered words. I had never before heard such spirited keyboard rhythms, such strange and fresh harmonies. The notes leapt from the old piano's sounding board and flew at my face. This was cheeky music, streetwise, exuberant, daring me to be anything less than totally overwhelmed by what it had to say.

Afterward, I sought Irving out at the refreshment table. "Who'd you say composed your second number?"

Irving had a moment of difficulty with the first syllable. On the second try, the name "Gershwin" emerged.

"Gershwin? Gershwin what?"

"George Gershwin."

The name held no significance for me. "What else has he written?"

"Come over to my house Saturday afternoon, I'll show you," Irving said.

Though we lived practically around the corner from each other, I wasn't certain I wanted to socialize with an older kid—he was fifteen, I was just turning thirteen—especially one constantly held up to me as an example of diligence and devotion bordering on musical saintliness. "I usually go to the Algoma on Saturday afternoons," I responded.

"Oh," Irving said, smiling, "I see." There was something about that smile . . . amusement, detachment, appraisal, dismissal . . . that made me feel reduced, as though I were standing before him clad in nothing but a diaper. A little cautiously, I asked, "What time did you have in mind?"

"Anytime after lunch."

The Cohen family were just rising from lunch when I knocked on their door that Saturday afternoon. They were setting the table for dinner some five hours later by the time I bid a reluctant "good night" and took my leave. During the interval between lunch and dinner, Irving, who was fortunate enough to own an electronic record player that operated through the speaker of his radio—a rarity in 1940—played and replayed *Rhapsody in Blue,* the Concerto in F, the Second Rhapsody, an orchestral suite from *Porgy and Bess,* the three piano preludes, the Cuban Overture, and *An American in Paris.* On his own piano, an immense upright that presided over the cramped Cohen living room like some dark monolith, Irving pounded out piece after piece from the Gershwin Song Book, a collection of the composer's hits—some of which I recognized from Astaire-Rogers films—arranged for concert performance, each more difficult to play than the last.

For the second time in my life, I had the sensation of having been drugged. Another case of instant addiction. I wanted to know everything there was to know about George Gershwin. "Here," said Irving, handing me a volume with a dull gray cover bearing a small cartoon of a pianist with grotesquely oversized hands spread like tentacles across the keyboard. I read the title aloud: *A Smattering of Ignorance.* The author was Oscar Levant, the same Oscar Levant I'd heard that day playing the Concerto in F with André Kostelanetz conducting.

"You can borrow it if you like," Irving said. "Read the chapter entitled 'My Life: Or the Story of George Gershwin.' I've read it so many times I can recite it from memory."

There is a natural tendency of writers to wax apocryphal when writing about themselves, and I am therefore tempted to claim that I reread Levant's account of his relationship with Gershwin a hundred times, when the truth is that I read it no more than a dozen or so times, proving once again that fact always pales alongside fiction. Still, it is no exaggeration to say that the opening paragraph took on the sanctity of a passage of Scripture, six lines of prose which Irving and I—who were becoming fast friends—repeated often by heart, including the punctuation!

> Long before I ever met George Gershwin, or even heard of him, he had begun to impinge on my life. Like the first theme in an elaborate rondo, his was a discomfitingly insistent motive constantly recurring in my orbit, eventually to reduce me from industry to inertia.

Indeed, now that Irving Cohen and I had figuratively met George Gershwin, he, and his biographer Oscar Levant too for that matter, began to impinge on *our* lives, but in a different way.

In the far north, where the calendar is dominated by winter, boys gifted with neither taste nor talent for rugged outdoor sports, such as Irving and I, were faced during leisure hours with two choices: to live like slugabeds or to develop a "kunstleben." Sloth, in our case, was out of the question. It was simply un-Jewish to sit when one could be standing, to stand when one could be walking, to walk when one could be running. No sons of hardworking entrepreneurs could afford the luxury of being horizontal except in the event of serious illness, and even then a doctor's certificate was required.

So a kunstleben it became. But not the bohemian existence one usually associates with the "artist's life" . . . a ramshackle garret through whose walls the pitiless elements pass in and out at will, a bare table, an empty pantry, a dilapidated spinet in one corner at which stoops a consumptive genius, the whole shabby scene illuminated by a lone flickering candle. No, the artist's life Irving and I envisioned was a life of penthouses overlooking Central Park furnished in black and chrome, private rooms on fast transcontinental trains heading for "the Coast," staterooms on transatlantic liners, standing ovations at Carnegie Hall, expensive Cuban cigars the size of dirigibles, chauffeur-driven Packards, camel-hair overcoats, headlines, headlines, and more headlines. In short, the life of George Gershwin.

We read everything we could lay our hands on that dealt even remotely with Gershwin, Levant, their families, friends, acquaintances, and mere hangers-on. On the eve of my bar mitzvah, I chose my first "adult" suit of clothes, a double-breasted item with pleated trousers similar to a suit Irving had acquired some months earlier. We took to wearing bar pins through our shirt collars and tightly knotted neckties. Thus outfitted, we aspired to look exactly like Gershwin and his well-heeled circle, though entering Curly Keenan's pool hall on Queen Street we could have been taken for a couple of teenage racketeers about to shake down the owner. At Capy's Grill on

Sunday afternoons we occupied a table of our own—a sort of Algonquin Round Table—where we amused ourselves (but none of the other restaurant patrons) by trading quips originally delivered by Alexander Woollcott, Franklin P. Adams, George S. Kaufman, as well as Levant himself, on *Information Please,* which we managed to pick up from a Detroit station on Irving's radio.

Irving continued to outshine me at the piano. I'd play the opening bars of Beethoven's *Appassionata;* Irving would immediately sit down and play it better. "You see," he would say afterward, quoting a famous Gershwin observation aimed at Levant, "that's the difference between talent and genius."

At times, when we were together at his piano or mine, Irving, in his quiet way, managed to monopolize the keyboard while I sat on the sidelines itching to demonstrate my own wizardry on the instrument. Afterward, paraphrasing an equally famous Levant observation about Gershwin, I would grumble, "An evening with Irving Cohen is an Irving Cohen evening."

In this northern hinterland, Cohen and I constructed a metropolitan life of our own, a vast urban landscape inhabited by a population of two. Today it was a purely imaginary city; tomorrow, or perhaps the day after tomorrow, it would be the real thing! The art we gazed at in magazines, the books we read, the music we listened to on Irving's record player or played ourselves . . . everything reinforced our determination that someday, some blessed day, we would get out of Sault Ste. Marie. And stay out.

Enter Father . . . *not laughing.*

"Are you crazy, or are you just out of your mind?" he demanded to know. "What's all this talk about being writers, artists, musicians? About living like princes in New York City? Here—" My father handed me a local telephone directory. "Show me in the yellow pages where there's an artist, a writer, a musician?"

"That's not fair," I countered. "You want to talk about the *New York City* yellow pages, that's a different story."

"Different nothing! New York City's got breadlines miles long. You know who's in those breadlines?"

"I know who's *not*," I replied. "George S. Kaufman's not. Neither is Oscar Levant or Jascha Heifetz. Neither is—"

"Never mind," my father cut in, waving my argument aside with a brusque sweep of his hand. "You're talking about people who are one in a million . . . no, one in *ten* million. For every Jascha Heifetz there are hundreds of fiddle players picking lice out of their hair."

I frowned, thoroughly bewildered. Almost five years had passed since that fateful night two brawny furniture movers had strained their vertebrae to the limits hoisting our piano up a long flight of stairs and into my bedroom . . . five years of lessons with Mr. Blackburn, God only knew how many hundreds of hours of practice, my father's hard-earned dollars that went to the teacher, the tuner . . . What was the point of it all? "I don't understand," I said.

"What's to understand?" my father said. "It's simple. Art is a hobby. Music is a hobby. Writing is a hobby. But medicine . . . medicine is a *profession!*"

Bewilderment turned to incredulity, then to anger. "I can't believe that's why I'm killing myself every day at the keyboard, just because music is a *hobby!*"

"But you're not killing yourself," my father insisted, "you're giving yourself *life*. No matter where you are, if there's a piano in the room, suddenly you are at the center of things. Any man who can entertain people the way you can will never be short of friends. You play for your own pleasure, you play for other people's pleasure, that's what it's all about, don't you see?"

This is what I saw: mornings in the operating room, saving one endangered life after another, colleagues at my side gasping in awe as my scalpel makes incisions where God Himself would fear to carve; in the afternoons, hospital rounds, grateful patients reaching toward me from their sickbeds hoping to touch the hem of my white linen coat, asking heaven's blessing on my hands, my stethoscope, my thermometer; a receptionist frantically juggling appointments ("I'm sorry but Dr. Torgov is booked solid till next spring"), my father parked across the street from my office conducting a secret surveillance, counting the patients that go in and come out, the latter clutching prescriptions; in the evenings I am the darling of the local salon set, plunking away for the amusement of my bank manager and the president of the town's Chamber of Commerce, all the "swells" in the room swaying to the irresistible beat, agreeing among themselves that the chap at the keyboard is not only the best goddamn doctor but the best goddamn piano player in—

In where? In this flyspeck of a town that could only be detected on the map with the aid of a magnifying glass? This defenseless municipality on whose outskirts winter lurked, threatening to attack all year round? These few blocks of low undistinguished buildings crouching under the smoke that poured from the steel mill in the West End? This Saturday-night place where life glowed for a few hours at the Algoma Theatre and the hockey arena and the beer parlors, like a flare, only to die out and become the deadliness of Sunday?

I saw no point in being a big fish in a small pond. "What's the use of being a doctor and driving an expensive Buick if the only place you get to drive it is up and down Queen Street?" I said.

"Buick Schmuick!" my father exploded. "We're not talking about cars. We're talking about respect . . . respect other people give you, and self-respect too. Have you seen where Dr. Sinclair lives? Where Dr. Grady lives? Where Dr. Roberts lives? Mansions! Solid brick, with lawns and gardens and fireplaces. And every single one in the East End. You want to know who lives in the *West* End, near the steel plant?"

"Here we go with the guessing games again," I said. "Okay, lemme see if I can guess—" I pretended to think hard.

"All the artists, writers, and musicians in Sault Ste. Marie live in the West End near the steel plant, right?" I smiled, like a poker player unfolding four aces.

The look my father gave me was the same look he gave to a suit or a coat that had loitered too long in his inventory and was about to be written off as unmarketable merchandise. "Okay," he said quietly, "be a wise guy, a smart aleck. Someday when you're stealing milk from the cats you'll remember my words. Believe me, sonny boy, there'll be plenty of blues and damn little rhapsodies."

"Someday," I shot back, "you're gonna eat your words when you visit me in my apartment twenty or maybe thirty stories above Fifth Avenue. I'll have not one but *two* Steinway grands and when we walk into a fancy restaurant everybody will stop eating and the waiters will fall all over us, just like they did with George Gershwin."

My father slapped his forehead with the palm of his hand. "Again with the Gershwin craziness! When will it end?"

For a time it seemed as though it would never end. We continued to slave away, Irving and I, he at his aged upright piano, I at mine, both of us expanding our reputations as musicians and our popularity among our peers. The only problem was this: Whenever Irving was invited to perform, he inevitably played Gershwin's *Rhapsody in Blue*. And whenever *I* was invited to perform, I inevitably played Gershwin's *Rhapsody in Blue*. Comparing program notes, we would cry aloud, borrowing a remark attributed to Oscar Levant's mother: "Again the *Rhapsody!*"

One day early in 1944 Irving called me. "Guess what," he said over the telephone. "I'm off to save humanity from the Huns."

"You're *what?*"

"My call-up came in today's mail. I'm supposed to report for a medical in two weeks. I'm thinking of signing up for the Navy."

"The Navy!" I shouted. "You can't even swim across your own bathtub. Besides, Jews don't go into navies. Name me one Jew that ever went into any navy."

"Okay. Irving Cohen."

The day Irving Cohen's train pulled out of the small station, its engine obscured by a giant cloud of steam, its dusty maroon passenger cars rattling obediently behind, it was really George Gershwin who was departing. Back at the station platform, Oscar Levant, empty and envious, waved listlessly until the caboose was out of sight.

At last there was an answer to my father's question "When will it end?" It ended then and there.

It is twenty years later now and I am driving my father to my home in a suburb of Toronto after his appointment with a chest specialist downtown. The car radio is on, tuned in to a late-afternoon newscast. "President Johnson today ordered more troops to be sent—"

"Turn the damn thing off," my father says in a low voice. "I've had enough news for one day." He reaches inside his coat and withdraws a cigarette, which he positions between his teeth in a way that always reminds me of Humphrey Bogart.

"I thought you were going to give those things up."

He smiles like a boy who enjoys committing a forbidden act. "Better you should keep your eyes on the road," he advises. Then, quietly, he adds, "Anyway, what the hell difference does it make now?"

"If my memory is correct," I say, "the doctor didn't exactly order you to smoke *more*. I mean, you're not going to make the situation any better by paving your lungs with tar."

Again the sly smile. "Oh," my father says, "so all of a sudden you're a doctor, eh? Son of a gun! And here I thought you graduated from law school."

The past hour or so at the doctor's office has been rotten and I'm in no mood to be teased. "It's nothing to kid about," I snap at my father. The sharpness in my voice is not unusual these days; it is the natural outgrowth of the decade just past, during which the character roles we play in our dialogues have become reversed. He has become to some extent the child. He is insubordinate in the face of his doctor's orders to halt his cigarette addiction, evasive when questioned about certain symptoms that suggest serious illness, almost insouciant in his defiance of medical advice, devil-may-care in his determination to live—and die—as he damn well pleases. I, on the other hand, have become the father, issuing stern-faced reprimands whenever he reaches for yet another Lucky Strike. I feel older than my years, repetitious, boring, and, worst of all, completely ineffective. With astonishing good nature, my father receives my biblical sermons on moderation and good clean living, then without pause he proceeds directly to do evil, lighting up even before I've managed to climb down from my pulpit.

Peering at him over my eyeglasses with the gravity of a school principal, I comment, "You know, if there was an Olympics for smokers, you'd win the gold every time."

He reacts with a burst of laughter that quickly infects me and in a moment we are both laughing at each other and at ourselves, and once more I face the fact that my crusade is utterly hopeless. Knowing that what I am about to ask will irritate him right through the roof of my car, I inquire, "Are you going to have the biopsy next week like the specialist suggested?"

"Are you crazy, or are you just out of your mind?"

My tone becomes snappier. "Answer my question first."

"Aha! It's the lawyer speaking again," he says. I cast a sidelong glance in his direction. His lips are tightly compressed as he attempts to stifle a grin. The man refuses to take me seriously. Across the windshield the words "wise guy" and "smart aleck" flash, projected there by memories of earlier conversations between us when it was *I* who refused to take *him* seriously.

"Tell me something," he says, breaking the silence after a couple of blocks. "I've never understood something about you lawyers. You start off in life claiming you don't want to be doctors because you can't stand the business of cutting people up. Then you become lawyers, and what do you do? You cut people up."

"I don't know what you're talking about," I lie, knowing perfectly well what he's talking about.

"I mean, you remind me of that fella on television . . . Perry Mason . . . you know, the one that's always cross-examining people in the witness box until they break down and confess." My father humphs, his customary warning signal that he is about to irritate *me*. "You enjoy a profession where people are at each other's throats all the time?"

"I manage to make a living at it, thank you." My voice is serrated now, like the edge of a paring knife. I remind him that I am happily married and have two fine children. "What's more," I add, "to the best of my knowledge, I haven't double-crossed a single client in all the ten years I've been practicing law."

He considers this for a moment while taking a long drag on his cigarette and exhaling smoke from every pore in his body, or so it seems. "It's still a dog-eat-dog business. I've had dealings with lawyers in my time and I know what I'm talking about. You turn and you twist and you aggravate and you *get* aggravated and who needs it. You saw that doctor today? Nobody argues with him. He looks in the X ray, and he tells you straight out what's doing in your chest, and nobody bullshits anybody. Thank you, leave a check with my nurse, and good luck to you. Next patient."

Not quite so, I think to myself. I saw the expression in the doctor's face, noticed that as he slid the X-ray photo out of the screening device his eyes were having difficulty meeting my father's, noticed too that his voice went slightly froggy when he talked about the odds. "Doctors have their own aches and pains too," I say.

"Aches and pains my ass. A doctor is not like a lawyer; he doesn't live and die with every case in his office."

"Then tell *me* something for a change," I say. "The trouble with your lungs . . . the coughing, the wheezing . . . it's been going on for years. How come, in all that time, you never once listened to your doctors . . . never once took their advice? Answer me that."

"See what I mean?" my father replies. "There you go again. Perry Mason."

The late-afternoon rush-hour traffic does nothing to relieve my growing impatience. On all sides, cars are pressing forward, their drivers testing one another in the nightly tournament of the roads. A motorist behind me, tailgating in his anxiety to beat me to the next red light, urges me to give way with a long blast of his horn. "Bastard!" I shout.

"Well, you wanted to live in a big city," my father says with a shrewd needling smile. "Thank God you didn't settle in New York. They carry guns in their cars there."

"I'd have had a chauffeur-driven limo at my disposal day and night."

My father remains skeptical. "I suppose you mean like George Gershwin?"

"Why not?"

"If Gershwin was alive today he'd probably be hiding in his apartment behind a steel door with twenty-nine locks. If he had to go to the corner store for milk he'd have to take a police dog along."

The mental picture of George Gershwin going to a corner store for milk strikes me as ludicrous, with or without a police dog; so ludicrous, in fact, that against my will I find myself chuckling.

"What's to laugh?" my father asks. "You think people like Gershwin didn't buy milk?"

"Good God! He had servants to look after such trivial matters. You don't honestly believe a George Gershwin would actually go to a grocery store and schlepp home a bag full of cornflakes and sliced bread, do you?"

"Don't kid yourself, sonny boy," my father replies. "George Gershwin was an ordinary man, like all ordinary men. He wasn't a god. If he'd been a god, he wouldn't have died on the operating table back in 1937. Gods don't die from brain tumors. Ordinary men do."

He pauses to extinguish the butt, squashing it into the pristine ashtray on the dashboard. The car is new, so new it still bears the heady automotive perfume of the showroom. I wince and, at the same time, make a sucking sound through my clenched teeth at the thought of the befouled ashtray. Ignoring this, my father ignites another Lucky Strike and asks, "Speaking of that Gershwin business, what do you hear from Irving Cohen these days? They tell me back in Sault Ste. Marie that he's got a very profitable business going for himself in Detroit."

From time to time—not often—Irving and I are in touch. He visits Toronto with his family, I visit Detroit with mine, we speak occasionally by long-distance telephone. "Irving's doing very well."

"They say he's in hospital supplies."

"Uh-huh."

"Makes a lotta sense," my father says, nodding in agreement with himself. "Anything to do with medicine, sickness, you can't go wrong."

I bite my lip. "Uh-huh."

"Being in the Navy during the war . . . that's what did it."

"Did what?"

"Opened his eyes. Made him see this lousy world the way it really is."

"Uh-huh."

Home at last, we run headlong into a frontal assault by my two young children, who strain upward to kiss their grandfather. It occurs to me that there will not be enough time for them to get to know him and that some years hence their memories of him will be sketchy at best. He will be their mystery grandfather, the man who was always generous and loving and who gave them hugs and candies and presents for their birthdays and for Chanukah, but anything else that he was or did they will only learn about from me.

I watch as, one at a time, they mount his knee and he bounces them up and down wildly, as though they are riding an unbroken bronco. All three are laughing, my father the hardest. I study his face and wonder, even at this precise moment, what paradoxes are parading back and forth in his mind, what inconsistencies are colliding head-on with each other in that brain.

Our small house is alive now with laughter and I want to say to him how phenomenal it is that, given time, we rise above the debris of our daydreams and find niches for ourselves somewhere between fantasy and reality where we can manage to breathe and hold out. I want to say this, but on second thought, better to hold my tongue. After all, I know what his reaction will be: "Are you crazy, or are you just out of your mind?"

MISSING: A MAN
WITH A BRIEFCASE

by Susan Allen Toth

*Susan Allen Toth was born in Iowa and is
professor of English at Macalester College in St.
Paul, Minnesota. She is the author of* Blooming:
A Small-Town Girlhood, Ivy Days, *and* How to
Prepare for Your High-School Reunion.

Almost all our family pictures show just the three
of us, my mother, my older sister Karen, and me. At first a
young wife in a floral dress and with neat braids, Mother stands
self-consciously before the camera. In her middle years, dressed
in trim suits, she changes to an upswept pompadour. Over the
years, as she relaxes, so does her hairdo, gradually turning into
a graying brisk bob. Karen and I appear in rompers, then
starched pinafores, eventually wedding dresses, and finally jeans
and baggy sweaters.

Someone is obviously missing from this sequence of snapshots. For years I thought we three were an ordinary family.
But now, studying the empty space, I know better. I see the
ghost who haunts it. For although he is invisible to the lens of
the camera, my father is standing beside us in every picture.
Only he does not age. Tall, lean, almost handsome except for
a Roman nose, he is always thirty-nine.

Here on my desk is his worn black briefcase, hauled out from under a dusty pile of high school annuals and college notebooks. The thick leather is glazed with cracks, and the clasps are coated with rust. When I asked my mother a few years ago if I could take this briefcase from her old trunk, I thought perhaps I would revive it and give it new life. Could I use it to carry books to my office? Even though it was heavy, could I perhaps stuff it with unfinished manuscripts and lug it on plane trips? My father might like that, I thought. His name is still there: EDWARD D. ALLEN, printed in gold leaf under the lock. Whenever I see his name in print, I have a faint sense of shock. After forty-two years, no one speaks or writes it anymore.

Of course, I didn't ever use his briefcase. It was too shabby and unwieldy. I kept it lying on my desk for many months, thinking each day I'd take it with me, before I finally let loose the string of that romantic but useless idea. Feeling a little guilty, I tucked the briefcase in my storage closet. Someday I suppose my daughter will have to toss it out.

I don't have much from which to reconstruct my father. Although I have an often alarming recall of many details of my life, my years with him are surprisingly blank, like an old-fashioned photograph album with only an occasional snapshot stuck there, a scene I seem to have mentally snapped and firmly glued down with corner mounts.

For a long time I didn't think losing my father had affected me very much. He died at thirty-nine, when I had just turned seven, and my mother, a strong, determined, and resourceful woman, took over the support and raising of Karen and me. Although my mother and I were very close when I was growing up, we didn't talk much about my father. We never set off our feelings like Roman candles—our heritage was Scandinavian and English, a blend that stands up better to cold weather than to dazzling heat—and we had to get on with our lives. My mother watched well over my sister and me, providing whatever she thought we needed—music lessons, bicycles, trips—and if someone had asked me, at eight or twelve or eighteen, what I had missed by not having a father, I don't think I could have told them.

Of course, I did notice his absence on Father's Day. I could ignore the official June day by walking quickly past the dime-store greeting-card aisle. But other kinds of Father's Days appeared at awkward times and places. Invite your father for Dad's Day at Camp! Take him to the Father-Daughter Dinner! Let him buy your corsage for the Dads-and-Daughters Dance! Living in a small town, I didn't have any friends who lacked a visible father, and I dreaded the events when I was supposed to produce one. Zac Dunlap, the kindhearted family man next door, was always glad to take me, but, uncertain what to say or do, I was on my company behavior—not, I realized, the way most kids acted with their fathers.

I was almost forty before I began to understand that, although my father had vanished so early, his influence had not. At thirty-nine, the age when he died, I found myself wracked by a strange and pervasive anxiety. Living beyond that milestone seemed odd, almost unthinkable, and perhaps impossible. As I struggled to understand my turbulent feelings, I gradually realized that, although I could not conjure up his face with a photograph, my father must have helped shape how I thought, how I felt, and who I was. For the first time, I asked myself what Edward D. Allen had really been like, and how we were related.

The clearest connection I could trace to my father was fear. A courageous man, he would hate knowing that. My mother has told me how bravely he endured his long illness, which began almost as soon as I was born. He had a brain tumor, but for many years no one recognized what it was. His symptoms resembled stroke or epilepsy. Sometimes, in the midst of a sentence, he would stop, blank-eyed; moments later he would resume, not realizing what had happened. Worse, he was struck by seizures. The word our family used was "spells." Once, in a mental snapshot so short it is a moment's click, my mother, father, sister, and I are sitting together in the dining nook of our small kitchen. It has a red-brick linoleum floor. "Hazel," my father says quietly to my mother, "I think I'm going to have a spell." He gets up from the table. Everything in my mind goes black for a moment, as it must have for him, and then I see him lying on the red linoleum, my mother bending over him. I do not know what happend next.

I do not remember any other "spells," though of course he had many of them. He also had terrible headaches; when I first was struck by a migraine, I thought I too had a brain tumor. But he continued his teaching, writing, and other professorial responsibilities. He was a proud man, my mother says, and he bore the agonizing knowledge that at any time, during a lecture or a meeting, he might lose control of himself. In another snapshot, my mother and I are walking down the steep polished-granite stairs inside the Agricultural Economics building at Iowa State College. My father's office is somewhere high above us. She is holding my hand tightly. "Watch your step," she says, and I hear a warning tone in her voice. I try to place my feet on the funny raspy-feeling strips that roughen the stair edges. Has she told me my father once fell here? Is that what I believe has caused his "spells"? In my memory, the stairs are cold and ominous.

Almost every day my father must have carried his heavy black briefcase up and down those stairs. He never gave up, my mother says. He did not like to talk about what was happening to him. I think I can see him, leaving home for his office, a tall lean man in a long overcoat, his hand firmly on the handle of the briefcase bulging with papers. It looked very important, an emblem of the College that he served so loyally. "He was a brilliant economist," my mother told me, "and he had a wonderful future ahead of him." When people spoke of my father in later years, they often echoed her. Among the remarkable group of young economists who worked at Iowa State in the early 1940s, most went on to make national and international reputations. Through the years I heard their names as a litany of achievement: Kenneth Boulding, Bill Nichols, Oswald Brownlee, Rainer Schickele. My father, I knew, should have been one of them.

So, not intending to, he left me his burden of unfulfilled promise. Without having to be asked, I picked it up. Like mountain climbers who gradually adjust to a rarefied atmosphere, children soon find the air of high expectations completely natural. From kindergarten, when I was embarrassed to bring home a report card because it had one minus among my pluses—under "Deportment," Miss Sawyer had written with unblinking severity: "Susan picks her nose"—I knew I needed to be a very good student. I was someone who ought to excel, someone with that exciting but demanding word "potential." Sometimes I was afraid that I would fail, that I too would not be able to redeem my promise.

But that fear came later. Another had hovered over my life from its beginning. I do not know how aware I was of my father's illness, of my mother's worry, of doctors, diagnoses, and medicines. Although I knew he had "spells," I did not know he was dying. Perhaps he didn't know himself. The summer before he died, a specialist at the University of Wisconsin, where my mother and father had gone for help, found a tiny pinpoint of a tumor in his brain. "Come back in six months, at Christmas," the doctor told him. But my mother says my father was so busy, so involved in his forthcoming book, so concentrated on his work at the College, that he didn't go back at Christmas. One bright July morning the following summer, they were having breakfast. My father suddenly threw up, a violent projectile vomiting, and when they called our family doctor, she advised them to go to Madison immediately.

If I was sitting in the kitchen that awful morning, I have locked the memory away in a dark closet without a key. I know I was sent to stay across the street with friends, while my sister Karen went to other neighbors. My father was ill, I was told, and he had gone to Madison—a city so remote in my imagination it might have been Oz—in order to get better. I don't believe I was very worried. The Zickefooses were a jolly family, and I was great friends with their daughter Kay, who was my age. On those hot July days, I'm sure we cut out paper dolls, hid under the lilacs, and ran through the sprinkler, just as we usually did.

One afternoon soon after my parents had left, Mrs. Zickefoose told me I had to pay a visit across the alley to the E. S. Allens—the *other* Edward Allens, not related, though I regarded them as an older aunt and uncle. Going to see E.S. and Aunt Minne was always a slightly exotic occasion; they were Quakers and pacifists, and Aunt Minne, who was German, still had an accent. Their house was filled with antique furniture and German knickknacks. Somehow it always felt dark and hushed, as if the curtains were drawn, and Aunt Minne's kitchen had a lingering aroma of unfamiliar pungent spices. The atmosphere was not frightening, just different, a little like church. But today, the way Mrs. Zickefoose spoke, I somehow didn't want to go the the Allens'.

Behind the E. S. Allens' house was a large garden, partly vegetables, but with lots of flowers. We had had a Victory garden once, and I can picture my father, in another mental snapshot, digging a pitchfork in the damp black dirt of early spring. I see the colorful Burpee's seed packets on stakes, marking each row, and the white string stretching over the deep furrows. I must have telescoped the time to midsummer, for I also see next to our garage another garden, a blur of rosy-red and white hollyhocks, sweet-smelling peonies, and orange nasturtiums. We had a small orchard too, in that narrow but deep city lot, and I remember my father once lifted me up into the white-flowering branches of the cherry tree. I sat there, perched above the whole world, while he worked among the lettuce and sweet corn below.

Walking to the Allens' house that afternoon, not wanting to hurry, not wanting to get there at all, I crunched the black cinders of the alley under my shoes. Despite the heat, I wasn't barefoot because I knew the cinders would hurt too much. Slowly I passed through their backyard garden, past what seemed like fields of daisies, petunias, and zinnias. I remember how brightly the sun shone.

My sister was there in the darkened living room, waiting for me. We sat next to Aunt Minne on the stiff-backed sofa. I do not remember how she led us toward what she had to say. It didn't take long. When she came to the end, I heard her words very clearly: "Your father was so sick they had to go to Madison. He had an operation in the hospital there, and during the night, he died."

I didn't completely understand what she had told us, but I knew she had pronounced something that had the sound of doom. I began to cry. Karen was tight-faced and silent; later, walking back through the blooming flowers of the back garden, I accused her of not caring enough. Even then I knew I was being mean, but with a shamed self-awareness, I realized I had cried partly because I knew I was expected to.

I never forgot Aunt Minne's last sentence: "And during the night he died." Far away and in a setting I couldn't imagine, my father had gone to sleep and never woke up. During the night, he had simply disappeared. Where had he gone? I'm sure I brushed aside as unreal any talk of heaven and angels. After the funeral, which my sister and I didn't attend—the grown-ups thought we were too young—we were taken to the cemetery. I remember the mound of fresh earth, heaped with flowers. My mother says I asked if Daddy was really down there, under the ground. This time I am sure my sister and I both wept.

"And during the night he died." It was such a matter-of-fact statement. How could Aunt Minne have said it better? Yet it haunts me still. I have never liked staying alone at night. Before my daughter was born, if my husband was going to be out of town, I occasionally drove across town to a friend's house to sleep. Even now, if I am by myself, I leave a few lights on, double-lock the doors, and keep the telephone nearby. I sometimes am reluctant to fall asleep. Lost in the night, my father closed his eyes and never opened them again.

So I grew up knowing how fragile and vulnerable were the people I loved. While I was not a brooding or depressed child—in fact, like my father, I usually showed a very cheerful face—I was a worrier. I still am. Not long ago, as my husband, James, and I were walking up the steps of the National Gallery in Washington, he suddenly stopped and gripped the railing. I paused too and looked at him anxiously. I am always edgy when we are traveling. He seemed far away from me, standing so silently on the steps, utterly preoccupied. "What is it?" I asked, reaching for his arm, wondering how I could get an ambulance and wishing I'd taken that Red Cross course in cardiopulmonary resuscitation. Hearing the urgency in my voice, James looked at me in surprise. "Nothing," he said, "except I was trying to remember where I left the car keys."

So I have to try to curb my catastrophic imagination. If I can stand far enough back from my frightening pictures, I can even sometimes see how funny-awful they are. Once a therapist asked me to go to a swimming pool and just float. "I want you to experience fully the feeling of being supported, of being held up without your having to make any effort," she explained. I dutifully went to the pool and floated, though I didn't much like it. I wanted to do laps; like my father, I'm used to keeping busy. Later I had to give the therapist a report. "And what did you think about?" she asked. I was embarrassed, but I had to answer truthfully. "Sharks," I said. "I thought about sharks."

I can see the fear my father left with me from another perspective, of course. Writers often turn things around and look at them from strange angles. Mine is one of gratitude, for I believe that when I became painfully aware of the possibility of sudden loss, I focused acutely and passionately on the world around me. I wanted to hold it close and never let it go. When my first two books of memoirs were published, readers assumed I had kept a journal. How else could I have remembered so much detail? Until they began asking me, I had not thought my memory was at all unusual. No, I hadn't kept a journal. I just kept those living pictures stored in my mind, piled in overfull bags spilling their contents onto the floor, until, by writing, I cleaned at least a corner of my attic and set it in order.

Fear was certainly not all my father gave me, however, and when I try to bring him back, I can focus on other pictures. On Sunday nights, my father liked to listen to the Jack Benny show. He stretched out on the sofa near the radio in the living room, and I climbed up to his lap and snuggled next to him. As he laughed, his stomach shook, and I rocked with the gentle waves of his laughter. Lying there on the sofa, I was sheltered and safe. Afterward, Mother often served us a special Sunday supper of soft-boiled eggs, Velveeta cheese, and milk toast. Though I didn't understand most of the jokes, I loved the Jack Benny show.

In the years since his death, several people have told me how much my father loved to laugh. "That's where you get your verve," my mother says to me wistfully. Old friends reminisce vaguely about how they enjoyed him, though few can think of any particular incidents I can grasp and make my own. Humor vanishes even more quickly than loosed balloons.

Though he could be lighthearted, my father believed in discipline. Once, going downstairs from my bedroom, I paused and looked over the banister into the kitchen. Mother was cooking oatmeal. Whatever I said—I didn't like oatmeal—brought my father swiftly out of the bathroom. "Don't let me ever hear you speak to your mother like that again," he said sternly. Another day, when I used some bad language—or was I "back-talking" again?—he took me into the bathroom and washed my mouth out with soap. I can still taste it, acrid and unpleasant. Just last week, when I hadn't thoroughly rinsed out a drinking glass, I spat out the soapy water with an instinctive revulsion and thought of my father.

I think of my father at other odd times. Although I haven't played tennis for years, he used to float into my mind during a game or even backboard practice. My mother told me when

I was quite young how he had enjoyed tennis. His old racket stayed on a shelf in our house for many years. One of my mother's pictures shows him smiling, racket in hand, tennis sweater flung casually over his shoulders. Like everything else my father did, he was very good at tennis. Thinking perhaps I'd inherited some genetic skills, I signed up for a tennis class in college, but I barely passed. I imagined my father dashing and lunging over the court; I puffed and lumbered.

My father had been light on his feet, a wonderful dancer. I never learned any steps beyond a basic fox-trot, and I stumbled over my partner's shoes. My parents loved to dance. When they went out as a young married couple with another pair of married friends, Mother remembers, still with some irritation, she'd get stuck with Dan, the other husband, who couldn't dance at all, because Dan's wife, Helen, insisted on waltzing around the floor with Edward. I know how Dan must have felt.

I followed him a little better in music. My father loved to sing too, and one of our most precious possessions was a 78 record, made by someone at the College, of a barbershop quartet that included my father. Over and over my sister and I would play "Ol' Man River," because for a few bars my father sang alone: "Hearts get weary and sick of tryin'." We held our breath and listened as hard as we could. That was our father's voice, rich and resonant, and, above all, alive.

I couldn't sing more than a few notes above middle C, but I did take piano lessons. My father's sister, Aunt Mary, had been a magnificent pianist, my mother said. Music ran in the family. She and my father liked concerts, and they had a small but prized collection of symphony records. On the piano was a thick volume of Gilbert and Sullivan songs, which my father had especially liked. Gathering all these clues, I made an effort to include music in my own life. When, at twenty, I sat alone in a cheap seat at the Sadler's Wells Theatre in London and entered eagerly into the D'Oyly Carte's production of *The Mikado*, I kept a paperback copy of the lyrics in my lap. I didn't want to miss a word.

A tennis racket, a book of Gilbert and Sullivan, a vision of my father whirling Helen Prince around the dance floor—these bits and scraps are not much from which to piece a coherent pattern. My father flashes in and out of my mind, yet each flash is illuminating. That is why I am frustrated that I cannot see him as a whole. I was an English major; I know what a well-rounded literary character should be like. I wish I could make my father into one. As a graduate student, I had some skill as a researcher, and I worked with primary source materials. So I have read the few letters my mother treasures, scrutinized the yellowed pages of the college newspaper he edited, and tried to read his posthumously published textbook. Our family was very proud of that book. I used to roll its title on my tongue, because it sounded so impressive: Allen and Brownlee, *The Economics of Public Finance*. I wasn't surprised that I couldn't understand it.

But my father has remained elusive, or, rather, frozen. He is captured only in those poses I have examined, again and again, in my mother's actual photograph album or in the one I have assembled in my mind. Sometimes I can enter my mother's black-and-white snapshots and briefly meet my father there. Daddy, his arm tucked in Mother's, poses on our front doorsteps, with my sister and me standing in front of them in our Sunday best. As I look at the picture, I can feel the touch of the soft velvet collar on my coat and the crispness of the plaid ribbon bows on my pigtails. Daddy stands knee-deep in the chilly water during our summer vacation at Lake Carlos. Afterward, I think I can see him stroking away from me, laughing and splashing, a strong swimmer moving easily through the water.

Why is it so difficult to bring my father back? I feel I ought to be able to do it, but I can't. I am left with random pieces, flashes, snapshots. Those people who still remember him tend to repeat the same phrases, over and over: "He was a wonderful man." "He had such a terrific sense of humor!" "What a tragedy he died so young." "He did so love you girls!" More, I think, I need more.

During the search I conducted in my early forties, my mother contributed an unexpected gift. When I was a toddler and Karen perhaps three, a neighbor who had acquired a movie camera—a rarity in those days—had shot a few minutes' footage of our family. Mother had it copied for Karen and me, and I promptly had my film transferred onto videotape. When I put it into our VCR, I thought that now, finally, I would see my father as he really was.

But I didn't. Although I was fascinated by the silent images, I didn't feel part of them. My father swung me up to his shoulders, where I grinned and clutched his hair. Karen grabbed one of my toys, and my mother bent over her, gently but reprovingly. My parents looked young and happy, and my sister and I were cute and wriggly. But I couldn't remember being there. I was less connected to that film than to the old familiar snapshots, Mother's and mine.

"Can you think of anything *bad* about my father?" I once asked my Uncle Don, his only brother. He and my aunt looked puzzled. There was an awkward pause. "It's just that he doesn't quite seem *real*," I tried to explain, but my words hung like discordant notes over the luncheon table, jarring them into silence. I knew then that I was asking questions no one could answer anymore.

My father's idealized portrait has hung, lit with a loving glow, in his family's and friends' memories for forty-two years: a tall, almost handsome, eager man, who knew how to laugh, who sang and danced and played tennis, who worked hard and brilliantly at his career. I grew up with this portrait, and I am glad I have it. But I long for a few flaws to make it come alive. I sometimes wonder if that is why I remember so vividly the taste of soap in my mouth.

Today, or tomorrow, I will pack away the old black briefcase. I am not sure when, if ever, I will look at it again. I won't need it. I have many different bags and satchels to carry my books and papers. My current favorite is a plastic "shopper" in a William Morris design that I found in a National Trust shop in England. I liked it so much I got an apron to match. The tote bag doesn't look very professional, but it is lightweight, waterproof, and very capacious. On top of a stack of papers, I can still jam a pair of shoes and a bag lunch. Besides, I like the twining leaves and flowers. If I had died when my daughter was only seven, could she reconstruct my personality from this flimsy satchel?

Though the black briefcase has not told me everything I want to know, it is not completely silent. A briefcase is the mark of a college professor; I became one. It once held my father's books and papers; my life sinks its deepest roots into all the books I have (at least partly) read and all the pieces of paper on which I have written. The man who carried that briefcase was someone I could talk to.

I could ask him about his work, his writing, and his teaching, and he could ask about mine. We could talk about families, my mother and sister, his granddaughters, my husband; about gardening; about summers at the lake. Maybe he would tell me stories about growing up as the youngest child of a Congregational minister in a small Iowa town, or his college years at Grinnell, or how he met and married my mother. He could explain how he managed to live with fear; what he felt when he left Karen and me to take the train to Madison, what he wished he could have said to us then. He could tell me about tennis, and music, and the economics of public finance. I'm sure we would laugh together, and we would talk, I think, for a very long time.

A CUNNING WOMAN

by Jonathan Yardley

*Jonathan Yardley is the book critic and a
columnist for* The Washington Post. *In the
academic year 1968–69 he was a Nieman Fellow
in Journalism at Harvard University and in 1981
received the Pulitzer Prize for Distinguished
Criticism. He is the author of* Ring: A Biography
of Ring Lardner *and* Our Kind of People: The
Story of an American Family.

Probably I was doomed from the start, from the moment in the summer of 1935 when Helen Marie Gregory was introduced to William Woolsey Yardley, somewhere on the campus of Harvard University: doomed to read books, even to write books, always to love books. The two young people who four years later would become my parents were not, in the received sense of the word, "bookish"; Helen Gregory, though shy, was lively and pretty and sociable, while Bill Yardley, though no athlete, was witty and handsome and liked his bourbon whiskey. Yet both had been lured to Harvard that summer by books, and for the half century of their marriage they were bound as much by books as by love and sex and children and property; in the household that they made together, it would have been more irreligious to hate books than to repudiate their shared Episcopalianism.

Eventually my father became, in the tiny world of people who collect old and rare books, a minor character. He was a schoolman who spent most of his career as headmaster—his actual title was "rector"—of a school for girls in southern Virginia called Chatham Hall. In the house on its campus where he and my mother reared their four children was a living room paneled in butternut and amply supplied with tall shelves; my father filled these with books in leather slipcases made by his own hand, the collective effect of which was both impressive and instructive.

By the late 1960s most of these books were the work of Anthony Trollope, an accumulation that by my father's reckoning was either—it depended on how boastful he felt at that particular moment—the world's best in private hands or its third best. When he auctioned most of the collection off upon his retirement in 1971, it brought him six times his $6,000 investment; this, so far as he was concerned, was sufficient proof of his acumen and standing as a bookman.

So Bill Yardley was the famous collector, and when friends of the family or parents of Chatham Hall girls spoke admiringly of the Yardleys' devotion to books and literature, most of that admiration was sent in his direction; he basked in it, as he basked in the sun that, I sometimes thought, shone solely to burnish his skin to the deep tan in which he took such immoderate satisfaction. Yet when, a few years later, the directors of the Redwood Library in Newport, Rhode Island, added a member of the Yardley family to their number, it was my mother rather than my father whom they chose. At the time the decision merely amused me, as I believe it did her as well, but I have since come to realize that the directors were right: my mother, in her quiet yet self-confident way, was the *real* book person in that house.

Not long ago I wrote a book about my mother and father, a work of nonfiction in which I attempted to re-create their lives from their own points of view: to see them not as my parents but as adults to whom parenthood was only one among the many duties and pleasures of well-lived lives. Because this was really their book rather than mine I chose to call them Bill and Helen rather than "my mother and father"; whether in other aspects of the book I succeeded is for others to judge, but in this choice I believe I was correct, as it put me on the sidelines—where in that context I most certainly belonged—and placed my parents entirely at center stage.

But here I want to speak not so much of Helen Gregory Yardly as of *my mother,* of the woman who was beyond question the most important person in my life—though in ways that even now, in my fiftieth year, I can explain only tentatively and incompletely—yet who, because she was often outshone by my father's incandescent glow, does not assume so large a role in my book as she deserves.

She was born in Brooklyn on November 22, 1913; on her birthday precisely a half century later she was aboard an airplane, flying with my father to Detroit, when the pilot came on the intercom to tell his passengers that John Fitzgerald Kennedy had just been shot to death in Dallas, and she rode the rest of the way in stunned, grieving silence. Her father, Alfred Gregory, was a self-made man, a lawyer who eventually achieved a senior partnership in the Wall Street firm of Hawkins & Delafield; years later a partnership in that same firm was assumed by Louis Auchincloss, which gave her immense pleasure because she loved his novels and felt that this afforded her a personal connection to them.

But the places of which Auchincloss wrote were only glancingly her own. Though Alfred Gregory became prosperous, he moved his family from Brooklyn, not into Auchincloss's world—the quiet brownstones of the East Sixties, the vast apartments of Fifth and Park avenues—but to a new suburb a few miles west of Newark called Maplewood. There my mother grew up among the children of the American middle class, attending a big public high school and participating in many, if not all, of its institutional rituals.

She was shy, and often she was more comfortable curled up with a book on the landing of the staircase in the big house on Mountain Avenue than she was in the company of girls and boys of her own age. She read prodigiously. Though the admissions office at Bennington College felt her tastes were "rather superficial," I think otherwise; as a teenager she read Tolstoy and Thackeray, Galsworthy and Maurois, as well as a now forgotten novelist named George Warwick Deeping, whose subjects included rivalries and resentments among social groups. Later, as a member of Bennington's first class, she extended her interest to Joyce and Hemingway and, above all, e. e. cummings. It is from her that I acquired such taste and tolerance for modernism as I possess; my father was most comfortable with a Victorian triple-decker, or a contemporary novel of manners by John P. Marquand or—a particular favorite, as his books always contained as much explicit sex as the market would bear—John O'Hara.

My mother was a rising senior at Bennington and my father a student in Harvard's graduate program in education when they were introduced that summer by a mutual friend. They fell in love in a great hurry. I don't know much about their courtship, but in my mind's eye I see them together at the Widener Library, or browsing in the stacks at the Old Corner Book Shop, a place they regularly visited on their frequent return trips to Boston in the half century that lay ahead of them. This isn't to say that in 1935 books and libraries were more important to them than the potent brew of romance and sexuality that drew them to each other, only that books were there at the beginning in Boston just as, in 1986, they were there at the end in Middletown, Rhode Island.

I think I know what my father saw in her, but of course I can only guess. She wasn't a beautiful woman, though over the years she grew prettier and more striking in a very Anglo-Saxon Protestant way, and her figure was more trim than full, and into the bargain in those days she hadn't figured out how to do her hair to best advantage. But things I've been told lead me to believe she was an enthusiastic participant in premarital petting adventures, and she was wonderful company. She was smart, though not brilliant, and she had a quick if unassertive wit; she'd begun to emerge a bit from her bookish cocoon, and she took pleasure in lively company, which Bill Yardley and his friends offered; she was endlessly curious about the world around her, though never in a self-absorbed way, and she had an appetite for the new that must have seemed briskly invigorating to her rather prematurely middle-aged beau.

A year later they were married, and three years after that they had me. By then my father had gotten a teaching position at a private school for boys in Pittsburgh, and the little family was established in residence in an apartment on its campus; free lodgings, in exchange for a dormitory master's duties, were part of their arrangement with Shady Side Academy. We lived there until I was three, and it is there that my first memory occurs: of being in a warm, bright kitchen with my mother and my grandmother Gregory, and of being quite blissfully happy.

That from this early hour I associate my mother with warmth may surprise some who knew her, especially perhaps those alumnae of Chatham Hall who, however much they may have admired her, regarded her as distant and somewhat forbidding. Indeed, both of my sisters, Jane and Sarah, often use the word "cool" in talking about her, and both of them wish that she had been more forthcoming with them emotionally—a feeling, I should add, that my brother, Ben, does not share, which may suggest she found it easier to bring up boys than girls.

Yet from my earliest days she always had all the love and care I needed; I cannot recall that I ever felt she had been inadequate when my demands on her were emotional rather than practical. This has nothing to do with my being her favorite—that, all four children agree, was Ben—or with my requiring a relatively small supply of such support; my blood tends to run more warm than cool, and I need as much tender loving as the next fellow. Rather, it is that from the beginning I always knew that she was there whenever and for whatever I needed her, and I always knew that, quite simply, she loved me—that whatever else in my world may ever have seemed uncertain, her love was secure.

This may seem an obvious matter, but it is not. Part of the Anglo-Saxon tradition on both sides of the ocean is emotional tentativeness and reticence, and my mother was very much of this tradition. She kept her feelings pretty much to herself, so you had to learn how to read her—gestures, smiles, inflections, body language—in order to figure out what was really in her heart. She absolutely hated giving verbal expression to her deepest emotions; toward the end of her life, when it became fashionable in the middle class for people to put all of their feelings right out there on the table, she visibly winced when someone said, "I love you," to her, and her reply in kind always seemed more dutiful than heartfelt.

What I seem somehow to have understood from an early age—heaven knows how or why—is that the way my mother expressed her love for me, and for the many other people whom she genuinely loved, was by being as true to herself as it was possible to be. She was dutiful, kind, self-effacing, considerate, empathic, responsive, but she was all of these things without ostentation. She thought—I am guessing at this, but it is a confident guess—that emotional display was essentially theatrical, and that what really counted was what one actually did: how, on her infrequent trips from Virginia to New York with my father, she always returned with a baseball book or a phonograph record for me; how, when I was sick, she always brought me ginger ale with a scoop of ice cream on top; how, when I was older, she knew that I secretly missed my Christmas stocking and always left a small package of paperback books outside my bedroom door.

This, to my mother, was love. So too—and this is part of what vexed my sisters—was the rigorously practical counsel with which she responded to anything even remotely approximating a family emergency. When my first marriage was breaking up she flew to North Carolina at my wife's request, but it wasn't to wail and moan and plead with us to patch things up; she wished we could and thought we ought to try, but if we couldn't, well, we'd better get on with the rest of our lives, and on that subject she had a few ideas.

For all of us, when comparable crises arose, she had comparable counsel: Jane when her own first marriage was dissolving, Sarah when she was in the throes of 1960s rebellion, Ben when he was trying to figure out what career seemed most appropriate and rewarding for him. In none of these conversations, in none of her letters, did her businesslike tone dissolve; yet in all of them she managed to convey that she said what she did because she loved us—even if, at times, it took a while for us to comprehend that particular message.

She was, throughout, a practical woman. The family's finances always were meager—we lived on a schoolmaster's salary and little else—but she delighted in managing them. She drew up lists and budgets in her neat hand, and she took pride in sticking to them. Her blood was Scots, and she had a bit of a tight streak, but she also had come to maturity in the Depression and well knew how thin could be the line that separated prosperity from need. As a girl she had been well-to-do, though hardly spoiled, and she had attended a college that charged the highest tuition in the country, yet when she married her impecunious English teacher she never complained about her reduced circumstances—never to my knowledge, that is—and seemed positively to rejoice in the challenge it afforded her; coming to the end of the month with all obligations paid and no debts outstanding was as much a thrill to her as coming in at four under par is to a nine-handicap golfer.

She was, in a word, cunning. It was one of her favorite words, and it was always used as a compliment. "Oh, isn't that cunning!" she'd exclaim over a successful paper by one of her children or a piece of needlework by a friend or a painting in a museum. The word as she employed it had nothing to do with wiliness or slyness. Rather she employed it to describe that which she found charming and beguiling, as well as in the usages that Webster ascribes to it: "possessed of or marked by knowledge, learning or lore . . . marked by dexterous or crafty use of some special skill, knowledge or other resource . . . marked by keen insight, practical analytic intelligence, resourcefulness or ability to anticipate, escape, elude."

To varying degrees all of those were my mother's qualities, yet I am possessed of remarkably few of them: a bit of learning and lore, to be sure, and a small skill at putting words together, but no dexterity—quite to the contrary!—and little practicality and not much analytic intelligence either. As I gaze at my mother's needlework in my living room—it is under glass, fitted into the top of a small table manufactured by my infuriatingly craftsmanly brother—I wonder how I, this clumsy man, could be the son of that ingenious and clever woman, and I am at a loss for words, save ones of gratitude.

Because my mother was so smart, industrious, and efficient, I often wondered what her life would have been like had she been born into my generation instead of her own; my sisters and brother have asked the same question and so, all of us believe, did she. The question has of course no answer, but for many women of her time it acquired a degree of urgency as, in their fifties and sixties, they watched their own daughters move out into the world of business and the professions. Couldn't *we* have done that? these women asked themselves, and: Isn't it outrageous that we were denied the opportunity, or that we denied it to ourselves?

That my mother asked herself these and other, related questions seems to me indisputable. We never really spoke on the subject, except once when my father seemed terminally ill and she discussed the possibility of supporting herself through her skill with figures, but from time to time—more frequently as she grew older—her behavior left little doubt that she felt she'd missed her chance. In retirement she took on several small, marginally remunerative part-time jobs, and derived a satisfaction from them that was all out of proportion to the work or its rewards: Look, she obviously was saying, see what *I* can do. As Jane and Sarah rejected mere housewifery for employment, the pleasure she took in their accomplishments was mixed with a not inconsiderable dose of envy; her interest in my professional life, and Ben's, was every bit as strong as her concern for our private happiness.

All of us think—on this our unanimity is emphatic—that she would have made a superb businesswoman or professional, or anything else she might have wanted to be. Not merely was she efficient and organized, she loved to run things: not to be the boss, but to *manage,* to make things come out right, to get all the right pieces on all the right squares. At Chatham Hall, once the four of us were more or less grown and gone, she turned her attentions to various school affairs with energy and zeal, and she did good work. Most notably she assumed management of the school's alumnae office, theretofore a moribund operation, and turned it into a going concern; its quarterly magazine, which she edited, became a lively and informative publication, far more than a mere alumnae-news and fund-raising sheet. She was proud of her alumnae work, and determined that it be recognized as her own rather than merely that of the wife of the rector.

Basking in Bill Yardley's reflected flory wasn't my mother's cup of tea, yet she did it for almost her entire adult life. Probably she let him know her feelings on the subject—here, I suspect, she threw caution, and Scots reticence, to the winds— but she spoke of it to no one else. At Chatham Hall, though, people sensed not merely frustration but even anger beneath her composed demeanor, and occasionally she let slip remarks that left little doubt she knew she could run the school every bit as well as he did, if in a different manner. But for the most part she kept whatever negative feelings she may have had under tight control; not merely was it in her nature to do so, but she was of a generation of middle-class women who had been reared in the conviction that their first duty must be to their husbands, and Helen Gregory Yardley always did her duty.

What she needed at Chatham Hall, and what she got too little of, was escape. Chatham, Virginia, is a lovely little town, but only in her final years there did it begin to shake its

Southern rural provincialism, and only then did she make real friends there; for much of the time in Chatham she was, I suspect, lonely. She was not especially close to her own sister and brothers, but she wanted to see them from time to time and they were far away; so too were New York and Boston and the world of Northeastern urbanity that she had known, even if not so well as she would have liked, before her marriage.

Since she had no means of physical escape, she fled instead into her books. In a corner of the big paneled living room stood the wing chair, covered in red damask, in which for hours each day and night she could be found, reading. *The New York Times* came in by mail, a couple of days late, and she read it through; she loved the crossword puzzle, which she solved efficiently, and she always read the engagement and wedding notices. She read *The New Yorker* and *The Atlantic* and *Harper's* and *The Manchester Guardian Weekly*: the magazines that an educated woman of her time and class would have been expected to read, except it was pleasure rather than duty that motivated her.

Most of all, she read books. Her reading was quick but never hasty; on the average she went through several volumes a week unless the distractions of school and family proved too forbidding. She patronized the little library in the town of Chatham and the larger one twenty miles away in Danville, she belonged to various book clubs at one time or another, and she built up a small library of titles that she read over and over. Behind her bed was a built-in bookshelf on which she kept a five-volume set of Jane Austen to which she regularly, and delightedly, returned; in the living room she had all that Trollope—she enjoyed him, though scarcely so much as my father did—and much else as well, including Thackeray and Dickens and other Victorian giants.

But I do not want to suggest that her reading was limited to the nineteenth century. To the contrary, she loved contemporary fiction, both American and British—like most Americans, she read little in translation—and kept up with it closely.

With varying degrees of admiration she read Faulkner and Styron, Marquand and Cozzens, Welty and Bowen, Cheever and Greene, Pym and Drabble. She liked popular fiction so long as it was intelligent and literate, as much of it was in her day; I remember the immense pleasure she took in *The Caine Mutiny,* and the equally great satisfaction she got from passing it along to me—I was then eleven years old—and seeing me share her enthusiasm.

When it came to my own reading, I never sensed that she thought I was "too young" for any of the books she herself had enjoyed and admired. Books were less salacious then than they are now, to be sure, but still a parent so inclined could have forbidden me Hemingway or Steinbeck or Algren. My mother not merely did not deny me these pleasures, she encouraged me in the pursuit of them; much of what she herself knew of the larger world she had learned through books, and she saw no reason why she should deny her son this world just because he happened to be several years short of his majority.

She gave me that gift, but she gave me something even more important as well: she made books seem a natural, necessary part of the life I wanted to live. My father's love of books was no less ardent than hers, but as with so much else in him it came with a measure of exhibitionism attached: the brilliant leather slipcases, the talk of New York dealers and auction houses, the public readings of Trollope he occasionally inflicted upon the Chatham Hall community. My mother didn't make a fuss about reading, she just did it, and in so doing she made it seem as essential and desirable to me as food and drink, happiness and love.

When, through a series of peculiar professional events, I became first a reviewer of other people's books and then the author of one of my own, the pleasure my mother took in this made all the labors and frustrations of my career worthwhile. Here, astonishingly, was a member of her own family actually making a living of sorts in a world she longed for, a world that had always seemed so distant and romantic to her. Soon enough I disabused her of *that* notion, but her pleasure was undiminished; when, in the 1970s, I was able to take her to an actual New York publishing party, and to introduce her to a few people whose words she had actually read in books and articles, she kept her cool—but the body language betrayed her happiness.

Whatever else she did, she read. In the winter of 1985, when a cancer was discovered in her lung and I came up to Rhode Island for a post-operative visit, I brought with me a large box, filled not with candy or fruit or gifts but with paperback mysteries of the genteel English variety that she so loved. For the eighteen months remaining to her the box rested on the floor of her bedroom; each time I visited I could see that the books had been moved around, that gradually—ever more gradually, as remission ended and the cancer began its final growth—she was making her way through them.

In the end reading, like everything else, hurt too much. Jane bought a small television set and placed it on a table at the foot of her bed, and for the last weeks of her life my mother mostly watched public broadcasting and the evening news. She wasn't reading a book when she died on September 2, 1986, and for that matter I do not know—I do not want to know— what was the last book she read. It wasn't Jane Austen, though the set was by her bedside. More likely it was Agatha Christie, or Ngaio Marsh, or Nicolas Freeling, or Josephine Tey: an old friend, a boon companion in the last days of a good life.